T0041437

The
Bolivian Diary

AUTHORIZED EDITION

ERNESTO CHE GUEVARA

The
Bolivian Diary

INTRODUCTION BY
FIDEL CASTRO

FOREWORD BY
CAMILO GUEVARA

Centro de Estudios
CHE GUEVARA

NEW YORK • OAKLAND • LONDON

Copyright © 1967, 2006 by Ernesto Che Guevara and Aleida March
All photographs copyright © Aleida March and the Che Guevara Studies Center

Preface © 2006 Camilo Guevara

Published by Seven Stories Press on behalf of Ocean Press, Melbourne, Australia, and the Che Guevara Studies Center, Havana. Direct all rights inquiries and permissions questions to rights@sevenstories.com.

All rights reserved. No part of this publication may be reproduced, stored in a retrieval system or transmitted in any form or by any means, electronic, mechanical, photocopying, recording or otherwise, without the prior permission of the publisher.

ISBN 978-1-64421-074-1 (paperback)
ISBN 978-1-64421-075-8 (ebook)

Also published by Seven Stories Press/Ocean Sur in Spanish as
El Diario del Che en Bolivia, ISBN 978-1-64421-139-7 (paperback);
ISBN 978-1-64421-077-2 (ebook)

Printed in the USA

9 8 7 6 5 4 3 2 1

CONTENTS

EDITOR'S NOTE

This edition of Che Guevara's *The Bolivian Diary* has been prepared by the Che Guevara Studies Center, Havana. It is based on the first authorized edition published in Spanish in 1968 by the Cuban Book Institute. Certain pages that did not appear in that first edition have now been incorporated. Those diary entries, originally withheld by the Bolivian government for "security" reasons, are dated: January 4, 5, 8, and 9; February 8 and 9; March 14; April 4 and 5; June 9 and 10; and July 4 and 5.

The text of the first edition has also been thoroughly checked and revised against facsimiles of the diary itself in order to clarify terms or words that were illegible. In the few remaining instances where this has not been possible, the text is marked "illegible in the original."

Che used a variety of noms de guerre or nicknames throughout the diary and sometimes the same person was referred to by several different names. For this reason, a glossary has been prepared to aid the reader.

Che's spelling of place names in the area of Bolivia in which the guerrilla force operated also varied, and this is reflected in the diary. Some of these names have been standardized to assist the reader, for example, in the case of the Ñacahuazú River.

Generally, however, the integrity of the original diary has been maintained.

Several key documents related to the Bolivian revolutionary movement at the time have been included as appendices. Throughout the diary, however, Che makes references to other documents that have not been reproduced here.

ERNESTO CHE GUEVARA

One of *Time* magazine's "icons of the century," Ernesto Guevara de la Serna was born in Rosario, Argentina, on June 14, 1928. He made several trips around Latin America during and immediately after his studies at medical school in Buenos Aires, including his 1952 journey with Alberto Granado, on the unreliable Norton motorbike described in his travel journal *The Motorcycle Diaries.*

He was already becoming involved in political activity and living in Guatemala when, in 1954, the elected government of Jacobo Árbenz was overthrown in a CIA-organized military operation. Ernesto escaped to Mexico, profoundly radicalized.

Following up on a contact made in Guatemala, Guevara sought out the group of exiled Cuban revolutionaries in Mexico City. In July 1955, he met Fidel Castro and immediately enlisted in the guerrilla expedition to overthrow Cuban dictator Fulgencio Batista. The Cubans nicknamed him "Che," a popular form of address in Argentina.

On November 25, 1956, Guevara set sail for Cuba aboard the yacht *Granma* as the doctor to the guerrilla group that began the revolutionary armed struggle in Cuba's Sierra Maestra mountains. Within several months, he was named by Fidel Castro as the first Rebel Army commander, though he continued ministering medically to wounded guerrilla fighters and captured soldiers from Batista's army.

In September 1958, Guevara played a decisive role in the military defeat of Batista after he and Camilo Cienfuegos led separate guerrilla columns westward from the Sierra Maestra (later described in his book *Reminiscences of the Cuban Revolutionary War*).

After Batista fled on January 1, 1959, Guevara became a key leader of the new revolutionary government, first as head of the Department of Industry of the National Institute of Agrarian Reform; then as president of the National Bank. In February 1961 he became minister of industry. He was also a central leader of the political organization that in 1965 became the Communist Party of Cuba.

Apart from these responsibilities, Guevara often represented the Cuban revolutionary government around the world, heading numerous delegations and speaking at the United Nations and other international forums in Asia, Africa, Latin America, and the socialist bloc countries. He earned a reputation as a passionate and articulate spokesperson for Third World peoples, most famously at the 1961 conference at Punta del Este in Uruguay, where he denounced US President Kennedy's Alliance for Progress.

As had been his intention since joining the Cuban revolutionary movement, Guevara left Cuba in April 1965, initially to lead a Cuban-organized guerrilla mission to support the revolutionary struggle in the Congo, Africa. He returned to Cuba secretly in December 1965, to prepare another Cuban-organized guerrilla force for Bolivia. Arriving in Bolivia in

November 1966, Guevara's plan was to challenge that country's military dictatorship and eventually to instigate a revolutionary movement that would extend throughout the continent of Latin America. He was wounded and captured by US-trained and run Bolivian counterinsurgency troops on October 8, 1967. The following day he was murdered and his body hidden. The diary he wrote during this period is published in this book.

Che Guevara's remains were finally discovered in 1997 and returned to Cuba. A memorial was built at Santa Clara in central Cuba, where he had won a major military battle during the revolutionary war.

CHRONOLOGY

June 14, 1928 Ernesto Guevara is born in Rosario, Argentina, of parents Ernesto Guevara Lynch and Celia de la Serna; he will be the eldest of five children.

January–July 1952 Ernesto Guevara travels around Latin America with his friend Alberto Granado.

March 10, 1952 General Fulgencio Batista carries out a coup d'état in Cuba.

July 6, 1953 After graduating as a doctor in March, Ernesto Guevara sets off again to travel through Latin America. He visits Bolivia, observing the aftermath of the 1952 revolution.

July 26, 1953 Fidel Castro leads an unsuccessful armed attack on the Moncada army garrison in Santiago de Cuba, launching the revolutionary struggle to overthrow the Batista regime.

December 1953 Ernesto Guevara meets a group of Cuban survivors of the Moncada attack in San José, Costa Rica.

December 24, 1953 Ernesto Guevara arrives in Guatemala, then under the popularly elected government of Jacobo Árbenz.

January–June 1954 While in Guatemala, he studies Marxism and becomes involved in political activities, meeting exiled Cuban revolutionaries.

August 1954 Mercenary troops backed by the CIA enter Guatemala City and begin massacring Árbenz supporters.

September 21, 1954 Ernesto Guevara arrives in Mexico City after fleeing Guatemala. He gets a job the Central Hospital.

July 1955 Ernesto Guevara meets Fidel Castro soon after the latter arrives in exile in Mexico City after his release from prison in Cuba. Che immediately agrees to join the planned guerrilla expedition to Cuba. The Cubans nickname him "Che," an Argentine term of greeting.

June 24, 1956 Che is arrested as part of a roundup by Mexican police of exiled Cuban revolutionaries.

November 25, 1956 Eighty-two combatants, including Che Guevara as troop doctor, sail for Cuba from Tuxpan, Mexico, aboard the small cabin cruiser *Granma*.

December 2, 1956 The *Granma* reaches Cuba at Las Coloradas beach in Oriente province but are surprised by Batista's troops at Alegría de Pío and dispersed.

December 21, 1956 Che's group (led by Juan Almeida) reunites with Fidel Castro and his group and they move deeper into the Sierra Maestra mountains.

January 17, 1957 The Rebel Army with some new peasant recruits successfully takes an army outpost in the battle of La Plata.

January 22, 1957 A significant victory over Batista's forces is scored at Arroyo del Infierno.

February 17, 1957 *New York Times* journalist Herbert Matthews interviews Fidel Castro in the Sierra Maestra. The same day, the first meeting is held between the urban underground and the guerrillas of the July 26 Movement since the start of the revolutionary war.

March 13, 1957 A group of students from the Revolutionary Directorate attack the Presidential Palace and seize a major Havana radio station. Student leader José Antonio Echeverría is killed in this attack.

May 27–28, 1957 The battle of El Uvero takes place, in which Che Guevara stands out among the combatants.

July 12, 1957 The rebels issue the Manifesto of the Sierra Maestra calling for a broad political front against General Batista and support for the Rebel Army.

July 21, 1957 Che Guevara is selected to lead the newly established second column (Column 4) of the Rebel Army and is promoted to the rank of commander.

July 30, 1957 Frank País, the young leader of the urban underground in Santiago de Cuba, is killed.

August 20, 1957 Fidel leads Column 1 (José Martí) in defeating Batista's forces in the battle of Palma Mocha.

September 17, 1957 Che's forces ambush army troops at Pino del Agua.

October, 1957 The rebels establish a permanent supply base at El Hombrito in the Sierra Maestra.

October 12, 1957 Batista launches a brutal campaign to destroy the Rebel Army in the Sierra Maestra.

November–December, 1957 The rebels respond with a "winter offensive" against Batista's army.

February 16-17, 1958 The Rebel Army wins a significant victory against Batista in the second battle of Pino del Agua.

March 1, 1958 Raúl Castro and Juan Almeida lead columns that open up second and third fronts in Oriente province.

April 9, 1958 A national general strike is defeated.

May 25, 1958 Batista launches a military offensive against the Rebel Army, but this fails after two and a half months of intensive fighting.

July 11–21, 1958 A decisive defeat is inflicted on Batista's army in the battle of El Jigüe, significantly expanding the rebels' operational zone in the Sierra Maestra.

August 31, 1958 Che Guevara and Camilo Cienfuegos lead invasion columns west from the Sierra Maestra toward central Cuba, opening new battle fronts in Las Villas province.

November 15, 1958 Fidel leaves the Sierra Maestra to direct the Rebel Army's final offensive in Santiago de Cuba. By the end of the month, Batista's elite troops are defeated at the battle of Guisa.

December 28, 1958 Che Guevara's Column 8 initiates the battle of Santa Clara and succeeds in taking control of the city within a few days.

January 1, 1959 Batista flees Cuba. Fidel enters Santiago de Cuba as the military regime collapses. Santa Clara falls to the Rebel Army.

January 2, 1959 Fidel Castro calls for a general strike and the country is paralyzed. The Rebel Army columns led by Che Guevara and Camilo Cienfuegos reach Havana.

January 8, 1959 Fidel Castro arrives in Havana.

February 9, 1959 Che Guevara is declared a Cuban citizen.

June 12–September 8, 1959 Che Guevara travels through Europe, Africa, and Asia; he signs various commercial, technical, and cultural agreements on behalf of the revolutionary government.

October 7, 1959 Che Guevara is designated head of the Department of Industry of the National Institute of Agrarian Reform (INRA).

November 25, 1959 Che Guevara is appointed president of the National Bank of Cuba.

March 5, 1960 At the funeral for the victims of a terrorist bombing on board the French ship *La Coubre,* Cuban photographer Alberto Korda snaps his famous photograph of Che Guevara.

March 17, 1960 President Eisenhower approves a CIA plan to overthrow the revolutionary government and to train a Cuban exile army to invade Cuba.

October 21, 1960 Che Guevara leaves on an extended visit to the Soviet Union, the German Democratic Republic, Czechoslovakia, China, and North Korea.

January 3, 1961 Washington breaks diplomatic relations with Cuba.

February 23, 1961 The revolutionary government establishes the Ministry of Industry, headed by Che Guevara.

April 15, 1961 As a prelude to the planned invasion by US-organized forces, planes attack Santiago de Cuba and Havana.

April 16, 1961 At a mass rally Fidel Castro proclaims the socialist character of the Cuban revolution.

April 17–19, 1961 One thousand five hundred Cuban-born mercenaries, organized and backed by the United States, invade Cuba at the Bay of Pigs but are defeated within 72 hours. Che Guevara is sent to command troops in Pinar del Río province.

August 8, 1961 Che Guevara condemns US President Kennedy's "Alliance for Progress" in a fiery speech to Organization of American States (OAS) Economic and Social Conference in Punta del Este, Uruguay, as head of Cuba's delegation. Cuba is subsequently expelled from the OAS.

February 3, 1962 President Kennedy orders a total trade embargo against Cuba.

August 27–September 7, 1962 Che Guevara makes his second visit to the Soviet Union.

October 1962 An international crisis breaks out after US spy planes discover Soviet missile installations in Cuba. Cuba responds by mobilizing its population for defense. Che Guevara is assigned to lead forces in Pinar del Río province in preparation for an imminent US invasion.

July 3–17, 1963 Che Guevara visits Algeria, recently independent under the government of Ahmed Ben Bella.

March 1964 Che Guevara meets with Tamara Bunke (Tania) to discuss her mission to move to Bolivia in anticipation of a future guerrilla expedition.

March 25, 1964 Che Guevara addresses the UN Conference on Trade and Development in Geneva, Switzerland.

November 4–9, 1964 Che Guevara visits the Soviet Union.

December 11, 1964 Che Guevara addresses the UN General Assembly meeting in New York, condemning the US war in Vietnam and supporting independence movements from Puerto Rico to the Congo.

December 17, 1964 Che Guevara leaves New York for Africa, where he visits Algeria, Mali, Congo (Brazzaville), Guinea, Ghana, Tanzania, and Egypt.

February 24, 1965 Che Guevara addresses the Second Economic Seminar of the Organization of Afro-Asian Solidarity in Algiers, controversially urging the socialist countries to do more to support Third World struggles for independence.

March 14, 1965 Che Guevara returns to Cuba and shortly afterwards drops from public view.

April 1, 1965 Che Guevara delivers a farewell letter to Fidel Castro. He subsequently leaves Cuba on a Cuban-sponsored internationalist mission in the Congo, entering through Tanzania.

April 18, 1965 In answer to questions about Che Guevara's whereabouts, Fidel Castro tells foreign reporters that Che "will always be where he is most useful to the revolution."

June 16, 1965 Fidel Castro announces Che Guevara's location will be revealed "when Commander Guevara wants it known."

October 3, 1965 Fidel Castro publicly reads Che Guevara's letter of farewell at a meeting to announce the central committee of the newly formed Communist Party of Cuba.

November 21, 1965 Che Guevara leaves the Congo, and begins writing up his account of the African mission, which he describes as a "failure."

December 1965 Fidel Castro arranges for Che Guevara to return to Cuba in secret. Che Guevara prepares for a Cuban-sponsored guerrilla expedition to Bolivia.

January 3–14, 1966 The Tricontinental Conference of Solidarity of the Peoples of Asia, Africa, and Latin America is held in Havana.

March 1966 The first Cuban combatants arrive in Bolivia to begin advance preparations for a guerrilla movement. Tania has already been working there since 1964.

July 1966 Che Guevara meets with Cuban volunteers selected for the mission to Bolivia at a training camp in Cuba's Pinar del Río province.

November 4, 1966 Che Guevara arrives in La Paz, Bolivia, in disguise, using the assumed name of Ramón Benítez.

November 7, 1966 Che Guevara and several others arrive at the farm on the Ñacahuazú River where the guerrilla detachment will be based. Che makes his first entry in his diary of the Bolivia campaign.

December 31, 1966 Che Guevara meets with the secretary of the Bolivian Communist Party, Mario Monje. There is disagreement over perspectives for the planned guerrilla movement.

March 23, 1967 The first guerrilla military action takes place in a successful ambush of Bolivian Army troops.

March 25, 1967 The formation of the Bolivian National Liberation Army (ELN) is publicly announced.

April 16, 1967 Publication of Che Guevara's "Message to the Tricontinental," which calls for the creation of "two, three, many Vietnams."

April 17, 1967 The guerrilla detachment led by Joaquín (Vilo Acuña) is separated from the rest of the unit. The separation is supposed to last only a few days but the two groups are never able to reunite.

April 20, 1967 French revolutionary Regís Debray and Ciro Bustos are arrested after having spent several weeks with the guerrilla unit in Bolivia. They are subsequently tried and sentenced to 30 years' imprisonment.

May 1967 US Special Forces arrive in Bolivia to train counterinsurgency troops of the Bolivian Army.

June 23-24, 1967 The Bolivian Army massacres miners and their families at the Siglo XX mines. This becomes known as the San Juan massacre.

June 26, 1967 The guerrillas ambush army troops at Florida.

July 1, 1967 President Barrientos publicly announces Che Guevara's presence in Bolivia.

July 6, 1967 The guerrillas occupy the town of Sumaipata.

July 26, 1967 Che addresses the guerrilla troops on the significance of the July 26, 1953, attack on the Moncada garrison.

July 31–August 10, 1967 The Organization of Latin American Solidarity (OLAS) conference is held in Havana. The conference supports guerrilla movements throughout Latin America. Che Guevara is elected honorary chair.

August 4, 1967 A deserter leads the Bolivian Army to the guerrilla's main supply cache. Documents discovered there lead to the arrest of key urban contacts.

August 31, 1967 Joaquín's detachment, which includes Tania, is ambushed and annihilated while crossing the Río Grande at Puerto Mauricio (Vado del Yeso).

September 14, 1967 Loyola Guzmán is arrested along with hundreds of others suspected of collaborating with the guerrilla movement.

September 22, 1967 The guerrillas occupy the town of Alto Seco.

September 26, 1967 The guerrilla group falls into a Bolivian Army ambush at Quebrada del Batán, near La Higuera.

October 8, 1967 The remaining 17 guerrillas are trapped by army troops and conduct a desperate battle in the Quebrada del Yuro (El Yuro ravine). Che Guevara is seriously wounded and captured.

October 9, 1967 Che Guevara and two other captured guerrillas (Willy and Chino) are murdered by Bolivian soldiers following instructions from the Bolivian government and Washington. The remains of Che Guevara and the other guerrillas are secretly buried in Bolivia.

October 14, 1967 Survivors of the battle of Quebrada del Yuro are ambushed at the fork of the Mizque and Río Grande rivers.

October 15, 1967 In a television appearance Fidel Castro confirms news of Che Guevara's death and declares three days of official mourning in Cuba. October 8 is designated the Day of the Heroic Guerrilla.

October 18, 1967 Fidel Castro delivers a memorial speech for Che Guevara in Havana's Revolution Plaza before an audience of almost one million people.

February 22, 1968 Three Cuban survivors (Pombo, Urbano, and Benigno) cross the Bolivian border into Chile, after traveling across the Andes on foot. They succeed in making it back to Cuba. Two Bolivians (Inti and Darío) stay in Bolivia and later reorganize the ELN.

Mid-March 1968 Microfilm of the pages of Che's Bolivian diaries arrives in Cuba.

July 1968 Che Guevara's *Bolivian Diary* is published in Cuba and distributed free of charge to the Cuban people. It is simultaneously published in many countries to counter the CIA campaign to discredit the revolutionary movement in Latin America. With an introduction by Fidel Castro, it becomes an instant international bestseller.

July 1997 Che Guevara's remains are finally located and returned to Cuba and buried along with the bodies of other guerrilla fighters found in Bolivia in a new memorial built in Santa Clara.

MAP OF BOLIVIA

SHOWING THE ZONE OF GUERRILLA OPERATIONS

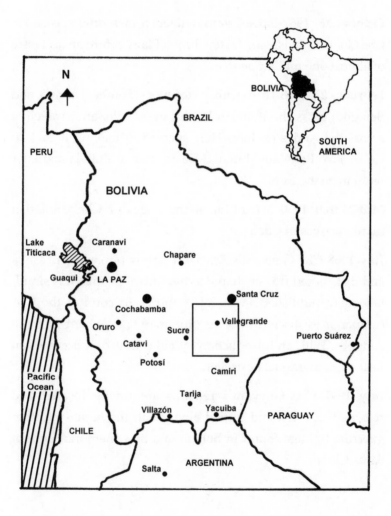

ZONE OF GUERRILLA OPERATIONS

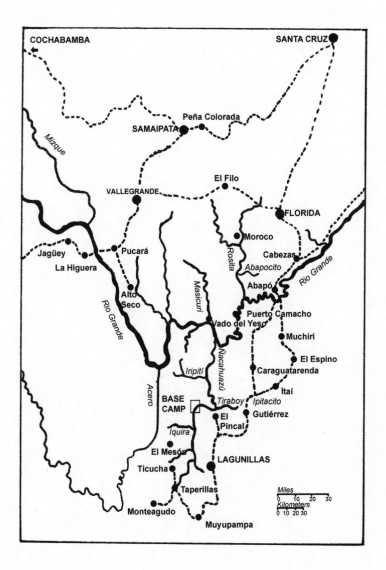

FOREWORD

Camilo Guevara

Santa Cruz, Bolivia
1967

Almost a year of intense warfare has transpired. Recently, due to a betrayal, Joaquín's group has fallen victim to an ambush in Vado del Yeso [Puerto Mauricio], and the encirclement of Che's troops tightens. They have decided to abandon the area in search of more suitable terrain, where they can more effectively develop the conditions to consolidate the guerrilla movement. It is the afternoon and soldiers are advancing; combat is imminent.

On the last page of the red diary, confiscated by the Bolivian military, is an entry dated October 7, 1967. It is barely possible to decipher the author's difficult handwriting: "The 11-month anniversary of our establishment as a guerrilla force passed in a bucolic mood, with no complications ..." These words in no way read as an epilogue to the heroic saga described in the diary, as there is not the slightest tone of discouragement, pessimism, or defeatism; on the contrary, these words appear to be a beginning, a prologue.

* * *

October 8 — A wounded prisoner is transferred to the tumble-down school at La Higuera, absorbed in his pain and almost unable to breathe. He can barely walk upright; he fights with the weight, accumulating over the past few months, which conspires against his shoulders. He has been weakened by calamity and illness, by the death of friends and compañeros, by the betrayal of some, by the unenviable responsibility he bears for the lives of those near and far away, by a yearning for his loved ones. The burden is equal to the sum of terrestrial forces. Yet his body is still upright and armed with conviction, preparing for another battle.

Later, bound against the adobe wall, waiting for the inevitable verdict, he silently observes the head guards. Some are more arrogant than others, assassins in the premature song of victory, who occasionally try to harass the man they consider their victim. But the respect he inspires and the power of his stony gaze deeply affects and confuses them, blocking any inclination toward cowardice. Nevertheless, they are poised to avenge this guerrilla's audacity in facing, with only 50 armed men, an entire army trained and financed by the empire and its Praetorian rangers.

His captors are faced with a tremendous dilemma. On the one hand, they hold one of the most legendary revolutionaries ever known, who can be paraded as proof of foreign aggression or an international communist plot. On the other hand, they know their captive is tenacious, a righteous man commanding solid arguments, who could transform any court into a public platform, so that any trial might become a dangerous political game with an uncertain outcome.

The National Liberation Army of Bolivia (ELN) has

dramatically announced its presence and carried out multiple actions, almost always successfully, with no effective response from the government. Neither national nor international public opinion is detached from these events: everywhere, a sympathetic atmosphere is developing, despite the fact that the expected mass incorporation of Bolivian peasants into the guerrilla ranks has yet not occurred. News reports emerging in recent days have provided the guerrilla fighters with enormous publicity. This is a very delicate moment and those interested in maintaining the status quo know it will be decisive.

A mood of vengeance abounds among the colorless, ignominious drones, who defend their "causes" with such unsubtle methods. If it is paradoxical to make a jail out of a school, it is simply futile (as well as inept and criminal), to seek to kill ideas with a rifle.

He is concerned about the fate of those who made it out of the battle alive, he wonders … In the brief moments of silence, struggling against the rope to alleviate the numbness in his arms and legs, he retreats into his memories, to the company of his wife, surrounded by their children, his relatives and closest friends, his Argentina, his Cuba, the world, and Fidel.

Undoubtedly, some will praise themselves or will be congratulated for having brought this "glory" to the Bolivian Army. The capture of Commander Guevara has been pure oxygen for the lifeblood and prestige of the regime — at least this is what they think. Should they have asked themselves: How can a future spirit be imprisoned in the past? How can an exemplar be incarcerated?

With his leg wounded, his rifle broken, and with no other weapon, they managed to capture this man, but only because he was a brother to his compañeros, a real man, a true revolutionary to the core, a human being moved only by great feelings of love.

He could have broken through the encirclement of soldiers surrounding him. Who could doubt his tactical genius? But he preferred to remain with those who could not defend themselves, his sick and wounded compañeros. He could have left Santa Cruz some time before, but he decided to wait, to continue the search and not abandon Joaquín's group. Precious time transpired, but he never dwelled on these lost days. He could have allowed Pelao and the Frenchman, who later demonized him, to attempt to reach the city through their own efforts, but he preferred to leave them where they were reasonably safe.

Such an intense, complete man does not fit within the narrow criteria of those who pass judgment on him. Certainly, there are those who fear him and criticize him—unwavering revolutionaries of after-dinner conversations, bureaucrats, ubiquitous cowards, opportunists, tyrants of the oligarchies and oligarchs of democracy. For different reasons they hide from him or try to hide him away behind the illusory mantel that utopias are unattainable. But others respect him—the majorities that in part or in full share his vision of the future. His grandeur is barely perceptible at the time of his capture, history will define it later.

Close by, during the evening hours, a small group of men have gathered in an area hemmed in by abrupt mountainous terrain. Some have fresh wounds, all are starving, thirsty, and exhausted beyond words, uncertainty etched on their faces. They desperately seek news on the whereabouts of their compañeros and their beloved commander via a portable radio. Taunted by a powerful intuition of disaster, they nervously move the dial in search of the more reliable radio stations, although naturally they regard any broadcast with tremendous reservation. They know from experience that radio news can be subtly manipulated, capitalizing on the guerrilla fighter's perennial need for information by laying mortal traps or by leading them in mistaken directions. This time, however, they are willing to resign themselves to the most elementary indication, and will act without measuring the consequences.

They will do whatever is necessary, in accordance with their ideas and their feelings of solidarity toward their brothers-in-arms. The desire to help them and to save the movement is stronger than any rational hesitation about a rescue mission. What is at stake is the ELN itself, in this initial formative stage, for which the fighters have already so often wagered their lives.

The possible evacuation of the guerrilla forces had been planned, including where they would meet in the event of a setback or forced retreat: if not here, there, and if not, farther over. They have fully complied with the previously agreed on plans. There is no reason to feel shame, but after so many months of fighting in Bolivian territory, some feel vulnerable, with an unjustified yet understandable sense of guilt. For others, it has been an entire lifetime of sharing the ups and downs of the struggle, the few provisions, and the many hopes, dreams, and fears—of surviving others, of risking one's life, of losing beloved friends and relatives. They feel the anguish and regret of a latent despair, silently wishing for the same fate as their compañeros, whatever that might be, and although they force optimism to remain uppermost in their minds, their hearts experience the shocking acknowledgment of what they had until now considered impossible.

The dramatic news is confirmed: Che has died in combat. His belongings are described in vivid detail and other information is given that only those close to the scene could have known. The reality engulfs them, overpowering their thoughts and the fiber of their bodies. What should they do? What is to be done? What are they doing there? Time presses upon them. The army has not abandoned its search for the guerrillas; in minutes or seconds, the soldiers might fall upon them. They have to act immediately. How many memories flood their minds, how many voices are still fresh in their ears? A phrase comes to mind, one of those that reduces great truths to a few words: "In a revolution, if it's a true revolution, you win or you die."

Perhaps there was another option, somewhere between an uncertain farewell and faith in the final goal, the "Hasta la victoria siempre" [Ever onward to victory] we have heard so often. What does it matter: If the struggle continues, independently of the great loss, Che and his compañeros will have won. If the struggle is abandoned, irrespective of the present or the future, his battle cry, specifically directed to the poor and other receptive ears, will fall as lifeless as his body.

Their decision will affect the course of history. Although it is the people who always have the final word, it is a favorable, unequivocal sign when the rank and file of the revolutionary movement adheres to the thought and actions of their leaders. The remaining members of the ELN make a pact, now famous, to fight to the end, to continue the struggle until the guerrilla movement's main objectives become reality. They are confident that a movement strongly rooted in Latin Americanism and Che Guevara's historical thought, will lead to new epic moments in the peoples' struggles for their redemption.

October 9—In that poor, little schoolhouse in La Higuera, a small space confines one of the most consequential human beings ever known. A great man patiently waits for death. The order to murder him comes from Washington; the underlings duly obey and with one bullet after another steal the vigor from the guerrilla fighter's body, a sad and terrible error.

Against their will, Che is transformed into a hardened symbol of resistance, a symbol of the fight for what is just, of passion, of the necessity of being fully human, multiplied infinitely in the ideals and weapons of those who struggle. This is what the front men and their omnipotent handlers fear.

They have never understood the absurdity of trying to destroy the essence of an audacious, creative spirit, an indefatigable and studious worker, a formidable leader who never ceased delivering blows against bureaucracy and aristocracy. They have never understood that it was, and always will be, impossible to undermine Che's conviction (which he himself embodied) that an individual human being can ascend to greater heights, can change for the better, and can make the society in which he or she lives a nobler place.

Che never ceased believing that revolutionaries, even if they are being massacred sadistically, should invoke the use of force only when absolutely necessary, and, even then, should never accompany it with cruelty. This idea is directly proportional to the condition of being a revolutionary.

Finally, without a trial, without a thought, the new man Che

Guevara represented is killed. But what is born is a yearning for the new human being who is neither an illusion nor a fantasy. The dream now emerges of a new human being who is constantly renewed, who sacrifices themselves for others, who grows beyond mediocrity, if only for an instant, to become different, better. A dream, dormant for many centuries, takes shape: an ethical, virtuous, selfless human being. This time, stripped of all myth and mysticism, this person must be fundamentally human.

Camilo Guevara March
Che Guevara Studies Center
July 2005

A NECESSARY
INTRODUCTION

Fidel Castro

It was Che's custom during his days as a guerrilla [during the 1956–58 Cuban revolutionary war] to carefully record his daily observations in a personal diary. During long marches over rugged and difficult terrain, in the midst of damp woods, when the lines of men, always hunched over from the weight of their packs, ammunition, and weapons, would stop for a moment to rest, or when the column would receive orders to halt and set up camp at the end of an exhausting day's march, you would see Che—as he was affectionately nicknamed by the Cubans from the beginning—take out a small notebook and, with the tiny and nearly illegible handwriting of a doctor, write his notes.

What he was able to save from these notes he later used in writing his magnificent historical narratives of the revolutionary war in Cuba—accounts full of revolutionary, educational, and human content.[1]

This time, thanks to his invariable habit of noting the main

---

1. Ernesto Che Guevara, *Reminiscences of the Cuban Revolutionary War* (New York: Seven Stories Press, 2022).

events of each day, we have at our disposal rigorously exact, priceless, and detailed information on the heroic final months of his life in Bolivia.

These notes, not really written for publication, served as a tool in the constant evaluation of events, situations, and people, and at the same time served as an outlet for the expression of his keenly observant and analytical spirit, often laced with a fine sense of humor. They are soberly written and form a coherent whole from beginning to end.

It should be kept in mind that they were written during those rare moments of rest in the midst of a heroic and superhuman physical effort, where he bore exhausting obligations as leader of a guerrilla detachment in the difficult first stages of a struggle of this nature, which unfolded under incredibly harsh material conditions. This reveals once more his method of work, his will of steel.

The diary, in the course of analyzing in detail the incidents of each day, takes note of the shortcomings, critical assessments, and recriminations that are part of and inevitable in the development of a revolutionary guerrilla struggle.

Inside a guerrilla detachment such assessments must take place constantly. This is especially true in the stage in which it consists of a small nucleus facing extremely adverse material conditions and an enemy infinitely superior in number, when the slightest negligence or the most insignificant mistake can be fatal. The leader must be extremely demanding, using each event or episode, no matter how insignificant it may seem, to educate the combatants and future cadres of new guerrilla detachments.

The process of training a guerrilla force is a constant appeal to each person's consciousness and honor. Che knew how to touch the most sensitive fibers in revolutionaries. When Marcos, after being repeatedly admonished by Che, was warned that he could be dishonorably discharged from the guerrilla unit, he replied, "I would rather be shot!" Later he gave his life heroically. Similar behavior could be noted among all those in whom Che placed confidence and those he had to admonish for one reason or another in the course of the struggle. He was a fraternal and humane leader, but he also knew how to be demanding and, at times, severe. But above all, and even more than with others, Che was severe with himself. He based discipline on the guerrilla's moral consciousness and on the tremendous force of his own example.

The diary also contains numerous references to [Régis] Debray; it reflects the enormous concern Che felt over the arrest and imprisonment of the revolutionary writer who had been given a mission to carry out in Europe—although at heart Che would have preferred him to have stayed with the guerrilla unit, which is why Che shows a certain uneasiness and, on occasion, some doubts about his behavior.

Che had no way of knowing the odyssey Debray experienced in the hands of the repressive forces, or the firm and courageous attitude he maintained in face of his captors and torturers. He noted, however, the enormous political significance of the trial and on October 3, six days before his death, in the midst of bitter and tense events, he wrote, "We heard an interview with Debray, very courageous when faced by a student acting as an agent provocateur." This was his last reference to the writer.

The Cuban revolution and its relation to the guerrilla movement are repeatedly referred to in the diary. Some may interpret our decision to publish it as an act of provocation that will give the enemies of the revolution — the Yankee imperialists and their allies, the Latin American oligarchs — arguments for redoubling their efforts to blockade, isolate, and attack Cuba.

Those who judge the facts this way should remember that Yankee imperialism has never needed a pretext to carry out its crimes anywhere in the world, and that its efforts to crush the Cuban revolution began as soon as our country passed its first revolutionary law. This stems from the obvious and well-known fact that imperialism is the policeman of world reaction, the systematic supporter of counterrevolution, and the protector of the most backward and inhuman social structures that still exist in the world.

Solidarity with a revolutionary movement may be taken as a pretext for Yankee aggression, but it will never be the real cause. To deny solidarity in order to avoid giving a pretext is a ridiculous, ostrich-like policy that has nothing to do with the internationalist character of today's social revolutions. To abandon solidarity with a revolutionary movement not only does not avoid providing a pretext, but in effect serves to support Yankee imperialism and its policy of dominating and enslaving the world.

Cuba is a small country, economically underdeveloped as are all countries dominated and exploited for centuries by colonialism and imperialism. It is located only 90 miles from the coast of the United States, has a Yankee naval base on its territory [Guantánamo], and faces numerous obstacles in attaining socioeconomic development. Grave dangers have threatened our country since the triumph of the revolution; but imperialism will never make us yield for these reasons, because the difficulties that flow from a consistently revolutionary line of action are of no importance to us.

From the revolutionary point of view, there is no alternative but to publish Che's Bolivian diary. It fell into the hands of [President René] Barrientos, who immediately sent copies to the CIA, the Pentagon, and the US government. Journalists with links to the CIA had access to the document inside Bolivia; having made photocopies of it, they promised to refrain, for the moment, from publishing it.

The Barrientos government and the top-ranking military officers have more than enough reasons not to publish the diary. It reveals the immense incapacity of their army and the countless defeats they were dealt by a handful of determined guerrillas who, in a matter of weeks, took nearly 200 weapons from them in combat. Furthermore, Che describes Barrientos and his regime in terms they deserve, with words that cannot be erased from history.

Imperialism also had its own reasons: Che and the extraordinary example he set are gaining increasing force in the world. His ideas, image, and name are banners of struggle against the injustices suffered by the oppressed and exploited; they evoke impassioned interest among students and intellectuals throughout the world.

In the United States itself, the Black [rights] movement and progressive students, both of which are continuing to grow in numbers, have made Che's figure their own. In the most combative demonstrations for civil rights and against the aggression in Vietnam, his image is brandished as a symbol of struggle. Few times in history, perhaps never before, has a figure, a name, an example become a universal symbol so quickly and with such impassioned force. This is because Che embodies, in its purest and most selfless form, the internationalist spirit that marks the world of today and that will characterize even more the world of tomorrow.

Arising from a continent yesterday oppressed by colonial powers, today exploited and held in backwardness and the most iniquitous underdevelopment by Yankee imperialism, there has emerged this singular figure who has become the universal symbol of revolutionary struggle, even in the metropolitan centers of the imperialists and colonialists.

The Yankee imperialists fear the power of this example and everything that may help to spread it. The diary is the living expression of an extraordinary personality; a lesson in guerrilla warfare written in the heat and tension of daily events, as flammable as gunpowder; a demonstration in life that the people of Latin America are not powerless in face of the enslavers of entire peoples and of their mercenary armies. That is its intrinsic value, and that is what has kept them from publishing it up to now.

Also among those who may be interested in keeping the diary unpublished are the pseudorevolutionaries, opportunists, and charlatans of every stripe. These people call themselves Marxists, communists, and other such titles. They have not, however, hesitated to call Che a mistaken adventurer or, when they speak more benignly, an idealist whose death marked the swan song of revolutionary armed struggle in Latin America. "If Che himself," they say, "the greatest exponent of these ideas and an experienced guerrilla fighter, died in the guerrilla struggle and his movement failed to free Bolivia, it only shows how mistaken he was!" How many of these miserable creatures were happy with the death of Che and have not even blushed at the thought that their stance and arguments completely coincide with those of imperialism and the most reactionary oligarchs!

That is how they justify themselves. That is how they justify their treacherous leaders who, at a given moment, did not hesitate to play at armed struggle with the underlying intention—as would be seen later—of destroying the guerrilla detachments, putting the brakes on revolutionary action, and imposing their own shameful and ridiculous political schemes, because they were absolutely incapable of carrying out any other line. That is how they justify those who do not want to fight, who will never fight for the people and their liberation. That is how they justify those who have made a caricature of revolutionary ideas, turning them into an opium like dogma with neither content nor message for the masses; those who have converted the organizations of popular struggle into instruments of conciliation with domestic and foreign exploiters; and those who advocate policies that have nothing to do with the genuine interests of the exploited peoples of this continent.

Che thought of his death as something natural and probable in the process; he made an effort to stress, especially in his last writings, that this eventuality would not hold back the inevitable march of the Latin American revolution. In his "Message to the Tricontinental," he reiterated this thought, "Our every action is a battle cry against imperialism ... Wherever death may surprise us, let it be welcome if our battle cry has reached even one receptive ear, if another hand reaches out to take up our arms ..."[2]

---

2. Ernesto Che Guevara, *Che Guevara Reader* (New York: Seven Stories Press, 2022).

Che considered himself a soldier in the revolution, with absolutely no concern as to whether he would survive it. Those who see the outcome of his struggle in Bolivia as marking the failure of his ideas can, with the same oversimplification, deny the validity of the ideas and struggles of all the great revolutionary precursors and thinkers; this includes the founders of Marxism, who were themselves unable to complete the task and to see in life the fruits of their noble efforts.

In Cuba, [José] Martí and [Antonio] Maceo were killed in combat; Yankee intervention followed, ending the War of Independence and frustrating the immediate objectives of their struggle. Brilliant advocates of socialist revolution, like Julio Antonio Mella, have been killed, murdered by agents in the service of imperialism. But these deaths could not, in the long run, block the triumph of a process that began 100 years ago. And absolutely nothing can call into question the profound justice of the cause and line of struggle of those eminent fighters, or the timeliness of their basic ideas, which have always inspired Cuban revolutionaries.

In Che's diary, from the notes he wrote, you can see how real the possibilities of success were, how extraordinary the catalyzing power of the guerrilla struggle. On one occasion, in the face of evident signs of the Bolivian regime's weakness and rapid deterioration, he wrote, "The government is disintegrating rapidly. What a pity we don't have 100 more men right now."

Che knew from his experience in Cuba how often our small guerrilla detachment had been on the verge of being wiped out. Whether such things happen depends almost entirely on chance and the imponderables of war. But would such an eventuality have given anyone the right to consider our line erroneous, and, in addition, to take it as an example to discourage revolution and inculcate a sense of powerlessness among the peoples? Many times in history revolutionary processes have been preceded by adverse episodes. We ourselves in Cuba, didn't we have the experience of Moncada just six years before the definitive triumph of the people's armed struggle?

From July 26, 1953 — the attack on the Moncada garrison in Santiago de Cuba — to December 2, 1956 — the landing of the *Granma* — revolutionary struggle in Cuba in the face of a modern, well-equipped army seemed to many people to lack any prospect for success; the action of a handful of fighters was seen as a chimera of idealists and dreamers who were "deeply mistaken." The crushing defeat and total dispersal of the inexperienced guerrilla detachment by Batista's troops on December 5, 1956, seemed to confirm entirely those pessimistic forebodings. But only 25 months later the remnants of that guerrilla unit had developed the strength and experience necessary to annihilate that same army.

In all epochs and under all circumstances, there will always be an abundance of pretexts for not fighting; but not fighting is the only way to never attain freedom. Che did not live as long as his ideas; he fertilized them with his blood. It is certain, on the other hand, that his pseudorevolutionary critics, with all their political cowardice and eternal lack of action, will outlive by far the evidence of their own stupidity.

Worth noting in the diary are the actions of one of those revolutionary specimens that are becoming typical in Latin America these days: Mario Monje, brandishing the title of secretary of the Communist Party of Bolivia, sought to dispute with Che the political and military leadership of the movement. Monje claimed, moreover, that he had intended to resign his party post to take on this responsibility; in his opinion, obviously, it was enough to have once held that title to claim such a prerogative.

Mario Monje, naturally, had no experience in guerrilla warfare and had never been in combat. In addition, the fact that he considered himself a communist should at least have obliged him to dispense with the gross and mundane chauvinism that had already been overcome by those who fought for Bolivia's first independence.

With such a conception of what an anti-imperialist struggle on this continent should be, "communist leaders" of this type do not even surpass the level of internationalism of the aboriginal tribes subjugated by the European colonizers in the epoch of the conquest.

Bolivia and its historical capital, Sucre, were named after the country's first liberators [Simón Bolívar and Antonio José de Sucre], both of whom were Venezuelan. And in this country, in a struggle for the definitive liberation of his people, the leader of the Communist Party of Bolivia had the possibility of enlisting the cooperation of the political, organizational, and military talent of a genuine revolutionary titan, a person whose cause was not limited by the narrow and artificial—not to mention unjust—borders of Bolivia. Yet he did nothing but engage in disgraceful, ridiculous, and unjustified claims to leadership.

Bolivia has no outlet to the sea, and therefore, for its own liberation and to avoid exposure to a cruel blockade, it more than any other country needs revolutionary victories by its neighbors. Che, because of his enormous authority, ability, and experience, was the person who could have accelerated this process.

In the period before a split occurred in the Bolivian Communist Party, Che had established relations with leaders and members, soliciting their help for the revolutionary movement in South America. Under authorization from the party, some members worked with Che for years on various assignments. When the split occurred, it created a special situation, given that a number of the people who had been working with him ended up in one or another group. But Che did not see the struggle in Bolivia as an isolated occurrence, rather as part of a revolutionary liberation movement that would soon extend to other countries in South America. He sought to organize a movement free of sectarianism, one that could be joined by anyone who wanted to fight for the liberation of Bolivia and of all the other peoples of Latin America subjugated by imperialism.

In the initial phase of preparing a base for the guerrilla unit, however, Che depended for the most part on the help of a group of courageous and discreet collaborators who, at the time of the split, remained in the party headed by Monje. Although he certainly felt no sympathy toward Monje, in deference to them he invited Monje to visit his camp first. He then invited Moisés Guevara, a leader of the mine workers and a political leader. Moisés Guevara had left the party to join in the formation of another organization, the one led by Oscar Zamora. He later left that group because of differences with Zamora, who proved to be another Monje. Zamora had once promised Che he would help in organizing the armed guerrilla struggle in Bolivia, but later backed away from that commitment and cowardly folded his arms when the hour of action arrived. After Che's death, Zamora became one of his most venomous "Marxist-Leninist" critics. Moisés Guevara joined Che without hesitation, as he had sought to do long before Che arrived in Bolivia; he offered his support and gave his life heroically for the revolutionary cause.

The group of Bolivian guerrillas who until then had stayed with Monje's organization also joined Che. Led by Inti and Coco Peredo, who proved to be courageous, outstanding fighters, they left Monje and decisively backed Che. But Monje, seeking revenge, began to sabotage the movement. In La Paz he intercepted well-trained communist militants who were on their way to join the guerrillas. These facts demonstrate that within the ranks of revolutionaries, men who meet all the conditions necessary for struggle can be criminally frustrated in their development by incapable, maneuvering, and charlatan-like leaders.

Che was a man never personally interested in posts, leadership, or honors; but he believed revolutionary guerrilla warfare was the fundamental form of action for the liberation of the peoples of Latin America, given the economic, political, and social situation in nearly all Latin American countries. Moreover, he was firmly convinced that the military and political leadership of the guerrilla struggle had to be unified. He also believed the struggle could be led only by the guerrilla unit itself, and not from the comfortable offices of bureaucrats in the cities. So he was not prepared to give up leadership of a guerrilla nucleus that, at a later stage of its development, was intended to develop into a struggle of broad dimensions in Latin America. And he certainly was not prepared to turn over such leadership to an inexperienced emptyhead with narrow chauvinist views. Such chauvinism often infects even revolutionary elements of various countries in Latin America. Che believed that it must be combatted because it represents reactionary, ridiculous, and sterile thinking.

"And let us develop genuine proletarian internationalism," he said in his "Message to the Tricontinental." "Let the flag under which we fight be the sacred cause of the liberation of humanity, so that to die under the colors of Vietnam, Venezuela, Guatemala, Laos, Guinea, Colombia, Bolivia ... to mention only the current scenes of armed struggle ... will be equally glorious and desirable for a Latin American, an Asian, an African, and even a European.

"Every drop of blood spilled in a land under whose flag one was not born is experience gathered by the survivor to be applied later in the struggle for liberation of one's own country. And every people that liberates itself is a step in the battle for the liberation of one's own people."

In the same way, Che believed fighters from various Latin American countries would participate in the guerrilla detachment, that the guerrilla struggle in Bolivia would be a school in which revolutionaries would serve their apprenticeship in combat. To help him with this task he wanted to have, together with the Bolivians, a small nucleus of experienced guerrilla fighters, nearly all of whom had been his comrades in the Sierra Maestra during the revolutionary struggle in Cuba. These were men whose abilities, courage, and spirit of self-sacrifice Che knew. None of them hesitated to respond to his call, none of them abandoned him, none of them surrendered.

In the Bolivian campaign Che acted with his proverbial tenacity, skill, stoicism, and exemplary attitude. It might be said that he was consumed by the importance of the mission he had assigned himself, and at all times he proceeded with a spirit of irreproachable responsibility. When the guerrilla unit committed a careless mistake, he quickly called attention to it, corrected it, and noted it in his diary.

Unbelievably adverse factors built up against him, such as the separation — supposed to last for just a few days — of part of the guerrilla detachment, a unit that included a courageous group of fighters, some of them sick or convalescent.

Once contact between the two groups was lost in very rough terrain, separation continued, and for endless months Che was preoccupied with the effort to find them. In this period his asthma — an ailment easily treated with simple medication, but one that, lacking the medication, became a terrible enemy — attacked him relentlessly. It became a serious problem, as the medical supplies that had been accumulated by the guerrillas beforehand had been discovered and captured by the enemy. This fact, along with the annihilation at the end of August of the part of the guerrilla detachment he had lost contact with, were factors that weighed considerably in the development of events. But Che, with his iron will, overcame his physical difficulties and never for an instant cut back his activity or let his spirits flag.

Che had many contacts with the Bolivian peasants. Their character — highly suspicious and cautious — would have come as no surprise to Che, who knew their mentality perfectly well because he had dealt with them on other occasions. He knew that winning them over to the cause required long, arduous, and patient work, but he had no doubt that in the long run they would obtain the support of the peasants.

If we follow the thread of events carefully, it becomes clear that even when the number of men on whom Che could count was quite small—in the month of September, a few weeks before his death—the guerrilla unit still retained its capacity to develop. It also still had a few Bolivian cadres, such as the brothers Inti and Coco Peredo, who were already beginning to show magnificent leadership potential.

It was the ambush in La Higuera [on September 26, 1967]— the sole successful action by the army against the detachment led by Che—that created a situation they could not overcome. In that ambush, in broad daylight, the vanguard group was killed and several more men were wounded as they headed for a peasant area with a higher level of political development—an objective that does not appear to have been noted in the diary but which is known through the survivors. It was without doubt dangerous to advance by daylight along the same route they had been following for days, with inevitably close contact with the residents of an area they were entering for the first time. It was certainly obvious that the army would intercept them at some point; but Che, fully conscious of this, decided to run the risk in order to help the doctor [Octavio de la Concepción de la Pedreja (El Médico)], who was in very poor physical condition.

The day before the ambush, he wrote, "We reached Pujio but there were people who had seen us down below the day before, which means we are being announced ahead of time by Radio Bemba [word of mouth] ... Traveling with mules is becoming dangerous, we are trying to make it as easy as possible for El Médico because he is becoming very weak."

The following day he wrote, "At 13:00, the vanguard set out to try to reach Jagüey and to make a decision there about the mules and El Médico." That is, he was seeking a solution for the sick, so as to get off the road and take the necessary precautions. But that same afternoon, before the vanguard reached Jagüey, the fatal ambush occurred, leaving the detachment in an untenable situation.

A few days later, encircled in the El Yuro ravine, Che fought his final battle.

Recalling the feat carried out by this handful of revolutionaries is deeply moving. The struggle against the hostile natural environment in which their action took place constitutes by itself an insuperable page of heroism. Never in history has so small a number of men embarked on such a gigantic task. Their faith and absolute conviction that the immense revolutionary capacity of the peoples of Latin America could be awakened, their confidence in themselves, and the determination with which they took on this objective—these things give us a just measure of these men.

One day Che said to the guerrilla fighters in Bolivia, "This type of struggle gives us the opportunity to become revolutionaries, the highest form of the human species, and it also allows us to emerge fully as men; those who are unable to achieve either of those two states should say so now and abandon the struggle."

Those who fought with him until the end have become worthy of such honored terms; they symbolize the type of revolutionary and the type of person history is now calling on for a truly challenging and difficult task—the revolutionary transformation of Latin America.

The enemy our forebears faced in the first struggle for independence was a decadent colonial power. Revolutionaries have as their enemy today the most powerful bulwark of the imperialist camp, equipped with the most modern technology and industry. This enemy not only organized and equipped a new army for Bolivia — where the people had destroyed the previous repressive military apparatus — and immediately sent weapons and advisers to help in the struggle against the guerrillas. It has also provided military and technical support on the same scale to every repressive force on the continent. And when these methods are not enough, it has intervened directly with its troops, as in the Dominican Republic.

Fighting this enemy requires the type of revolutionaries and individuals Che spoke of. Without this type of revolutionary and human being, ready to do what they did; without the spirit to confront the enormous obstacles they faced; without the readiness to die that accompanied them at every moment; without their deeply held conviction in the justice of their cause and their unyielding faith in the invincible force of the peoples, against a power like Yankee imperialism, whose military, technical, and economic resources are felt throughout the entire world — without these, the liberation of the peoples of this continent will not be attained.

The people of the United States themselves are beginning to become aware that the monstrous political superstructure that reigns in their country has for some time no longer been the idyllic bourgeois republic the country's founders established nearly 200 years ago. They are increasingly subjected to the moral barbarism of an irrational, alienating, dehumanized, and brutal system that takes from the people of the United States a growing number of victims in its wars of aggression, its political crimes, its racial aberrations, the miserable hierarchy it has created among human beings, its repugnant waste of economic, scientific, and human resources on its enormous, reactionary, and repressive military apparatus—in the midst of a world where three-quarters of humanity live in underdevelopment and hunger.

Only the revolutionary transformation of Latin America will enable the people of the United States to settle their own accounts with imperialism. At the same time, and in the same way, the growing struggle of the people of the United States against imperialist policy can become a decisive ally of the revolutionary movement in Latin America.

An enormous differentiation and imbalance occurred in the Americas at the beginning of this century. On one side a powerful and rapidly industrializing nation, in accordance with the very law of its social and economic dynamics, was marching toward imperial heights. On the other side, the weak and stagnant countries in the Balkanized remainder of the Americas were kept under the boot of feudal oligarchies and their reactionary armies. If this part of the hemisphere does not undergo a profound revolutionary transformation, that earlier gap will seem but a pale reflection of not just the enormous present unevenness in finance, science, and technology, but rather of the horrible imbalance that, at an increasingly accelerated rate, the imperialist superstructure will impose on the peoples of Latin America in the next 20 years.

If we stay on this road, we will be increasingly poor, weak, dependent, and enslaved to imperialism. This gloomy perspective also confronts, to an equal degree, all the underdeveloped nations of Africa and Asia. If the industrialized and educated nations of Europe, with their Common Market and supranational scientific institutions, are worried about the possibility of being left behind, and contemplate with fear the perspective of being converted into economic colonies of Yankee imperialism, what does the future have in store for the peoples of Latin America?

This is unquestionably the real situation that decisively affects the destiny of our peoples. What is urgently needed is a deep-going revolutionary transformation that can gather together all the moral, material, and human forces in this part of the world and launch them forward so as to overcome the economic, scientific, and technological backwardness of centuries; a backwardness that is greater still when compared with the industrialized world to which we are tributaries and will continue to be to an even greater degree, especially to the United States. If some liberal or bourgeois reformist, or some pseudorevolutionary charlatan, incapable of action, has a different answer; and if, in addition, that person can provide the formula, the magic road to carrying it out, that is different from Che's conception — one that can sweep away the oligarchs, despots, and petty politicians, that is to say, the servants, and the Yankee monopolists, in other words, the masters, and can do it with all the urgency the circumstances require — then let them stand up to challenge Che.

But no one really has an honest answer or a consistent policy that will bring genuine hope to the nearly 300 million human beings who make up the population of Latin America. Devastatingly poor in their overwhelming majority and increasing in number to 600 million within 25 years, they have the right to the material things of life, to culture, and to civilization. So the most dignified attitude would be to remain silent in face of the action of Che and those who fell with him, courageously defending their ideas. The feat carried out by this handful of guerrila fighters, guided by the noble idea of redeeming a continent, will remain the greatest proof of what determination, heroism, and human greatness can accomplish. It is an example that will illuminate the consciousness and preside over the struggle of the peoples of Latin America. Che's heroic cry will reach the receptive ear of the poor and exploited for whom he gave his life; many hands will come forward to take up arms to win their definitive liberation.

On October 7, Che wrote his last lines. The following day at 1 p.m., in a narrow ravine where he proposed waiting until nightfall in order to break out of the encirclement, a large enemy force made contact with them. The small group of men who now made up the detachment fought heroically until dusk. From individual positions located on the bottom of the ravine, and on the cliffs above, they faced a mass of soldiers who surrounded and attacked them. There were no survivors among those who fought in the positions closest to Che. Since beside him were the doctor in the grave state of health mentioned before, and a Peruvian guerrilla who was also in very poor physical condition, everything seems to indicate that until he fell wounded, Che did his utmost to safeguard the withdrawal of these comrades to a safer place. The doctor was not killed in the same battle, but rather several days later at a place not far from the Quebrada del Yuro [El Yuro ravine]. The ruggedness of the rocky, irregular terrain made it difficult—at times impossible—for the guerrillas to maintain visual contact. Those defending positions at the other entrance to the ravine, some hundreds of meters from Che, among them Inti Peredo, resisted the attack until dark, when they managed to lose the enemy and head toward the previously agreed point of regroupment.

It has been possible to establish that Che continued fighting despite being wounded, until a shot destroyed the barrel of his M-2 rifle, making it totally useless. The pistol he carried had no magazine. These incredible circumstances explain how he could have been captured alive. The wounds in his legs kept him from walking without help, but they were not fatal.

Moved to the town of La Higuera, he remained alive for about 24 hours. He refused to exchange a single word with his captors, and a drunken officer who tried to annoy him received a slap across the face.

At a meeting in La Paz, Barrientos, Ovando, and other top military leaders coldly made the decision to murder Che. Details are known of the way in which the treacherous agreement was carried out in the school at La Higuera. Major Miguel Ayoroa and Colonel Andrés Selich, rangers trained by the Yankees, ordered warrant officer Mario Terán to proceed with the murder. Terán, completely drunk, entered the school yard. When Che, who heard the shots that had just killed a Bolivian [Willy] and a Peruvian guerrilla fighter [Chino], saw the executioner hesitate, he said firmly, "Shoot! Don't be afraid!" Terán left, and again it was necessary for his superiors, Ayoroa and Selich, to repeat the order. He then proceeded to carry it out, firing a machine gun burst at the belt down. A statement had already been released that Che died a few hours after combat; therefore, the executioners had orders not to shoot him in the chest or head, so as not to induce fatal wounds immediately. This cruelly prolonged Che's agony until a sergeant, also drunk, killed him with a pistol shot to the left side of his body. Such a procedure contrasts brutally with the respect shown by Che, without a single exception, toward the lives of the many officers and soldiers of the Bolivian Army he took prisoner.

The final hours of his existence in the hands of his contemptible enemies must have been very bitter for him, but no one was better prepared than Che to be put to such a test.

The way in which the diary came into our hands cannot be told at this time; suffice it to say it required no monetary payment. It contains all the notes he wrote from November 7, 1966, the day Che arrived in Ñacahuazú, until October 7, 1967, the evening before the battle in the El Yuro ravine. There are a few pages missing, pages that have not yet reached our hands; but they correspond to dates on which nothing of any importance happened, and therefore do not alter the content of the diary in any way.[3]

Although the document itself offers not the slightest doubt as to its authenticity, all photocopies have been subjected to a rigorous examination to establish not only their authenticity but also to check on any possible alteration, no matter how slight. The dates were compared with the diary of one of the surviving guerrilla fighters; both documents coincided in every aspect. Detailed testimony of the other surviving guerrilla fighters, who were witnesses to each of the events, also contributed to establishing the document's authenticity. In short, it has been established with absolute certainty that all the photocopies were faithful copies of Che's diary.

---

3. These pages are now incorporated in this edition.

It was a laborious job to decipher the small and difficult handwriting, a task that was carried out with the tireless assistance of his compañera, Aleida March.

The diary will be published almost simultaneously in France by the publishing house of François Maspero; in Italy by Feltrinelli publishers; in the Federal Republic of Germany by Trikont Verlag; in the United States by *Ramparts* magazine; in France, a Spanish edition, by Ediciones Ruedo Ibérico; in Chile by the magazine *Punto Final*; in Mexico by Editorial Siglo XXI; and in other countries.

Hasta la victoria siempre! [Ever onward to victory]

Written for the first authorized edition of Che's The Bolivian Diary
published in July 1968.

The Bolivian Diary

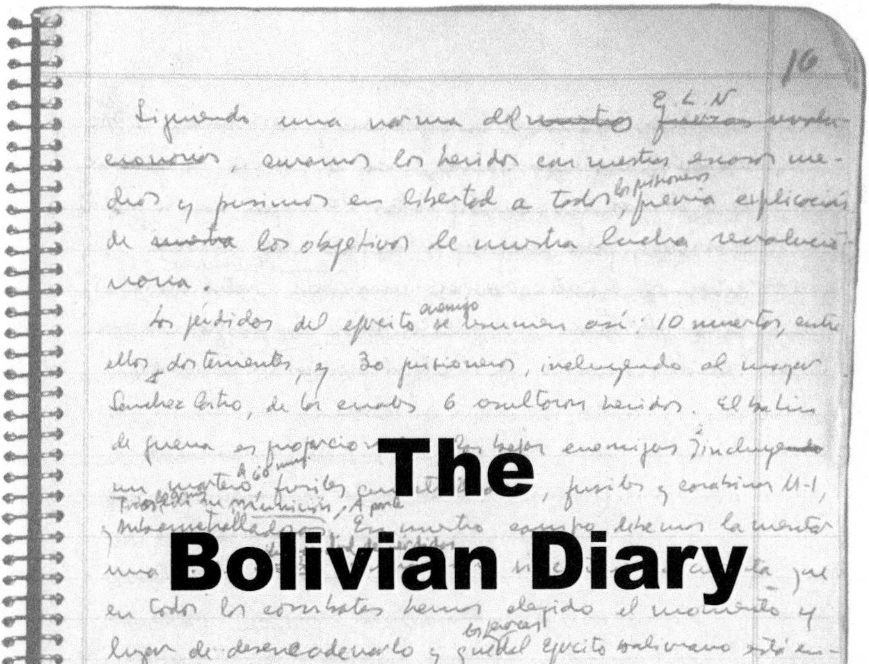

NOVEMBER 1966

November 7

Today begins a new phase. We arrived at the farm at night. The trip went quite well. After we got to Cochabamba, conveniently disguised, Pachungo and I made some contacts and then traveled by jeep for two days, in two vehicles.

As we approached the farm, we stopped and continued in only one vehicle to avoid arousing the suspicion of the neighboring landowner,[1] who is muttering that our business must be devoted to manufacturing cocaine. Oddly enough, the ineffable Tumaini is apparently identified as the chemist of our group. On discovering my identity on the way to the farm during the second trip, Bigotes almost drove into a ditch, leaving the jeep nearly hanging over it. We walked about 20 kilometers, reaching the farm after midnight, where there are three workers from the [Bolivian Communist] party.[2]

Bigotes indicated he was ready to work with us, whatever the party does, but he is loyal to Monje, whom he respects and

---

1. Ciro Algarañaz Leigue was the owner of the Pincal farm, the nearest farm to the area used as the first guerrilla base.
2. This refers to Apolinar Aquino Quispe (Apolinario, Apolinar, or Polo); Serapio Aquino Tudela (Serapio or Serafín); and Antonio Domínguez Flores (Antonio or León).

seems to like. According to him, Rodolfo is similarly disposed, as is Coco, but we should try to get the party to join the struggle. I asked him to help us and to refrain from mentioning anything to the party until the arrival of Monje, who is on a trip to Bulgaria; he agreed to both things.

November 8

We spent the day in the undergrowth by the creek, barely 100 meters from the house. We were pestered by *yaguasas*[3] that were very annoying even though they do not bite. So far, there have been *yaguasas*, *jejéns*,[4] mosquitoes, *mariguís*,[5] and ticks.

Bigotes got his jeep out with the help of Algarañaz and went to buy a few things, such as pigs and chickens.

I was thinking of writing down the latest developments, but I will leave that for next week, when we expect the second group to arrive.

November 9

An uneventful day. With Tumaini, we explored the area following the course of the Ñacahuazú River (in reality, a creek),[6] but we did not find its source. It runs through a steep gully that is apparently mostly deserted. With appropriate discipline, we could be there for some time.

In the afternoon, heavy rain forced us to leave the

---

3. Small insect, similar to a gnat.
4. Insect smaller than a mosquito, but with a more irritating bite.
5. A yellow insect with large wings.
6. Known also as the Ñacaguazu, which has various spellings throughout the diary, including Ñacahuasi, Ñacahuasu, Ñacahuazú, Ñancahuazu, and Ñancahuazú, Ñacahuasú, Ñancahuasú, and Ñacahuaso.

undergrowth and head toward the house. I removed six ticks from my body.

November 10

Pachungo and Pombo went off exploring the area with one of the Bolivian compañeros, Serafín. They went a bit farther than we had and found the fork in the creek, in a little gully that seems to be good. When they returned, they hung around the house and Algarañaz's driver saw them when he brought back the men and the purchases they had made. I blew my top, and we decided to move to the undergrowth tomorrow, where we will make a permanent camp. Tumaini can be seen, because they already know him and they will think he is just another farmhand. Everything is deteriorating rapidly; we have to see if we can at least get our men here. I will be more relaxed when they are here.

November 11

We spent an uneventful day at the new camp, on the other side of the house where we sleep.

The insect plague is a torment, and we have to shelter in our hammocks with mosquito nets (which only I have).

Tumaini went to visit Algarañaz and bought some things from him: chickens and turkeys. It seems he does not have too many suspicions yet.

November 12

A day with nothing new. We explored the area briefly to prepare the land where we will set up our camp when the six from the second group arrive. The place chosen is 100 meters from the clearing, on a rise and close to a hollow where we could dig caves to store food and other things. By now, the first of the three groups from the two divisions of the party should be arriving. At the end of the coming week, they should make it to the farm. My hair is growing, although very sparsely, and the gray hairs are turning blond and beginning to disappear; my beard is returning. In a few months, I will be myself again.

November 13

Sunday. Some hunters went past our place—farmhands working for Algarañaz. They are backwoodsmen, young, single, and ideal recruits, who have an intense hatred for their boss. They told us that by the river eight leagues away, there are houses and some ravines with water. Nothing else of note.

November 14

A week at the camp. Pachungo is unhappy and finding it hard to adapt, but he should get over it soon. Today we began to dig a tunnel to hide anything that might be compromising. We will cover it with sticks and grass to keep it as dry as possible. First, we dug a hole one and a half meters deep, and from there began digging the tunnel.

November 15

We are still working on the tunnel: in the morning Pombo and Pachungo, and in the afternoon Tumaini and me. By the time we stopped working at 6:00, we had already dug two meters. We think we will finish it tomorrow and be able to place everything compromising in there. During the night, the rain forced me out of my hammock, which got wet because the nylon cover is too small. Nothing else worth mentioning.

November 16

The tunnel is finished and camouflaged; now we only have to conceal the path; we will move things to our little house and tomorrow store them away, covering the opening with branches and mud. The diagram of the tunnel, known as No. 1, is in Document I.[7] The rest was uneventful; from tomorrow it is reasonable to expect news from La Paz.

November 17

The tunnel is filled with the articles that could be compromising for those staying in the house, along with some canned food; it is quite well hidden.

Nothing new from La Paz. The lads from the house spoke with Algarañaz, from whom they bought some supplies, and he insisted again that he be included in the cocaine factory.

November 18

No news from La Paz. Pachungo and Pombo went back to explore the creek, but are not convinced that this would be the best place for the camp. On Monday, we will explore the area with Tumaini. Algarañaz came to repair the track used to carry rocks up from the river; he spent quite some time doing this. It

---

7. Not all documents referred to in the diary are included here.

seems he is not suspicious about our presence here. Everything continues monotonously; the mosquito and tick bites are getting infected and turning into bothersome sores. It is starting to get a little chilly in the early morning.

November 19

No news from La Paz. No news here; we spent Saturday lying low, as it is the day the hunters are around.

November 20

Marcos and Rolando arrived at noon. Now we are six. Immediately, they began to tell us stories from their trip; they were late because they received our message a week ago. They still came faster than anyone else, via São Paulo. We do not expect the other four to arrive before next week.

Rodolfo came too and made a good impression on me. Apparently he is even more willing than Bigotes to break completely from everything. Papi had told both him and Coco that I was here, violating instructions; it seems to have been a case of jealousy of authority. I wrote to Manila[8] with some recommendations (Documents I and II), and to Papi, answering his questions. Rodolfo went back at dawn.

November 21

First day of the expanded group. It rained heavily, and we were drenched as we moved to our new location. We are now settled. The tent turned out to be a canvas tarp used for trucks;

---

8. Code used to refer to Cuba.

it leaks, but gives some protection. We have hammocks with nylon covers. More weapons have arrived; Marcos has a Garand, and Rolando will be given an M-1 from the cache. Jorge stayed with us, but in the house; he is directing the work there to improve the farm. I asked Rodolfo for an agronomist who can be trusted. We will try to keep up this front for as long as possible.

November 22

Tuma, Jorge, and I walked along the river (Ñacahuazú) to inspect the creek we had discovered. The river was unrecognizable after the rain from the day before, and it took a lot of effort to get to where we wanted — a little rivulet that is concealed just where it meets the river. With proper preparation, it could be a permanent camp. We returned just after 9:00. Nothing new here.

November 23

We set up a lookout from where we can watch the little house at the farm so that we will be alerted if there is an inspection or some unwelcome visitor. As two men left to scout the area, the rest of us did three hours' sentry duty. Pombo and Marcos explored the terrain extending from our camp to the creek, which is still flooded.

November 24

Pacho and Rolando left to explore the creek; they should be back tomorrow.

At night, two of Algarañaz's farmhands stopped by while "taking a walk." It was an unusual visit. Nothing strange happened, but Antonio was still out exploring, as was Tuma, who officially lives at the house. Reason given: hunting.

Aliucha's[9] birthday.

November 25

News came from the lookout that a jeep with two or three passengers was approaching. They turned out to be part of an antimalaria campaign and left immediately after taking blood samples. Pacho and Rolando came back very late at night. They had found the creek that was on the map; they had also followed the river until they found some abandoned fields.

November 26

Because it was Saturday, we all stayed in our quarters. I asked Jorge to explore the riverbed on horseback to see how far it went; the horse was not around, so he went on foot to ask Don Remberto[10] for one of his (20 to 25 kilometers away). By nightfall he had still not returned. No news from La Paz.

November 27

Jorge still has not returned. I gave the order to maintain a watch all night, but at 9:00 the first jeep arrived from La Paz. Coco brought Joaquín, Urbano, and Ernesto, a Bolivian medical student who will stay with us. Coco left and returned later with Ricardo, Braulio, and Miguel, and another Bolivian, Inti, who also will stay. There are now 12 insurgents, with

---

9. Aleida Guevara March, his second daughter.
10. Don Remberto Villa, owner of the Ñacahuazú farm, who sold it to Roberto Peredo (Coco).

Jorge acting as owner; Coco and Rodolfo will be in charge of making contacts. Ricardo brought an unfortunate message: Chino is in Bolivia and wants to send 20 men and come to see me. This is inadvisable because it would internationalize the struggle before we can count on Estanislao's support. We agreed that Chino could go to Santa Cruz where Coco would pick him up to bring him here. Coco left at dawn with Ricardo, who took the other jeep to carry on to La Paz. Coco will go by Remberto's place to see what happened with Jorge. During my first conversation with Inti, he told me he did not think that Estanislao would join the struggle, but Inti himself seemed determined to cut ties.

November 28

In the morning Jorge had still not shown up, and Coco had not come back either. Later they returned; all that had happened was that he had stayed with Remberto.

Rather irresponsible. In the afternoon, I met with the Bolivian group to discuss the Peruvian offer to send 20 men; everyone agreed they should be sent, but after the action had begun.

November 29

We went to check out the river and to explore the creek that will be the site of our next camp. Tumaini, Urbano, Inti, and I made up the group. The creek is quite safe, but very muddy. We will try to look for another one that is an hour away. Tumaini had a fall and apparently fractured his ankle. We reached the camp at night, after taking some measurements at the river. No news here; Coco left for Santa Cruz to wait for Chino.

November 30

Marcos, Pacho, Miguel, and Pombo set off with instructions to explore a creek farther away; they should be gone for two days. Heavy rains. Nothing new at the house.

Analysis of the month

Everything has gone quite well; my arrival was without incident; half the troops have arrived, also without incident, although they were somewhat delayed; Ricardo's main collaborators are joining the struggle, come what may. The general outlook seems good in this remote region and everything indicates that we could be here for practically as long as necessary. The plans are: to wait for the rest of the troops, increase the number of Bolivians to at least 20, and then commence operations. We still need to see how Monje reacts and how Guevara's people conduct themselves.

DECEMBER 1966

December 1

The day passed uneventfully. Marcos and his compañeros returned at night, their trip having lasted longer than it should have, roaming around the hills. At 2:00, I was told that Coco arrived with a compañero;[1] I will leave it for tomorrow.

December 2

Chino arrived early, quite effusive. We spent the day chatting. The substance is: he will go to Cuba to inform them in person of the situation, and that five Peruvians can join us in two months, after we see some action. Two will come now to stay for a while: a radio technician and a doctor. Chino asked for weapons and I agreed to give him a BZ, some Mausers, and grenades; and I will purchase an M-1 for them. I also decided to assist them in sending five Peruvians, who would establish the necessary connections for sending arms to a region near Puno, on the other side of the Titicaca. He told me about his troubles in Peru, including a daring plan to free Calixto,[2] which seems unrealistic to me. He thinks that some survivors of the guerrilla

---

1. Aniceto Reinaga Gordillo (Aniceto).
2. A reference to Héctor Béjar Rivera, the leader of the National Liberation Army (ELN) in Peru who had been arrested and imprisoned.

movement are active in that area, but he is not certain because no one has been able to make it there to see.

The rest of the conversation was anecdotes. He said goodbye with the same enthusiasm he had when he arrived; he took some of our photos with him to La Paz. Coco has been instructed to organize the contacts with Sánchez[3] (whom I will see later) and to contact the head of the president's information office, who is Inti's brother-in-law and who has offered to help. The network is still in its infancy.

December 3

Uneventful. There were no scouting expeditions because it is Saturday. The three farmhands went to Lagunillas to run errands.

December 4

Uneventful. Everyone is quiet since it is Sunday. I give a little talk about our approach to the Bolivians who will be coming and about the war.

December 5

Uneventful. We were thinking of going out, but the day was a washout. There was a minor false alarm when Loro fired a few shots without warning.

December 6

We set out to begin work on the second cave at the first creek.

---

3. A reference to Peruvian journalist Julio Dagnino Pacheco who served in La Paz as a liaison for the National Liberation Army of Peru.

This was Apolinar, Inti, Urbano, Miguel, and me. Miguel came to replace Tuma, who has still not recovered from his fall. Apolinar has requested to join the guerrilla unit, but first he wants to straighten out some things in La Paz; I told him it was ok, but that he should wait a while. Around 11:00 we got to the creek, we made a camouflaged path, and searched for a suitable place for the cave; but it is all rock and the creek dries up at one point, continuing through steep banks of solid rock. We gave up the exploration until tomorrow; Inti and Urbano went off to hunt deer because our food supply is very limited and has to last until Friday.

December 7

Miguel and Apolinar found a suitable place and devoted themselves to digging the tunnel, but the tools are inadequate. Inti and Urbano returned empty-handed, but at nightfall Urbano shot a turkey with an M-1. As we already had food prepared, we have left it for tomorrow's breakfast. Today, in fact, completes our first month here, but for the sake of convenience I will give the summaries at the end of each month.

December 8

With Inti, we went to a ridge that overlooks the creek. Miguel and Urbano continued digging the shaft. In the afternoon, Apolinar relieved Miguel. Nightfall brought Marcos, Pombo, and Pacho, who was falling behind and very tired. Marcos asked me if I could remove him from the vanguard if he did not improve. I marked down the path to the cave that is drawn in Diagram No. 2. I left them with the most important tasks to perform during their stay. Miguel will stay with them and we will return tomorrow.

December 9

We came back slowly in the morning, arriving close to 12:00. Pacho was given orders to stay behind when the group returns. We tried to make contact with Camp 2, but failed. There is no other news.

December 10

The day passed uneventfully, except for the first batch of bread baked in the house. I spoke with Jorge and Inti about some urgent tasks. No news from La Paz.

December 11

The day passed uneventfully, but at night Coco turned up with Papi. He brought Alejandro, Arturo, and Carlos, a Bolivian. As usual, the other jeep remained on the road. Later they brought the doctor, Moro; Benigno; and two Bolivians, both *Cambas*[4] from the Caranavi farm.[5] We spent the night engaged in the usual conversation about the trip and talked about the absence of Antonio and Félix, who should have been here by now. A discussion with Papi led to the decision that he should make two more trips to bring Renán and Tania. We will dispose of the [safe] houses and empty the caches to give $1,000 to Sánchez,

---

4. Orlando Jiménez Bazán (Camba) and Julio Méndez Korne (Ñato). The term *Cambas* refers to the indigenous people of the eastern region of Bolivia.
5. The farm belonged to the guerrillas and was located in the Caranavi area of the Nor Yungas province, state of La Paz.

who will keep the van. We will sell a jeep to Tania and keep the other one. We need to make an arms run; I gave the order that everything be transported in one jeep to avoid switching from one to another and being spotted doing so. Chino left for Cuba, apparently very enthusiastic, and wants to return here when he comes back. Coco stayed to get food in Camiri, and Papi left for La Paz. A dangerous incident occurred: the Vallegrandino,[6] a hunter, discovered some footprints; he saw our tracks, apparently spotted one of us, and found a glove Pombo had dropped. This changes our plans and we should be more careful. The Vallegrandino will go off tomorrow with Antonio to show him where he sets his traps to catch tapirs. Inti let me know his reservations about the student Carlos, who began to talk about Cuba's participation as soon as he arrived, and he had already said he would not take up arms if the party did not participate. Inti said that Rodolfo had sent him here, but that there had been a misunderstanding.

December 12

I spoke to the whole group, taking them to task about the reality of war. I emphasized the importance of a united command and discipline, and I warned the Bolivians of the responsibility they would bear in violating the discipline of the party's line by adopting another one. I made the following assignments: Joaquín as military second in command; Rolando and Inti as political commissars; Alejandro as head of operations; Pombo, services; Inti, finances; Ñato, provisions and armaments; and Moro, medical services, for the moment.

---

6. Tomás Rosales, from Vallegrande, Bolivia.

Rolando and Braulio went off to tell the group either to stay put while waiting until the Vallegrandino had set his traps, or to go exploring with Antonio. At night they returned; the traps are not too far from here. They got the Vallegrandino drunk, and he was very happy with a bottle of *singani*[7] inside of him when he left for the night. Coco returned from Caranavi where he had bought the necessary food, but some people from Lagunillas saw him and were surprised by the quantity he had purchased.

Later on, Marcos arrived with Pombo. Marcos had a gash above his eyebrow received while cutting a stick; he was given two stitches.

December 13

Joaquín, Carlos, and El Médico [Ernesto] left to meet up with Rolando and Braulio. Pombo went with them but with instructions to return today. I gave the order to cover the path and to make another that, branching off from the first, will end at the river. This tactic was so successful that when Pombo, Miguel, and Pacho tried to return, they got lost.

I spoke with Apolinar, who will go to his house in Viacha for a few days, giving him money for his family and advising him to maintain absolute secrecy. Coco departed at nightfall, but three hours later the alarm was sounded when whistles, noises, and a dog barking were heard — it turned out to be him, lost in the woods.

---

7. Clear brandy made from grapes.

December 14

An uneventful day. The Vallegrandino came by the house to check his traps, which he had set yesterday, contrary to what he had said before. Antonio was shown the path we had cleared in the woods so he could take the Vallegrandino that way in order to avoid suspicion.

December 15

Nothing new. Preparations were made to leave (eight men) and to move permanently to Camp 2.[8]

December 16

Pombo, Urbano, Tuma, Alejandro, Moro, Arturo, Inti, and I started out in the morning, heavily loaded down; it took us three hours to get there.

Rolando stayed with us, and Joaquín, Braulio, Carlos, and El Médico[9] returned. Carlos has shown himself to be a good hiker and a good worker. Moro and Tuma discovered a cave by the river with very large fish in it; they caught 17, plenty for a good meal. Moro hurt his hand on a catfish. We looked for a place to dig the second cave, as we have finished the first one, and then stopped work until tomorrow. Moro and Inti tried to hunt tapir by spending the night lying in wait.

December 17

Moro and Inti only caught a turkey. We—Tuma, Rolando,

8. Although this appears indistinctly with Arabic and Roman numerals, it refers to the same camp.
9. Freddy Maymura Hurtado (Ernesto).

and I—devoted ourselves to digging the second cave, which should be ready by tomorrow. Arturo and Pombo searched for a place to position the radio and then worked on clearing the access path, which is pretty rough. At night it began to rain and continued until the morning.

December 18

It rained all day but we still worked on the cave, which needs only a little more digging to be two and a half meters deep. We inspected a hill to find a place to install the radio. It seems good enough, but the tests will tell.

December 19

Today was also rainy, so a hike not appealing; at about 1:00 Braulio and Ñato arrived with the news that the river could be crossed even though it was deep. As we were leaving, we ran into Marcos and his vanguard, who had come to establish themselves. He will remain in command, and was ordered to send over three to five men, if he could. We completed the hike in just over three hours.

At 12:00 tonight, Ricardo and Coco arrived bringing Antonio and Rubio (they could not get tickets last Thursday) and Apolinar, who has come to stay with us permanently. In addition, Iván came along to discuss a range of matters.

We stayed up practically all night.

December 20

We continued to discuss various points and were organizing everything when a group led by Alejandro turned up from Camp 2. They said that on a path near the camp a deer had been shot and a string had been tied on its leg. Joaquín had passed by there an hour earlier but had not mentioned anything. We presumed that the Vallegrandino had taken it there, and then for some unknown reason, left it and ran off. A guard was posted at the rear and two men were stationed to catch the hunter if he came by. Later we learned that the deer had been dead for quite some time and was full of worms, and when Joaquín returned, he confirmed that he had seen it. Coco and Loro took the Vallegrandino to the little animal where he verified that he had wounded it several days before. The matter was thus settled.

We resolved to speed up communication with our Information Office contact, whom Coco had neglected, and to ask Megía to serve as a liaison between Iván and our Information contact. He will maintain communication with Megía, Sánchez, Tania, and someone from the party who has not yet been chosen. This may be someone from Villamontes, but this has not yet been finalized. A telegram came from Manila indicating that Monje will be coming from the south.

They set up a contact system, but I was not satisfied because it shows how truly suspicious of Monje his compañeros are.

At 1:00 in the morning La Paz will inform us if they have gone to collect Monje.

Iván has the opportunity to do some business but his poorly forged passport is preventing him; the next step is to improve the document and write to our friends in Manila to expedite it.

Tania will come soon to receive instructions; I will probably send her to Buenos Aires.

It is definitely decided that Ricardo, Iván, and Coco will leave Camiri by plane and the jeep will stay here. When they return, they will call Lagunillas to tell them they have arrived. Jorge will go at night to check for any news and will pick them up when they come. At 1:00, we could not get a signal from La Paz. They left for Camiri at daybreak.

December 21

Loro did not leave me the maps that the scout had made, so I was left without knowing what type of road there is to Yuqui. We started out in the morning and made our way without any setbacks. We will try to have everyone here for the 24th, the day we plan to have a party.

We crossed paths with Pacho, Miguel, Benigno, and Camba who were in charge of carrying the equipment. At 5:00 in the afternoon, Pacho and Camba returned without the equipment, which they had left hidden in the woods because it was so heavy. Five men from here will go tomorrow to retrieve it. The supply cave has been completed; tomorrow we will start one for the radio.

December 22

We started work on the cave for the radio operator. At first, we had a lot of success with loose dirt, but then we hit a slab of rock we could not break through.

They brought the equipment, which is very heavy, but we have not been able to try it yet because we have no gasoline. Loro said that he had not sent maps as the report had been verbal, but he will come tomorrow to present it.

December 23

We left with Pombo and Alejandro to explore terrain to the left. We have to clear it, but it gives the impression of being an easy walk. Joaquín arrived with two compañeros, explaining that Loro did not come because a pig had escaped and he went to find it.

There is no news of the Lagunillero's[10] trip.

In the afternoon, the pig arrived, quite a large one, but we still need to organize the drinks. Loro is incapable of even managing these things; he seems very disorganized.

December 24

The day was devoted to the Christmas Eve celebration. There were people who had to take two trips and arrived late, but at last we were all together and had a good time, with some people getting a bit drunk. Loro told me that the Lagunillero's trip was not fruitful and resulted in only a few minor notes that were very imprecise.

December 25

Back at work; there were no trips to the first camp, which has been baptized C26 at the suggestion of the Bolivian doctor. Marcos, Benigno, and Camba set off to make a path along the ridge to our right. They returned in the afternoon with the news that they had sighted a sort of barren pampa a two-hour walk away; tomorrow they will take a closer look. Camba came back with a fever. Miguel and Pacho made some diversionary

---

10. Mario Chávez.

paths on the left bank and an access track to the radio cave. Inti, Antonio, Tuma, and I continued working on the radio cave, but it is very difficult because we keep running into solid rock. The rear guard is in charge of setting up the camp and finding a lookout point to observe access areas on both sides of the river; the location is very good.

December 26

Inti and Carlos went off to explore up to the point called Yuqui on the map; the trip should take two days. Rolando, Alejandro, and Pombo are still working on the cave, which is extremely difficult. Pacho and I left to inspect the paths cleared by Miguel, as it is useless to continue with the one on the ridge. The access path to the cave is very good and difficult to find. Two snakes were killed, plus another one yesterday; apparently there are quite a lot. Tuma, Arturo, Rubio, and Antonio went hunting while Braulio and Ñato did guard duty at the other camp. They came back with the news that Loro had flipped the jeep over; they also had a note announcing the arrival of Monje. Marcos, Miguel, and Benigno went to work on the path on the ridge, but did not return all night.

December 27

We set off with Tuma to try to find Marcos; walking for two and a half hours before reaching the edge of a ravine that descended to the west on the left side. We followed his tracks from there, climbing down steep rocky slopes. I thought we could get back to the camp this way, but hours passed and it was still not in sight. After five in the afternoon, we reached the Ñacahuazú, about five kilometers below Camp 1; at 7:00 we got to the camp. There we found out that Marcos had spent last night there. I did not send any messenger as I presumed that Marcos would have told them about my possible route. We saw the jeep, quite a wreck. Loro had gone to Camiri to get some spare parts. According to Ñato, he fell asleep at the wheel.

December 28

Just as we were leaving for the camp, Urbano and Antonio arrived looking for me. Marcos had gone with Miguel to clear a path along the ridges to the camp and had not yet returned; Benigno and Pombo had gone looking for me on the same track we had taken. When I got to the camp, I found Marcos and Miguel, who had slept on the ridge as they could not make it to the camp. The former complained about the way I had been treated. Apparently, the complaint was about Joaquín, Alejandro, and El Médico [Moro]. Inti and Carlos had returned without finding any inhabited houses, only an abandoned one that presumably is not the point marked as Yaki on the map.

December 29

With Marcos, Miguel, and Alejandro, we went to the barren hill to get a better idea of the situation. It seems to be where the Pampa del Tigre begins, a range of barren hills of the same height, located at an altitude of about 1,500 meters. We should forget about the terrain to the left because it arcs toward the Ñacahuazú. We climbed down and reached the camp within an hour and 20 minutes. Eight men were sent to get supplies, but they could not carry everything back. Rubio and El Médico [Ernesto] relieved Braulio and Ñato. Braulio had cleared a new path before he came back; the track leads from the river along some rocks and enters the woods on the other side through some other rocks, so no footprints are left. No work was done on the cave. Loro left for Camiri.

December 30

Despite the rainfall that had caused the river to rise, four men went to clear out everything from Camp 1, which is now empty. There is no news from the outside. Six men went to the cave and in two trips stored away everything that belongs there.

The oven could not be finished because the clay is too soft.

December 31

At 7:30 El Médico [Ernesto] arrived with the news that Monje was there. I went to meet him with Inti, Tuma, Urbano, and Arturo. The reception was cordial, but tense; the obvious question, what are you here for? hung in the air. He was accompanied by Pan Divino, the new recruit, Tania, who came to receive instructions, and Ricardo, who will now stay with us.

The conversation with Monje began with generalities but came down to his fundamental position, summarized by three basic conditions:

1) He will resign from the leadership of the party, but he will at least ensure it remains neutral and he will recruit cadres for the struggle.
2) He will head the political-military struggle for as long as the revolution is taking place in Bolivian territory.
3) He will handle relations with other South American parties, and try to convince them to support liberation movements. (He used Douglas Bravo as an example.)

I responded, saying that the first point was up to him, as secretary of the party, although I considered his position to be a grave error.

It was vacillating and compromising and protected those who should be condemned by history for abandoning their principles. Time will prove me right.

Concerning the third point, I had no objections to his attempting this, but it was doomed to fail. To ask Codovila to support Douglas Bravo was like asking him to condone an uprising in his own party. Time will be the judge here too.

On the second point, there was no way I could accept his proposal. I had to be military chief and would not accept any ambiguity on this. Here the discussion got stuck and went around and around in a vicious circle.

We left it that Monje would think it over and talk to his Bolivian compañeros. We moved on to the new camp and there he spoke with everyone, presenting the ultimatum that they could either stay or support the party; everyone opted to stay, which he seemed to take quite hard.

At 12:00, we made a toast, pointing out the historical importance of this date. I replied, taking advantage of his words and marking this moment as the new Cry of Murillo[11] of the revolution on this continent, saying that our lives meant nothing when faced with the fact of the revolution.

Fidel sent me the attached messages.

---

11. Pedro Domingo Murillo was a Bolivian patriot who led the first struggle for independence from Spain in 1809.

Analysis of the month

The team of Cubans has been successfully completed; morale is good and there are only minor problems. The Bolivians are doing well, although few in number. Monje's attitude can delay the development on the one hand, but on the other, can free me from political constraints. Apart from waiting for more Bolivians, the next steps are to speak with Guevara and with the Argentines Mauricio and Jozami (Masetti and the dissident party).

JANUARY 1967

January 1

In the morning, with no further discussion, Monje informed me that he was leaving and would present his resignation to the party leadership on January 8. According to him, his mission was over. He left looking like he was being led away to the gallows. My impression was that when Coco told him that I would not budge on strategic matters, he held onto this point to force the break, because his arguments are inconsistent.

In the afternoon, I brought everyone together to explain Monje's position and to announce that we would unite with all those who want to make the revolution happen. I predicted difficult times ahead and days of moral anguish for the Bolivians, and that we would try to solve problems through collective discussions or through the commissars.

I worked out the details of Tania's trip to Argentina to speak with Mauricio and Jozami and to bring them back. I worked out Sánchez's tasks with him and resolved to leave Rodolfo, Loyola, and Humberto in La Paz for now. Loyola's sister[1] will stay in Camiri and Calvimonte[2] in Santa Cruz. Mito[3] will

---

1. Vicenta Guzmán Lara.
2. This refers to a member of the Bolivian Communist Party.
3. A Peruvian revolutionary whose identity has not been revealed.

travel through the Sucre region to see where he might establish himself. Loyola will take charge of the finances and has been sent 80,000 pesos, 20,000 of which will go toward a truck that Calvimonte will buy. Sánchez will contact Guevara to have a meeting with him. Coco will go to Santa Cruz to meet with Carlos's brother[4] and put him in charge of receiving the three who will come from Havana. I wrote Fidel the message that is in Document CZO II.

January 2

We spent the morning encoding the letter. The others (Sánchez, Coco, and Tania) left in the afternoon when Fidel's speech was over. He talked about us in a way that makes us feel even more committed, if that is possible.

In the camp we worked only on the cave. The rest went to retrieve things from the first camp. Marcos, Miguel, and Benigno left to scout out the north; Inti and Carlos went to explore the Ñacahuazú until they ran into people (presumably in Yuqui); Joaquín and El Médico [Moro] will scout the Yaqui River up to its source or until they encounter people. They all have a maximum of five days.

The men arrived back from the camp with the news that Loro had not returned after dropping off Monje.

January 3

We worked on making a roof for the cave, but did not finish it. We will do it tomorrow. Only two men went to pick up a load and they brought back the news that everyone had left

---

4. Olga Vaca Marchetti, Carlos's sister.

last night. The rest of the compañeros devoted themselves to making the roof for the kitchen, which is ready now.

January 4

A day without major news; people went to get supplies. We finished the roof of the cave for the radio operator. We postponed target practice because of rain.

January 5

We continued transporting supplies. Several trips still have to be made. The cave was finished with all its additions (including a smaller cave for the generator). We tested the rear guard's rifles and some of those belonging to the center group; all are good except for Apolinario's rifle. The scouting parties have all returned. Inti and Carlos walked along the Ñacahuazú until they came across some people; they found several houses, among them those belonging to two landowners of medium-sized plots, one of whom has 150 cows and lives in Lagunillas. There is a small village called Iti from where there is a road from La Herradura to Lagunillas. From there they went to Ticucha, connected by a truck route to Vaca Guzmán. They returned by a trail that goes as far as the Iquira River, the one we call Yaqui. The point called Yuqui is a cattle ranch close to this camp, abandoned by its inhabitants because of an epidemic among the livestock. Joaquín and El Médico [Moro] followed the Iquira until they came to an impassable cliff; they did not meet anyone but saw tracks. Marcos, Miguel, and Benigno continued along the ridges until they reached an inaccessible point, cut off by a cliff.

We have a new recruit: a little turkey hen caught by Inti.

January 6

In the morning, Marcos, Joaquín, Alejandro, Inti, and I went along the bare ridge. At that point, I decided the following: Marcos, with Camba and Pacho, would try to reach the Ñacahuazú from the right, avoiding people; Miguel, with Braulio and Aniceto, would look for a way across the ridge to clear a main path; and Joaquín, with Benigno and Inti, would search for a track to the Frías River, which, according to the map, runs parallel to the Ñacahuazú, on the other side of the terrain that must be the Pampa del Tigre.

In the afternoon Loro arrived with two mules that he had bought for 2,000 pesos; a good buy as the animals are tame and strong. Braulio and Pacho were sent for so that they can leave tomorrow; Carlos and El Médico [Ernesto] will relieve them.

After the class, I launched into a little tirade about the qualities required of a guerrilla force and the need for greater discipline; I explained that our mission, above all else, was to become a model nucleus, one of steel. I explained the importance of study as indispensable for the future. Then I met with those who held responsibilities: Joaquín, Marcos, Alejandro, Inti, Rolando, Pombo, El Médico [Moro], Ñato, and Ricardo, explaining why I had chosen Joaquín as second in command, pointing out some of Marcos's repeated errors. I criticized Joaquín's attitude during the incident with Miguel on New Year's and I explained some of the tasks we needed to accomplish to improve our organization. At the end, Ricardo told me of an incident with Iván, where in the presence of Tania, they had insulted each other and Ricardo had ordered Iván out of the jeep. These disagreeable incidents between compañeros are hurting our work.

January 7

The scouts departed. The *góndola*[5] consisted of only Alejandro and Ñato; the rest devoted themselves to tasks within the camp; the generator was installed along with all of Arturo's things; a small additional roof was made for the cave and a water supply was fixed up by making a little bridge across the creek.

January 8

Sunday. With eight people on the *góndola*, almost everything was brought over. Loro announced a trip to Santa Cruz that was not planned, apparently to find harnesses for the mules. There were no classes or activities of any kind. It was my turn for guard duty outside, in very inclement weather.

January 9

It rained; everything is wet. The flooded river is impassable, so we were unable to relieve the sentries at the old camp.

No other news today.

January 10

We changed the regular sentries at the old camp; Rubio and Apolinar relieved Carlos and El Médico [Ernesto]. The river is still flooded, but is going down. Loro went to Santa Cruz and has not returned.

With El Médico (Moro), Tuma, and Antonio, who is to stay in charge of the camp, I climbed up to the Pampa del Tigre,

---

5. The term *góndola* is often used in Bolivia for buses and other means of public transportation. The guerrilla movement used the term to refer to trips on which provisions were brought back to the camps.

where I explained to Antonio his tasks for tomorrow, including the exploration of what could possibly be a creek located to the west of our camp. From there we looked for a junction with Marcos's old path, which we found with relative ease. At nightfall six of the scouts arrived: Miguel, with Braulio and Aniceto; Joaquín, with Benigno and Inti. Miguel and Braulio discovered a tributary to the river that cuts across the ridge and came across another one that could be the Ñacahuazú. Joaquín went down to the river that we think is the Frías and followed it for a while. It seems to be the same river that the other group followed, which tells us that our maps are very bad because they show the two rivers divided by a chain of hills and then flowing separately into the Río Grande. Marcos still has not returned.

A message arrived from Havana, announcing that Chino leaves on the 12th with the doctor, and the radio technician; Rhea[6] will leave on the 14th. It does not mention our two remaining compañeros.

January 11

Antonio left with Carlos and Arturo to explore the adjacent creek; he returned at night with the only concrete news that the creek fed into the Ñacahuazú in front of the cattle ranch where we hunt. Alejandro and Pombo devoted themselves to the preparation of maps in Arturo's cave. When they returned, they told me that my books had become wet, and some of them were ruined, and that the radio equipment was wet and

---

6. Humberto Rhea Clavijo, a Bolivian doctor who collaborated with the guerrillas.

had rusted. On top of this, the two radios were broken—a sad reflection on Arturo's competence.

Marcos arrived during the night; he had followed the Ñacahuazú a long way downstream and still never reached where it joins with the supposed Frías. I am not at all sure about these maps, or about the identity of this last waterway.

We began the study of Quechua,[7] led by Aniceto and Pedro.

Day of the *boro*.[8] Fly larvae were removed from Marcos, Carlos, Pombo, Antonio, Moro, and Joaquín.

January 12

The *góndola* was sent to retrieve the last items. Loro still has not returned. We did some practice exercises, climbing the hills by our creek, but it took us more than two hours to go up the sides and only seven minutes up through the center; that is the place to set up our defense.

Joaquín told me that Marcos's feelings were hurt during the meeting the other day when I mentioned the mistakes he had made. I should talk with him.

January 13

I spoke with Marcos; his complaint was that I had criticized him in front of the Bolivians. His argument had no basis; however, his emotional state deserves attention; the rest was unimportant.

He made reference to some disparaging remarks Alejandro

---

7. Quechua is the native language widely spoken in Bolivia, especially in the territory of the ancient Inca empire.
8. A fly that deposits its larva under the skin when it bites.

had made about him. We cleared this up with Alejandro, and apparently the comments were simply idle gossip. Marcos calmed down a bit.

Inti and Moro went off hunting but caught nothing. Some teams left to work on a cave in a place the mules can get to, but this did not work and we decided to build a little sunken hut instead. Alejandro and Pombo studied the defense of the entrance and marked the area for trenches; tomorrow they will continue the task.

Rubio and Apolinar returned and Braulio and Pedro went to the old camp. No news of Loro.

January 14

Marcos, with all the members of his vanguard, except Benigno, went downstream to build the hut; they were going to come back at night, but returned at noon due to rain, without finishing the hut.

Joaquín led a group that began digging trenches. Moro, Inti, Urbano, and I left to clear a path around the edge of our position along the terrain to the right of the creek, but we went the wrong way and had to pass along quite dangerous cliffs. At noon it began to rain and we suspended all activities.

No news of Loro.

January 15

I stayed at the camp, drawing up some instructions for the cadres in the city. Because it was Sunday, we worked only half a day. Marcos and the vanguard worked on the hut, and the rear guard and the center group dug the trenches. Ricardo, Urbano, and Antonio tried to improve the trail we started yesterday but failed because there is a large rock face between the ridge and the hill beside the river.

No trip was made to the old camp.

January 16

Work continued on the trenches that are still not finished. Marcos almost completed his work, making a great little hut. El Médico [Ernesto] and Carlos relieved Braulio and Pedro, who brought news that Loro had arrived with mules, but he never showed up, although Aniceto went to meet him.

Alejandro is showing signs of malaria.

January 17

Not much activity today. The frontline trenches and the hut were finished.

Loro came to report on his trip; when I asked him why he had gone, he answered that he thought it was understood that he would go, although he confessed that he was visiting a woman there; he brought the harnesses for the mules, but could not make them cross the river.

No news of Coco; it is becoming quite alarming.

January 18

The day started out cloudy, so I did not inspect the trenches. Urbano, Ñato, El Médico (Moro), Inti, Aniceto, and Braulio left on the *góndola*. Alejandro did not work because he felt unwell.

A while later, it began to rain heavily. Loro came through the downpour to tell me Algarañaz had spoken with Antonio, saying he was skilled in many things and offering to collaborate with us, with cocaine or whatever. This shows that he now suspects there is something more going on. I gave instructions to Loro to make a commitment to him, without offering too much—only payment for what he brings in his jeep—and to threaten to kill him if he betrays us. Due to the heavy downpour, Loro set out immediately to avoid being cut off by the river.

The *góndola* had not arrived by 8:00, so I gave them the go-ahead to eat the rations of those absent, and the food was devoured. A few minutes later, Braulio and Ñato arrived, reporting that the flooding had surprised them on the road; they had all tried to continue but Inti had fallen in the water, losing his rifle and getting bruised. The others decided to spend the night there, while the two returned with some difficulty.

January 19

The day began routinely, working on the defenses and improving the camp. Miguel came down with a high fever and has all the symptoms of malaria. I felt like I was coming down with something, but nothing developed.

At 8:00 in the morning the four stragglers showed up, bringing a good supply of *choclos*[9]; they had spent the night huddled around a fire. We will wait for the river to go down before trying to recover the rifle.

Close to 4:00 in the afternoon, when Rubio and Pedro had already gone to relieve the pair of guards at the other camp, El Médico [Ernesto] showed up saying that there were police officers there. Lieutenant Fernández[10] and four police officers in civilian clothes had arrived in a rented jeep, looking for

---

9. *Choclos* are baby corn.
10. Carlos Fernández González, a Bolivian police officer.

the cocaine factory. They only searched the house and some unusual things caught their attention, such as the carbide for our lamps that we had not yet taken to the cave. They confiscated Loro's pistol but left him the Mauser and the .22; they made a big fuss about taking a .22 from Algarañaz, which they showed to Loro. They left after warning that they knew everything and that we had better take them into account. Loro could reclaim the pistol in Camiri, said Lieutenant Fernández, "if he did not make a fuss and came to talk to me." He asked about the "Brazilian." Loro was told not to get too friendly with the Vallegrandino and Algarañaz, who are probably the spies and the ones who tipped them off. He went to Camiri under the pretext of getting his pistol back, but in reality he was trying to connect with Coco (I doubt that he is at liberty). He should keep to the woods as much as possible.

January 20

I inspected the positions and gave orders to carry out the defense plan that had been explained the night before, a plan based on a quick defense of the area bordering the river. This area can also be used as a base for a counterattack by the vanguard group, along the paths that run parallel to the river and that lead to the rear guard.

We were thinking of making several practice runs but the situation in the old camp is still compromised, and now a *gringo*[11] has appeared, shooting rounds with an M-2; he is Algarañaz's "friend" and will spend a 10-day vacation at his

---

11. The *gringo* was Cristian Reese, a Bolivian of German descent who lived in Lagunillas.

place. Scouting parties will be sent out to explore and to move the camp to a point closer to Algarañaz's house; if the situation blows up, we will make our presence known to that person before leaving the area.

Miguel still has a high fever.

January 21

We conducted the drill, which fell short in some things, but in general went well. We need to practice the withdrawal, which was the weakest aspect of the exercise. Afterwards, teams were dispatched: one, with Braulio in charge, to clear a path parallel to the river to the west, and another, led by Rolando, to do the same to the east. Pacho went to the barren hill to try the two-way radios and Marcos left with Aniceto to try to find a path that would allow us to watch Algarañaz closely. Everyone should return before 2:00, except Marcos. Clearing the paths and testing the radios turned out well. Marcos returned early because the rain blocked all visibility. Pedro arrived in the rain, bringing Coco and three new recruits: Benjamín, Eusebio, and Wálter. The first, who is from Cuba, will become part of the vanguard because he has knowledge of weapons; the other two will be in the rear guard. Mario Monje spoke to three others coming from Cuba, dissuading them from joining the guerrillas. Not only did he not resign from the party leadership, but he also sent a document to Fidel, attachment D. IV. I received a note from Tania about her departure and Iván's illness, and another note from Iván, which is attachment D. V.

During the evening I met with the whole group and read [Monje's] document to them, pointing out inaccuracies in his points (a) and (b), along with a little tirade of my own. They seemed to respond well. Of the three new arrivals, two seem to be solid and aware; the youngest is an Aymará peasant who seems to be very sound.

January 22

A *góndola* of 13 people, plus Braulio and Wálter, went to relieve Pedro and Rubio, returning in the afternoon without having brought the full load. Everything is quiet over there. On the way back, Rubio had a dramatic fall but was not seriously hurt.

I wrote to Fidel (#3) to explain the situation and to test the mail drop. I should send it to La Paz with Guevara if he comes to Camiri for the meeting on the 25th.

I wrote instructions for the urban cadres (Document III).[12] Due to the *góndola*, there is no activity in the camp. Miguel is getting better, but Carlos now has a high fever.

A tuberculin test was administered today. Two turkeys were caught; a small animal was trapped, but its foot was severed and it was able to escape.

January 23

We split up the tasks, some working within the camp and some exploring. Inti, Rolando, and Arturo went to look for a place for a possible hideout for the doctor and any wounded. Marcos, Urbano, and I went to explore the hill in front to find a place from which Algarañaz's house could be watched; we found one and can see it quite well.

Carlos still is running a fever, typical of malaria.

---

12. "Instructions to Urban Cadres." See Appendices.

January 24

The *góndola* left with seven men, returning early with the whole load and some corn; this time it was Joaquín who took a bath in the river, losing his Garand, but then finding it again. Loro is coming back and is now in hiding; Coco and Antonio are still away—they should return tomorrow or the next day with Guevara.

One of the paths was improved so that, in case we need to defend these positions, we can surround the soldiers. At night, we reviewed the other day's drill, correcting some of our errors.

January 25

We set off with Marcos to explore the path that, in case of attack, would lead us to the enemy's rear guard; it took almost an hour to get there, but the location is very good.

Aniceto and Benjamín went to try to transmit from the hill overlooking Algarañaz's house, but they got lost and were not able to communicate; we need to repeat this exercise. Work began on another cave for our personal gear. Loro came back and joined the vanguard. He spoke with Algarañaz and told him what I had said. Algarañaz admitted that he had sent the Vallegrandino to spy but denied turning us in. Coco had scared the man away from the house, since he had been sent by Algarañaz to spy. Manila sent a message reporting that everything had been received and that Kolle will go to where Simón Reyes is already waiting. Fidel said he would hear them out, but will be hard on them.

January 26

We had barely started on the new cave when word came that Guevara was on his way with Loyola; we set off for the little house at the intermediate camp and they arrived at 12:00.

I set out my conditions to Guevara: the dissolution of the group, no ranks for anyone, no political organization at this point, and the avoidance of polemics over differences on international and national policy. He accepted everything with great humility, and so after a frosty start, relations with the Bolivians have become friendly.

Loyola made a very good impression on me; she is very young and softly spoken, but one can tell she is very determined. She is about to be expelled from the [Communist Party] youth group, but they are trying to get her to resign first. I gave her the instructions for the [urban] cadres and another document, and I repaid the money we had already spent, which was almost 70,000 pesos. We are going to be short of money soon.

Dr. Pareja[13] was named head of the urban network, and Rodolfo[14] will come to join us within two weeks.

I sent a letter with instructions to Iván (D. VI).

I ordered Coco to sell the jeep, but to stay in contact with the farm.

At around 7:00, as night was falling, we said good-bye. They will leave tomorrow night and Guevara will come again with the first group between the 4th and the 14th of February; he said that he could not come sooner because of communication

---

13. Wálter Pareja Fernández. In practice, Pareja did not head the urban network, but he did collaborate with it.
14. Rodolfo Saldaña was never able to join the guerrilla movement.

problems and because the men are taking time off to enjoy the carnivals.

More powerful radio transmitters are on the way.

January 27

A strong *góndola* was sent that brought back nearly everything, but there is still a load left. At night, Coco and the visitors left; they will stay in Camiri, and Coco will go on to Santa Cruz to arrange the sale of the jeep, some time after the 15th.

We are still working on the cave. A *tatú*[15] was caught in the traps. We are finishing preparing the supplies for the trip; the plan is to leave when Coco returns.

January 28

The *góndola* has cleaned out the old camp and brought the news that the Vallegrandino had been caught hanging around the cornfield, but he escaped. Everything indicates it is time for a decision about the farm.

Now the supplies are ready for a 10-day march, and we have settled on a date: one or two days after Coco returns on February 2.

January 29

A day of absolute idleness, except for the cooks, hunters, and sentries.

Coco came back in the afternoon, having gone to Camiri and not Santa Cruz. He dropped off Loyola, who will continue on to

---

15. *Tatú* is an armadillo.

La Paz by plane, and Moisés, who will go to Sucre by *góndola*.
They set Sunday as the day to make contact.

February 1 will be our departure date.

January 30

The *góndola* of 12 men carried the majority of the supplies;
there is still a load for five men. The hunters returned empty-
handed.

The cave for our personal items is finished; it did not turn
out so well.

January 31

Last day at camp. The *góndola* cleaned out the old camp and the
sentries were withdrawn. Antonio, Ñato, Camba, and Arturo
will remain; their instructions are: to make contact at least every
three days; as long as there are four of them, two will be armed;
sentry duty must not be neglected at any time; the new recruits
will be instructed in our general rules, but should not know
more than is absolutely necessary; all the personal items will be
removed from the camp and the weapons hidden in the woods,
covered by a tarp. The cash reserve will remain in the camp
permanently, on someone's person. They will keep watch over
the paths already made and the neighboring creeks. In case
they have to withdraw suddenly, two will go to Arturo's cave:
Antonio and Arturo himself; Ñato and Camba will withdraw to
the creek and one of them will run to leave a warning at a site
we will choose tomorrow. If there are more than four men, one
group will take care of the supply cave.

I spoke to the troops, giving them final instructions for the
march. I also gave final instructions to Coco (D. VII).

Analysis of the month

As I expected, Monje's position was at first evasive and then treacherous.

The party has taken up arms against us and I do not know where this will lead, but it will not stop us and maybe, in the end, it will be to our advantage (I am almost certain of this). The most honest and militant people will be with us, although they are going through a more or less severe crisis of conscience.

Up to now, Guevara has responded well; we will see how he and his people act in the future.

Tania departed, but the Argentines have shown no sign of life and neither has she. Now the real guerrilla phase begins and we will test the troops; time will tell what they can do and what the prospects for the Bolivian revolution are.

Of everything that was envisioned, the slowest has been the incorporation of Bolivian combatants.

FEBRUARY 1967

February 1

The first phase was carried out. The men arrived somewhat tired, but in general, did well. Antonio and Ñato came up to work out the passwords and to bring my backpack and that of Moro, who is recovering from malaria.

We established a system to alert each other by putting messages in a bottle under a bush close to the path.

Joaquín, in the rear guard, is struggling with his load, and this is holding up the whole group.

February 2

A slow, arduous day. El Médico [Moro] delayed the march a bit, but in general the pace is slow. At 4:00 we came to the last site with water and camped there. The vanguard was ordered to march to the river (presumably the Frías) but they too failed to maintain a good pace.

It rained during the night.

February 3

It was raining at daybreak, so our departure was delayed until 8:00. Just as we were heading off, Aniceto arrived with some rope to help us through the difficult passes; shortly afterwards, the rain started again. We reached the creek at 10:00, drenched, and decided not to continue any further today. The creek cannot be the Frías; it is simply not indicated on the map.

Tomorrow the vanguard will set out, led by Pacho, and we will communicate every hour.

February 4

We walked from the morning until 4:00 in the afternoon, with a two-hour break at noon to eat some soup. The path follows the Ñacahuazú; it is relatively good but so rough on our shoes that several compañeros are already almost barefoot.

The troops are fatigued but they have responded very well. I was relieved of nearly 15 pounds and can walk with ease, although the pain in my shoulders becomes unbearable at times.

We have not encountered any recent signs of people along the river, but we should come across populated areas any time now, according to the map.

February 5

Unexpectedly, after walking five hours in the morning (12 to 14 kilometers), the vanguard notified us that they had encountered animals (a mare and her foal). We halted and ordered a scouting expedition so we could avoid an area that might be populated. We debated over whether we had reached the Iripití[1] or at the junction with the Saladillo, marked on the map. Pacho returned with the news that there was a river many times larger than the Ñacahuazú and that it was impassable. We went there and

---

1. A tributary of the Ñacahuazú River.

found ourselves facing the real Río Grande; moreover, it was overflowing. There are signs of life but they are rather old and the tracks lead to dense undergrowth where there are no signs of traffic.

We camped in a bad spot, close to the Ñacahuazú, to make use of its water; tomorrow we will explore both sides of the river (east and west) to become familiar with the area and the other group will try to cross it.

February 6

A calm day to restore our strength. Joaquín left with Wálter and El Médico [Moro] to explore along the course of the Río Grande; they walked eight kilometers without discovering a way across and found only a creek with salt water. Marcos walked a little upstream and did not reach the Frías; Aniceto and Loro went with him. Alejandro, Inti, and Pacho tried unsuccessfully to swim across the river. We moved about a kilometer back, looking for a better campsite. Pombo is rather sick.

Tomorrow we will begin building a raft to try to cross the river.

February 7

The raft was made under Marcos's direction; it turned out very large and difficult to maneuver. At 1:30 we went to the spot from which we could cross, and at 2:30 we began to do so. The vanguard made it in two trips and the third trip took half the center group, along with my clothes, but not my backpack. When they went back again to take the rest of the center group across, Rubio miscalculated and the river took the raft way downstream—it could not be saved, and fell apart. Joaquín began to build another that was ready by 9:00, but it was not necessary to cross at night because it had not rained and the water level was still dropping. Of the center group, Tuma, Urbano, Inti, Alejandro, and I remain here. Tuma and I slept on the ground.

February 8

At 6:30 the rest of the center group began the crossing. The first section of the vanguard went at 6:00 and when the center group made it, everyone crossed; once the entire rear guard made it over, the center group left at 8:30. The rear guard was instructed to hide the raft and then follow behind. The path became rough and we had to clear it with machetes. At 6:00, thirsty and hungry, we came to a creek with a little pond, where we decided to camp; there are many pig tracks here.

Braulio, Aniceto, and Benigno walked about three kilometers to the river and came back with the news that they had seen tracks made by *abarcas*[2] and by three animals, one with horseshoes; all are recent.

February 9

When we had walked more than half an hour, it occurred to me to leave the path, which was heading uphill, and to follow the creek, and in a while we came across a cornfield; I sent Inti and Ricardo to investigate, and then pandemonium broke out. The marker we had left for those behind us was missed, and they thought I was lost; groups went in all directions. The vanguard found a house and waited there for me. Inti and Ricardo ran

---

2. *Abarcas* are sandals made from hide.

into some small boys and went to the house of a young peasant[3] with six children, who received them very well and gave them a lot of information. During the second conversation, Inti told him that he was the head of the guerrillas and he bought two pigs to make *huminta*.[4]

We stayed in the same place eating corn and pork. We made *ponche*[5] in the early morning, but left it for the following day.

February 10

Posing as one of Inti's assistants, I went to talk to the peasant. The performance was not particularly effective because Inti was so shy.

The peasant is true to type—unable to help us, but also incapable of seeing the harm he can cause us, and for this reason, potentially dangerous. He told us about other peasants, but we could not be entirely confident about his information because he was not very specific.

El Médico [Moro] treated the children who had worms and a mare had kicked one of them; then we headed off.

We spent the afternoon and evening making *huminta* (it is not very good). At night we gathered everyone together and I made a few observations about the next 10 days. First, I am thinking of a hike of 10 days or more toward Masicuri, so that all the compañeros can actually see the soldiers for themselves; and then we would try to return along the Frías to be able to explore another trail.

(The peasant's name is Rojas.)

---

3. Honorato Rojas.
4. A typical Bolivian meal made of baby corn, similar to tamales.
5. A drink made from hot milk, sugar, and liquor.

February 11

The old man's birthday: 67.[6]

We continued down a clearly marked path along the river-bank, until it became rather difficult to get through, and every now and again we would lose the trail as it seemed nobody had passed through this area in a while. At midday we got to a point where it disappeared completely, next to a large river that suddenly made us doubt again whether it was the Masicuri or not. We stopped at a creek while Marcos and Miguel went upstream to explore. Inti, with Carlos and Pedro, did the same downstream, trying to find the mouth. They found it, and confirmed that it was the Masicuri, whose nearest ford seemed to be farther downstream, where they had seen several peasants loading horses in the distance. They have probably seen our tracks, so from now on we will have to take greater care. We are one or two leagues from Arenales, according to what the peasant told us.

Altitude = 760 meters.

February 12

We walked the two kilometers rapidly on the path made by the vanguard yesterday. From here, the trail took a while to clear. At 4:00 in the afternoon, we hit a main road that seems to be the one we have been looking for. There was a house on the other side of the river, ahead of us, but we decided not to go there, and instead we looked for another house on this side that should belong to Montaño, whom Rojas recommended. Inti and Loro went there but they found no one, although there

---

6. Birthday of his father, Ernesto Guevara Lynch.

were signs that it was the right place.

At 7:30 we set off on a night march that served to show how much there is to learn. At around 10:00, Inti and Loro returned to the house, bringing not so good news: the man was drunk and not very welcoming; he had nothing but corn. He had got drunk at Caballero's[7] house on the other side of the river, where the ford is. We decided to sleep in the little patch of trees nearby. I was completely exhausted; the *humintas* had not agreed with me and I had not eaten anything all day.

February 13

The dawn let loose a downpour that lasted all morning, flooding the river. The news is better: Montaño is the owner's son—about 16 years old. His father was not there and will be away for a week; he gave us a lot of specific information about the ford, which he says is a league away. A section of the road follows the left bank, but only for a short distance. The only house on this side is that belonging to Pérez's brother, a small farmer whose daughter is the girlfriend of a member of the army.

We moved on to a new camp, beside the creek and a cornfield. Marcos and Miguel made a shortcut to the main road.

Altitude = 650 meters. (Stormy weather.)

February 14

A quiet day, spent at the same camp. The lad from the house came by three times: once to tell us that some people had crossed from the other side of the river looking for some pigs,

---

7. Evaristo Caballero was the mayor of Arenales.

but would not come our way. We paid him extra money for the damage we had done to his cornfield.

The *macheteros* spent the entire day slashing without coming across a single house; they estimate they completed about six kilometers, which is half of our work for tomorrow.

We decoded a long message from Havana, the main news being about the meeting with Kolle, who claimed he had not been informed our undertaking was on a continental scale and, if this was the case, they were ready to collaborate in a plan and wanted to discuss details with me; Kolle himself, Simón Rodríguez, and Ramírez[8] will come here. The message also stated that Simón had declared his decision to help us independently of what the party decides.

Besides this, there is news that the Frenchman,[9] traveling with his own passport, will arrive in La Paz on the 23rd, and will stay with either Pareja or Rhea. Part of the message has yet to be decoded. We will see how to deal with this new conciliatory offensive. Other news is that Merci turned up with no money, claiming it was stolen; misappropriation is suspected, although something more serious cannot be ruled out. Lechín[10] is going to ask for money and training.

February 15

Hildita's birthday: 11.[11]

---

8. Refers to Humberto Ramírez, a leader in the Bolivian Communist Party. The meeting never took place because military action was triggered and afterward all contact was lost.

9. Jules Régis Debray.

10. Juan Lechín Oquendo, key leader of the Bolivian Workers Confederation.

11. Birthday of his oldest daughter, Hilda Guevara Gadea.

A peaceful day on the march. At 10:00 in the morning we caught up to where the *macheteros* had stopped; it was a slow hike after that. At 5:00 in the afternoon, we were informed that a cultivated field was ahead and at 6:00 this was confirmed. We sent Inti, Loro, and Aniceto to talk with the peasant, who turned out to be Miguel Pérez, the brother of Nicolás, who is a rich peasant. But Miguel is poor and exploited by his brother, so much so that he seems ready to collaborate with us. We did not eat because it was so late.

February 16

We walked a few meters to avoid the brother's curiosity and we camped on high ground overlooking the river 50 meters below. The position is good as far as protecting us from surprise attacks is concerned, but it is rather uncomfortable. We began preparing a large quantity of food for the journey across the mountain range toward the Rosita.

The afternoon brought strong and persistent rain that fell all night, delaying our plans. It flooded the river and left us isolated once again. We will lend the peasant $1,000 so he can buy and fatten some pigs; he has capitalist ambitions.

February 17

Rain fell all morning: 18 hours of rain. Everything is wet and the river is very high. I sent Marcos, with Miguel and Braulio, to look for a trail to the Rosita; they returned in the afternoon after having cleared a four-kilometer path. They reported that there was some terrain ahead similar to that which we call the Pampa del Tigre. Inti feels ill, from stuffing himself too much.

Altitude = 720 meters. (Unusual weather conditions.)

February 18

Josefina's birthday: 33.[12]

Partial failure. We hiked slowly, following the pace of the *macheteros,* but by 2:00 they had reached a level plateau where machetes were no longer needed; we slowed down further, and at 3:00 arrived at a water hole where we set up camp, hoping to cross the plateau in the morning. Marcos and Tuma went off to explore, returning with very bad news: the entire hill is surrounded by steep rocky cliffs, making it impossible to descend; there is no alternative but to turn back.

Altitude = 980 meters.

February 19

A lost day. We went down the hill until we came to the creek; we tried to climb along its banks, but this was impossible. I sent Miguel and Aniceto to see if they could climb a rocky cliff and cross to the other side, but without success. We wasted the day waiting for them; they returned later stating that the cliffs were the same: impassable. Tomorrow we will try to climb to the last ridge just past the creek, the one that leads to the west (the others descend to the south, where the hill ends).

Altitude = 760 meters.

February 20

A day of slow, uneven progress. Miguel and Braulio went up the old path and got to the little creek by the cornfield; from there they lost the way and returned to the creek at nightfall.

---

12. Birthday of his wife, the revolutionary combatant Aleida March de la Torre.

When we reached the next creek, I sent Rolando and Pombo to explore it up to the point where it meets a rocky cliff. They had not returned by 3:00, so we took the track Marcos had been making, leaving behind Pedro and Rubio to wait for them. We arrived at 4:30 at the creek by the cornfield, where we set up camp. The explorers did not return.

Altitude = 720 meters.

February 21

A slow hike up the creek. Pombo and Rolando returned with the news that we could cross the other creek, but Marcos had already explored it and it seemed just like this one. We headed off at 11:00, but at 13:30 we encountered some ponds with very cold water that we could not wade across. Loro was sent to explore and took so long that I sent Braulio and Joaquín from the rear guard. Loro returned with the news that the creek widened farther up and was easier to cross, so we decided to go ahead without waiting to see what Joaquín would find. At 6:00, while we were setting up camp, Joaquín brought the news that we could climb the ridge to a very accessible path. Inti is unwell; he has gas pains for the second time in a week.

Altitude = 860 meters.

February 22

The whole day was spent climbing steep ridges through dense undergrowth. After such an exhausting day we decided to camp without reaching the top; I sent Joaquín and Pedro to attempt it alone and they came back at 7:00 saying it would take at least three hours to slash a way through.

Altitude = 1,180 meters.

We are at the source of the creek that runs into the Masicuri, but headed south.

February 23

A bad day for me. I was exhausted and moved through willpower alone. Marcos, Braulio, and Tuma left in the morning to work on the path, while we waited in the camp. We decoded a new message reporting that my message had been received through the French mail drop. We set out at noon, with the sun strong enough to split rocks, and a little later, when we reached the crest of the highest hill, I felt faint; from then on, I kept going from sheer determination. The highest point in this area is 1,420 meters, a summit that overlooks a wide area that includes the Río Grande, the mouth of the Ñacahuazú, and part of the Rosita. The topography is different from what is marked on the map: after a clear dividing line, the ground abruptly falls to a kind of wooded plateau, eight to 10 kilometers wide, at the end of which the Rosita flows. Then there is another range of similar heights to this chain and a plain that can be seen far in the distance.

We decided to descend a different way, which was passable but very steep, to follow a creek that leads to the Río Grande, and from there to the Rosita. It appears there are no houses along the riverbank, contrary to what is marked on the map. After an infernal hike, without water and with night already falling, we camped at 900 meters.

In the early hours of yesterday I heard Marcos telling a compañero to go to hell, and saying it again to someone else during the day. He needs to be spoken to.

February 24

Ernestico's birthday: 2.[13]

An arduous and unproductive day. Very little progress was made, without water because the creek we are following is dry. At 12:00, the *macheteros* were relieved because they were exhausted. At 2:00 in the afternoon it rained a bit and we filled the canteens; a little later we found a small pool of water, and at 5:00 we camped on a ledge beside the water. Marcos and Urbano continued to explore and Marcos returned with the news that the river is only a few kilometers away, but the path by the creek is very bad because it turns into a swamp.

Altitude = 680 meters.

February 25

Bad day. We made very little progress and, to make matters worse, Marcos went the wrong way and we lost the whole morning; he had gone off with Miguel and Loro. At 12:00, he communicated this to us, asking for a replacement and a radio, so Braulio, Tuma, and Pacho went. After two hours, Pacho returned saying that Marcos had sent him back because the radio reception was poor. At 4:30 I sent Benigno to tell Marcos that if he had not found the river by 6:00, he should return; after Benigno left, Pacho called me over to tell me that he had had an argument with Marcos, who he said had been domineering while giving orders, threatening him with a machete and hitting him with the handle in the face; when Pacho had come back and told him that he could not go any farther, Marcos

13. Birthday of Ernesto Guevara March, the youngest of his children.

again threatened him with a machete, pushed him around, and ripped his clothes.

Given the seriousness of the incident, I called over Inti and Rolando, who confirmed the bad atmosphere existing in the vanguard because of Marcos's personality, and also reported some insolence on Pacho's part.

February 26

I spoke with Marcos and Pacho in the morning, asking for an explanation, and I became convinced that Marcos had insulted and mistreated Pacho, and might have threatened him with the machete, but had not hit him. Pacho, for his part, is prone to insulting others and has an innate tendency to bravado, which has been demonstrated at other times.

I waited until everyone was assembled and talked about the importance of our effort to get to the Rosita; I explained these kinds of deprivations were an introduction to what was in store for us and that because of an inability to adapt to our new circumstances some shameful incidents had arisen, such as had occurred between the two Cubans. I criticized Marcos for his attitude and made it clear to Pacho that another incident like the last would lead to his dishonorable discharge from the guerrilla force. Pacho had first refused to continue with the radio and then had returned without telling me about the incident, and later he had probably lied when he said Marcos had hit him.

I told the Bolivians that if anyone felt unable to continue, they should refrain from using deceitful methods to be discharged; they should come to me and then they could leave the guerrilla force in peace.

We continued walking, trying to reach the Río Grande and then follow its course; we made it and were able to walk along it for just over a kilometer, but then we had to climb away from it because we could not get past a rocky cliff. Benjamín had fallen behind, having difficulties with his backpack and was physically exhausted; when he caught up, I ordered him to continue, which he did for 50 meters; but then he lost the trail on the climb and went on to a ledge to locate it. When I ordered Urbano to help him find the way, he made a sudden movement and fell into the water. He did not know how to swim. The current was so strong he was dragged away as he tried to gain his footing; we ran to save him, but as we were taking off our clothes, he disappeared under the water. Rolando swam toward him and tried to dive under, but the current carried him away. After five minutes we gave up hope. He was a weak lad, not cut out for this at all, but he had a great determination to succeed. The test was beyond him, his physique did not match his will. Now we have had our baptism of death on the banks of the Río Grande, in such an absurd way. We camped at 5:00 in the afternoon without finding the Rosita. We ate the last ration of beans.

February 27

After another exhausting day, marching along the riverbank and climbing rocky cliffs, we reached the Rosita River. It is bigger than the Ñacahuazú and smaller than the Masicuri, and its waters are of a reddish hue. We ate the last of our reserve rations and have not seen any signs of life nearby, despite our close proximity to populated areas and roads.

Altitude = 600 meters.

February 28

Partial rest day. After breakfast (tea) I gave a brief talk, analyzing the death of Benjamín and telling some stories from the Sierra Maestra. Then the scouts set off to explore: Miguel, Inti, and Loro went up the Rosita, with instructions to walk for three and a half hours, which was what I believed was required to reach the Abapocito River, but this was not the case because there was no path. They found no recent signs of life. Joaquín and Pedro climbed up to the woods ahead of us, but they saw nothing—no path, not even a trace of a path. Alejandro and Rubio crossed the river but did not find a path either, although their search was superficial. Marcos directed the construction of a raft, which, as soon as it was finished, was used to cross at a bend in the river into which the Rosita flows. Five men's backpacks were taken across, but they took Miguel's and left Benigno's, and did the opposite thing with the men themselves. To make matters worse, Benigno left his shoes behind.

The raft could not be recovered and the second one is not finished, so we will wait to cross tomorrow.

Analysis of the month

Although I have no news of what is happening at the camp, everything is going reasonably well, with some exceptions, fatal in one instance.

From the outside, there is no news of the two men who should have arrived to complete the group; the Frenchman should be in La Paz by now and should come to the camp any day. I have no news of the Argentines or Chino. Messages are being communicated well in both directions. The party's position remains vacillating and two-faced, to say the very least, although when I speak with the new delegation and hear the latest explanation, this will be clearer.

The march has been going well enough, although it has been seriously affected by the accident that cost Benjamín his life. The men are still weak and not all of the Bolivians are able to hold up; the last few days of hunger have dampened their enthusiasm, which was already obvious after the group was divided.

Of the Cubans, two of those with little experience, Pacho and Rubio, have not responded well. Alejandro has done extremely well; of the old timers, Marcos is a constant headache and Ricardo is not up to speed. The rest are doing well. The next phase will be combat, and that will be decisive.

MARCH 1967

March 1

It began to rain at 6:00 in the morning. We postponed crossing the river until it stopped, but the rain got heavier and continued until 3:00 in the afternoon, by which time the river was flooded and we did not think it prudent to try to cross. Now the river is very high, with no sign of ebbing soon. I moved into an abandoned *tapera*[1] to escape the rain and set up a new camp there. Joaquín stayed where he was. At night I was told that Polo finished off his can of milk, and Eusebio had had his milk and sardines, so now, as punishment, they will not eat when the others get their rations. A bad sign.

March 2

It was rainy at daybreak and the troops were restless, especially me. The river rose higher still. We decided to leave the camp as soon as the rain stopped and to continue parallel to the river, taking the same trail that had brought us here. We left at 12:00, bringing along a good provision of palm hearts. At 4:30 we stopped, having left our path to follow an old one, which we then lost. No news of the vanguard.

---

1. *Tapera* is a Guaraní term — used to describe an abandoned or derelict house or cabin.

March 3

We set off with enthusiasm, walking well, but the hours took their toll and our pace slackened; we had to change paths and walk along higher ground because I was afraid of another accident in the area where Benjamín had fallen. It took us four hours to travel the same distance that had taken less than a half an hour lower down. At 6:00 we reached the bank of the creek where we set up camp; with only two palm hearts left, Miguel and Urbano, and later Braulio, went off to look for some more farther away, returning at 9:00 at night. We ate around midnight; palm hearts and fruit from the *corojo* palm (called *totai* in Bolivia) are saving the day.

Altitude = 600 meters.

March 4

Miguel and Urbano left in the morning and cleared the path with machetes all day, returning at 6:00 in the afternoon having progressed about five kilometers and seen a plain we would be able to walk across; but there is no place to camp, so we decided to stay here until the trail can be lengthened. The hunters caught two little monkeys, one parrot, and one pigeon—this was our meal, along with the palm hearts that are abundant by this creek.

Troop morale is low and our physical strength is deteriorating day by day; I am showing signs of edema in my legs.

March 5

Joaquín and Braulio went with the *macheteros* in the rain, but they are both weak and did not make much progress. Twelve palm hearts were collected and some small birds were caught, which allowed us to save the canned food for one more day and to keep the palm hearts for two more days.

March 6

A day of intermittent hiking until 5:00 in the afternoon. Miguel, Urbano, and Tuma were the *macheteros*. Some progress was made and in the distance we can see some terrain that might be near the Ñacahuazú. Only a little parrot was caught and this was given to the rear guard. Today we ate palm hearts with meat. We have three very basic meals left.

Altitude = 600 meters.

March 7

Four months. The troops are more discouraged with each passing day, seeing the end of our provisions but not of our journey. Today we advanced between four and five kilometers along the riverbank, and finally we found a promising trail. Our meal: three and a half small birds and the rest of the palm hearts. Tomorrow and the next day, it will be canned food alone, one-third per head; after that, milk will be it.

We will need two or three more days to reach the Ñacahuazú.

Altitude = 610 meters.

March 8

Day of little walking, full of surprise and tension. At 10:00 in the morning we left the camp without waiting for Rolando, who was hunting. We had only walked an hour and a half when we met up with the *macheteros* (Urbano, Miguel, and Tuma) and the hunters (El Médico [Moro] and Chinchu), who had caught a whole bunch of parrots, but then saw a water tank across the river and stopped. I went to check out the place after giving the order to set up camp; it appeared to be an oil pumping station. Inti and Ricardo, pretending to be hunters, jumped into the water to have a look. They were fully dressed and tried to make it in two stages, but Inti ran into problems and almost drowned; Ricardo saved him, and finally they made it to the bank, attracting a lot of attention. They failed to make the warning before they disappeared. They had begun to cross at noon, and when I left at 15:15 there was no sign of them. The whole afternoon passed without their return. The last one on guard duty came back at 21:00 and had still not seen any sign of them.

I was very concerned at having two valuable compañeros at risk and no one knew what had happened. We decided that our best swimmers, Alejandro and Rolando, would go over tomorrow to find out.

We ate better than we did other days — despite the lack of palm hearts — because there was an abundance of parrots and the two little monkeys Rolando had killed.

March 9

We began preparing for the crossing early, but it was necessary to make a raft, which delayed us considerably. At 8:30 the sentries announced that they had seen half-naked people on the other side, so we postponed the crossing. A little path had been made that led to the other side, but it went through a clearing where we could be seen; we had to cross during the early morning, taking advantage of the fog over the river. Close to 16:00, after an exasperating watch that for me had lasted since 10:30, our providers (Inti and Chinchu) jumped into the river, ending up far downstream. They brought back pork, bread, rice, sugar, coffee, some canned food, ripe corn, etc. We treated ourselves to a little feast of coffee and bread and authorized the consumption of a can of condensed milk that we had been keeping in reserve. They explained they had shown themselves every hour so that we could see them, but to no avail. Marcos and his people had passed by three days ago and Marcos apparently behaved in his usual manner, showing off his weapons. The engineers at the oil plant did not know exactly how far away the Ñacahuazú is, but they guessed it is about a five-day walk; if that is true then our provisions will be sufficient. The oil pump is part of a pumping installation they are constructing.

March 10

We set out at 6:30, walking 45 minutes until we caught up with the *macheteros*. At 8:00 it began to rain, which continued until 11:00. Effectively, we walked three hours, making camp at 5:00. Some hills can be seen that might be the Ñacahuazú. Braulio went scouting and returned with the news that there is a path and the river runs straight to the west.

Altitude = 600 meters.

March 11

The day began auspiciously. We walked more than an hour on a perfect trail, but then it suddenly disappeared. Braulio took a machete and struggled onward until he reached a sandy area. We gave him and Urbano some time to clear the way and when we were about to follow them, without warning, rising water blocked our way as the river rose one or two meters.

We were thus separated from the *macheteros* and forced to clear a path through the woods. We stopped at 13:30 and I sent Miguel and Tuma to find the vanguard and to give them the order to return if they could not get to the Ñacahuazú or another good site.

They returned at 18:00, having walked about three kilometers, until reaching a steep rocky cliff. Apparently, we are close, but these last days will be very difficult if the river does not go down, and this is unlikely. We walked four to five kilometers.

A disagreeable incident arose because the rear guard's sugar supply has run low and the suspicion is that either less was distributed or Braulio has been taking certain liberties. I must talk to him.

Altitude = 610 meters.

March 12

We walked the stretch that had been cleared yesterday in an hour and 10 minutes. On catching up to Miguel and Tuma, who had left first, they were already searching for a way around a steep cliff. This took all day; our only activity was to catch four small birds that we ate with rice and mussels. We have two meals left. Miguel stayed on the other side and it seems he has found a way to the Ñacahuazú.

We walked some three to four kilometers.

March 13

From 6:30 to noon we scaled the infernal cliffs, following the trail that Miguel had made in a heroic effort. We thought that we had found the Ñacahuazú when we ran into some bad stretches and made very little progress in five hours. We set up camp in a downpour at 17:00. The men are very tired and a bit demoralized once again. There is only one meal left. We walked some six kilometers but very little of it was worthwhile.

March 14

Almost without realizing it, we reached the Ñacahuazú. (I was—am—exhausted, as if a boulder had fallen on me.) The river is rough and no one really wants to try to cross it, but Rolando volunteered and got across easily. He began his trip back to base at exactly 15:20. I expect it will take him two days.

We ate our last meal: *mote*[2] with meat, so now we are dependent on what we hunt. At this moment, we have one small bird and have heard three shots. El Médico [Moro] and Inti are out hunting.

Altitude = 600 meters.

We heard parts of Fidel's speech in which he makes blunt criticisms of the Venezuelan communists and harshly attacks the position of the Soviet Union on Latin American puppets.

March 15

The center group crossed the river, bringing along Rubio and El Médico [Ernesto] to help us. We thought we could get to the mouth of the Ñacahuazú but we have three men among us who do not know how to swim, and a heavy load. The current dragged us nearly a kilometer and the raft could not be used

---

2. Boiled corn kernels, a Quechua dish eaten in some parts of Latin America.

to cross again, as was our intention. Eleven of us are now on this side, and tomorrow El Médico [Ernesto] and Rubio will go back across. We caught four sparrow hawks, which was our meal — not as bad as expected. Everything got wet and the skies remain full of rain. The men's morale is low; Miguel has swollen feet and several others have a similar condition.

Altitude = 580 meters.

March 16

We decided to eat the horse because swollen feet is now an alarming problem. Miguel, Inti, Urbano, and Alejandro all have various symptoms; I am extremely weak. We made an error in our calculations thinking that Joaquín would cross over here, but he did not. El Médico [Ernesto] and Rubio tried to cross over to help them and were swept downstream and out of sight; Joaquín asked for authorization to cross and I agreed; then his group, too, was lost downstream. I sent Pombo and Tuma to go after them, but they did not find them, returning at night. Since 17:00 we have gorged ourselves with the horsemeat. Tomorrow we will probably suffer the consequences. I estimate that today Rolando should be arriving at the camp.

Message 32 has been completely decoded, reporting the arrival of a Bolivian who will join us, with another load of Glucantine, an antiparasitic medication for leishmania. Up to now we have had no cases.

March 17

Another tragedy before our first test in combat. Joaquín turned up mid-morning; Miguel and Tuma had gone to find him, carrying large pieces of meat. It was a real odyssey: they said they could not control the raft and it was carried down the Ñacahuazú until it struck a whirlpool and overturned several times. The final outcome was that several backpacks were lost, as was almost all the ammunition, six rifles, and one man: Carlos. Carlos was thrown into the whirlpool along with Braulio but they met different fates: Braulio made it to the bank and could see Carlos being dragged under, unable to resist. Joaquín had already reached the shore farther downstream, and did not see him being swept away. Up to now, Carlos was considered the best man of the Bolivians in the rear guard, for his seriousness, discipline, and enthusiasm.

The lost weapons are: a Brno, belonging to Braulio; two M-1s, (Carlos's and Pedro's); three Mausers, (Abel's, Eusebio's, and Polo's). Joaquín informed me that he had seen Rubio and El Médico [Ernesto] on the other side and had ordered them to build a little raft and to return. At 14:00 they showed up with a long tale about their trials and tribulations; they were naked and Rubio was barefoot. Their raft had broken apart in the first whirlpool; they made it to the bank almost at the same place that we had.

Our departure is set for early tomorrow and Joaquín will leave at midday. I hope to have more news tomorrow during the course of the day. The morale of Joaquín's troops seems good.

March 18

We took off early, leaving Joaquín to finish digesting his food and to cure his half of the horsemeat; he had instructions to leave when they felt strong enough.

I had a struggle to maintain a certain reserve of meat against the wishes of those who wanted to finish it off. By mid-morning, Ricardo, Inti, and Urbano had fallen behind and we had to wait for them, although I had intended to rest only when we reached the camp from where we had begun. In any event, we are not traveling very well.

At 14:30 Urbano showed up with a *urina*[3] Ricardo caught, which gave us some comfort and a reserve of horse ribs. At 16:30 we arrived at what should have been the halfway point, and we slept there. Several men are lagging behind and in bad moods: Chinchu, Urbano, and Alejandro.

March 19

In the morning those of us in the lead made headway; we stopped at 11:00 as agreed, but once again Ricardo and Urbano, and this time Alejandro, too, fell behind. They arrived at 13:00 with another *urina* also caught by Ricardo; Joaquín was with them. There was an incident in which words were exchanged between Joaquín and Rubio, and I had to be harsh with Rubio without being certain he was guilty.

I decided to proceed to the creek in any case, but a small plane was circling overhead, which was hardly a good sign; furthermore, I was worried about the lack of news coming from the base camp. I thought that the stretch would take longer, but despite the low energy of the troops, we arrived at 17:30. We were received there by the Peruvian doctor, Negro,[4] who had come with Chino and the telegraph operator.[5] He told us that Benigno was waiting for us with food, that two of Guevara's

---

3. A small deer.
4. Restituto José Cabrera Flores (Negro or El Médico), Peruvian doctor.
5. Lucio Edilberto Galván Hidalgo (Eustaquio).

men had deserted,[6] and that the police had raided the farm. Benigno explained he had left to meet us with the food and had crossed paths with Rolando three days ago. Benigno spent two days at this place but did not want to go farther because the army could be advancing down the river, as the small plane had been circling for three days. Negro had witnessed the attack on the farm by six men. Neither Antonio nor Coco were there: Coco had gone to Camiri to find another group of Guevara's men and Antonio had left immediately afterwards to warn him about the desertion. I received a long report from Marcos (D. VIII) in which he explains his actions in his own way; he had gone to the farm against my express orders. There were also two reports from Antonio explaining the situation. (D. IX and X.)

At the base camp now are the Frenchman, Chino, his compañeros, Pelado, Tania, and Guevara with the first part of his group. After eating a sumptuous dinner of rice, beans, and *urina*, Miguel went to look for Joaquín, who has not yet turned up, and to find Chinchu, who is lagging yet again. Miguel returned with Ricardo, and Joaquín showed up at dawn; now we are all together here.

March 20

We started out at 10:00, making good time; Benigno and Negro went ahead with a message for Marcos putting him in charge of defense and to leave administrative matters to Antonio. Joaquín left after having concealed our tracks leading to the

---

6.   Refers to two Bolivians, Vicente Rocabado Terrazas (Orlando) and Pastor Barrera Quintana (Daniel).

creek, but he took his time; he brought back three barefoot men. We were taking a long break at 13:00 when Pacho appeared with a message from Marcos. This message expanded on information in the first one from Benigno, but was now more complicated, because apparently the guards, 60 of them, had come along Vallegrandino's path and had seized one of our messengers, Salustio, one of Guevara's men. They took one mule and we lost the jeep. There was no news from Loro, who had been watching the little house. We decided to continue on, in any case, to Oso Camp [Bear Camp], so named because a bear had been killed there. We sent Miguel and Urbano to prepare food for the hungry troops and we ourselves arrived at nightfall. Dantón, Pelao, and Chino were at the camp, along with Tania and a group of Bolivians who used the *góndola* to bring food and then left. Rolando had been sent to organize the withdrawal of everything; a climate of defeat prevailed. A little later a Bolivian doctor who had recently joined us arrived with a message for Rolando, stating that Marcos and Antonio were at the water hole, and that he should go there to talk to them. I sent the same messenger back to tell them that war is won by bullets, and that they should return immediately to the camp and wait for me there. Everything gives the impression of utter chaos; no one knows what to do.

I had an initial talk with Chino. He asked for $5,000 every month for 10 months; in Havana they had told him to come and discuss it with me. He brought a message that Arturo could not decode because it was very long. I told him I agreed in principle, provided that in six months they take up arms. He thinks he will need 15 men, with him as leader in the Ayacucho area. We agreed, furthermore, that he would get five men now and 15 more after a period of time, and they would be sent with weapons after having been trained in combat. He should send me a pair of medium-range transmitters (40 miles) and we will work out a code to use for keeping in permanent contact. He seems very enthusiastic.

He also brought several reports from Rodolfo that are already out-of-date. We heard that Loro was back, saying he had killed a soldier.

March 21

I spent the day in talks and discussions with Chino, going over some points, and with the Frenchman, Pelao, and Tania. The Frenchman brought news we had already heard about Monje, Kolle, Simón Reyes, etc. He came to stay, but I asked him to go back and organize a support network in France, stopping first in Cuba, which coincides with his desire to get married and to have a child with his compañera. I must write letters to Sartre[7] and B. Russell[8] so they can organize international support for the Bolivian liberation movement. He should also talk to a friend who will organize all channels of support, fundamentally financial, medical, and electronic—the latter in the form of an electrical engineer and equipment.

Pelao, of course, is ready to receive my orders and I proposed to him that he act as a kind of a coordinator, working for now only with the groups led by Jozami, Gelman, and Stamponi, and sending me five men to begin training. He is to send my

---

7. Jean-Paul Sartre, French philosopher and writer who met Che during his first visit to Cuba in 1960.
8. Bertrand Russell, English philosopher and mathematician who presided over the International Tribune on US war crimes in the Vietnam War.

greetings to María Rosa Oliver[9] and the old man.[10] I will give him 500 pesos to send off and 1,000 to get around with. If they accept, they should begin exploratory activities in northern Argentina and send me a report.

Tania made her contacts and the people came, but, according to her, she had to drive them here in a jeep, and although she intended to stay only one day, things got complicated. Jozami could not stay the first time, and the second time no contact was made because Tania was here. She talked about Iván with considerable disdain—I do not know what is at the bottom of it all. We received Loyola's account balance up to February 9 ($1,500). (She also informed us she had left the leadership of the youth group.)

Two reports from Iván were received; one was of no interest, only containing information about a military school, with some photos attached, and the other reported on other matters, but also of no great importance.

The main thing is that he could not decode the written message (D. XIII). A report was received from Antonio (D. XII) where he tries to justify his position. We heard a radio broadcast in which a death was announced, followed by a retraction, which indicates that what Loro said was true.

March 22

At [illegible in the original] we set out, abandoning the [illegible in the original] camp, with some food precariously stored [illegible in the original]. Our group, consisting of 47 people, counting visitors and all, made it downstream by 12:00.

---

9. María Rosa Oliver, an Argentine writer.
10. This refers to his father.

On arrival, Inti informed me of several disrespectful acts Marcos had committed; I exploded and told Marcos that if this were true, he would be thrown out of the guerrilla force; he answered he would rather be shot.

Orders were given to set up an ambush with five men ahead at the river and to dispatch a scouting expedition of three men: Miguel and Loro, with Antonio in charge. Pacho went to the observation post on the barren hill that overlooks Algarañaz's house, but he saw nothing. The scouts returned at night and I gave them a full blast. Olo reacted very emotionally and denied the charges. The meeting was explosive and ill-timed, with no good result. It is not clear what Marcos said. I sent for Rolando to resolve once and for all the problem of the new recruits in terms of their numbers and distribution, as there are now more than 30 of us in the center group who are hungry.

March 23

A day of military events. Pombo wanted to organize a *góndola* to get provisions, but I opposed it until we clarified the matter of Marcos's replacement. Just after 8:00, Coco rushed in to report that a section of the army had fallen into our ambush. At this point the outcome has been three 60-mm mortars, 16 Mausers, two BZs, three Uzis, one .30-caliber machine gun, two radios, boots, etc. There were seven dead, 14 healthy prisoners, and four wounded, but we could not secure any provisions. An operations plan was captured, which revealed a plan to advance from both directions along the Ñacahuazú, making contact mid-way. We rapidly moved our troops to one side, with Marcos, and almost the entire vanguard at the end of the path of operations, while the center group and part of the rear guard remained in defensive positions; Braulio set up an ambush at the end of the other path of operations. We will spend the night this way to see if tomorrow the famous Rangers turn up. Two prisoners — a major[11] and a captain[12] — talked like parrots.

We decoded the message sent with Chino. It describes Debray's trip, the sending of $60,000, Chino's requests, and explains why they had not written to Iván. I also received a communication from Sánchez, which reports on the possibilities for setting up Mito at various points.

March 24

The total haul is the following: 16 Mausers, three mortars with 64 shells, two BZs, 2,000 Mauser rounds, three Uzis with two clips each, and one .30-caliber machine gun with two cartridge belts. There are seven dead and 14 prisoners, including four wounded. Marcos was sent to explore but did not come up with anything; but planes are bombing close to our house.

I sent Inti to speak with the prisoners for the last time and to set them free, taking all the clothes we can use, but the two officers were questioned separately and went off with their clothes. We told the major that they had until 12:00 on the 27th to remove the dead bodies and offered a truce for the entire area of Lagunillas if he stayed here, but he said that he was retiring from the army.

The captain said he had just rejoined the army a year ago at the request of people from the party and that he had a brother studying in Cuba; he gave us the names of two other officers who would be willing to collaborate. When the planes began

---

11. Bolivian Army Major Hernán Plata Ríos.
12. Bolivian Army Captain Augusto Silva Bogado.

bombing they got a terrible fright, and it also scared two of our men: Raúl and Wálter. The latter had also been cowardly in the ambush.

Marcos scouted the area but found nothing. Ñato and Coco went upstream with the "reject group"[13] to carry supplies, but the men had to be brought back because they did not want to walk. They must be discharged.

March 25

The day passed uneventfully. León, Urbano, and Arturo were sent to a point from which to observe access to the river from both sides. At 12:00 Marcos withdrew from his ambush position and the rest remained concentrated at the main ambush site. At 18:30 with nearly all personnel present, I made an analysis of our expedition and its significance, reviewing Marcos's errors and demoting him, and then named Miguel as head of the vanguard. At the same time I announced the discharge of Paco, Pepe, Chingolo, and Eusebio, telling them that they would not eat if they do not work; I suspended their tobacco ration and redistributed their personal things among other compañeros more in need. I referred to Kolle's plan to come here and hold discussions at the same time as those members of the youth organization who are here with us are being expelled, saying that we are interested in action—words are of no importance. I announced we would look for a cow and that study classes would be resumed.[14]

I informed Pedro and El Médico [Ernesto] they have almost achieved full status as guerrilla fighters, and gave Apolinar

---

13. Che uses the word *resaca*, literally flotsam, dregs, driftwood.
14. Quechua and French were taught, as were political and cultural classes.

some encouragement. I criticized Wálter for being too soft during the trip, for his attitude in combat, and for the fear he showed of the planes; he did not react well. I went over some details with Chino and Pelado, and gave the Frenchman a long oral report on the situation. In the course of the meeting, the group adopted the name National Liberation Army of Bolivia, and a public statement about the meeting will be made.

March 26

Inti set off early with Antonio, Raúl, and Pedro to look for a cow near Ticucha, but saw troops about three hours from here so they turned back, apparently without being seen. They reported that the soldiers had a sentry in a clearing and something like a house with a shiny roof from which they saw eight men leave. They were close to the river we used to call the Yaqui. I spoke with Marcos and sent him to the rear guard — but I do not expect his conduct to improve much.

We ran a small *góndola* and placed lookouts at the usual posts; from the observation point at Algarañaz's house, 30 to 40 soldiers were seen, as well as a helicopter landing.

March 27

Today there was a spate of broadcasts filling the airwaves, producing a flurry of press announcements, including a press conference with Barrientos.[15] The official report includes one more death than we account for and states that men were wounded and later shot. They said that we suffered 15 dead and four prisoners, two of them foreigners; they also mention

---

15. General René Barrientos Ortuño, president of Bolivia.

a foreigner who shot himself and discuss the composition of the guerrilla force. It is obvious that either the deserters or the prisoner spoke, but we do not know exactly how much they said and how they said it. Everything seems to indicate that Tania has been identified, which means we have lost two years of good and patient work. The departure of the people is very difficult now, and when I told Dantón this, he did not seem very amused. We will see in the future.

Benigno, Loro, and Julio set out to find a trail to Pirirenda; this should take them two or three days, and their instructions are to get there without being seen and then to move on to Gutiérrez. The reconnaissance plane dropped some paratroopers that the sentry reported had landed in our hunting ground; Antonio and two others were sent to investigate and to try to take prisoners, but there was nothing.

We had a meeting of the general command during the evening where we worked out plans for the days ahead. Tomorrow we will send a *góndola* to the little house to pick up some corn, and then another to buy supplies in Gutiérrez; then we will stage a small diversionary attack, possibly in the woods against vehicles traveling between Pincal and Lagunillas.

Communiqué No. 1 was drafted, which we will try to send to journalists in Camiri (D XVII).

March 28

The radio continues to be saturated with news about the guerrillas; it is reported that we are surrounded by 2,000 men in a radius of 120 kilometers and that they are closing in and bombing us with napalm; we supposedly have had 10 to 15 casualties.

I sent Braulio with nine men to try to look for some corn. They returned at night with a bunch of crazy reports:

1) Coco, who had left earlier to warn us, disappeared.

2) At 16:00 they arrived at the farm, where they had discovered the cave had been ransacked; they had spread out to gather things when seven men from the Red Cross appeared, along with two doctors and several unarmed soldiers, who were all taken prisoner and told that the truce had expired, but then allowed to continue their work.

3) A truckload of soldiers turned up and instead of shooting them, our troops made them promise to withdraw.

4) The soldiers withdrew in a disciplined way, and our men accompanied the health workers to the rotting corpses, but they were unable to carry them away and said that they would come tomorrow to burn them.

They confiscated two horses from Algarañaz and then they returned, leaving Antonio, Rubio, and Aniceto where the animals could not go on; when they went looking for Coco, he showed up—apparently he had fallen asleep.

Still no news from Benigno.

The Frenchman made a statement, with too much vehemence, about how useful he could be abroad.

March 29

A day of little action but an extraordinary amount of news: the army provides a wide range of information that, if true, could be very valuable. Radio Habana already reported the news, and the Bolivian government announced its support for

Venezuela in presenting the case against Cuba before the OAS [Organization of American States]. There is one news item that disturbs me: there was a clash in the Tiraboy ravine in which two guerrillas were killed. That is the way to Pirirenda, where Benigno went to explore and he should have returned by now, but has not. The order was not to go through the ravine, but in recent days my orders have been repeatedly ignored.

Guevara has advanced very slowly in his work; he was given dynamite but all day they could not detonate it. A horse was killed and everyone ate lots of meat, although it has to last us four days; we will try to bring the other one here, but it might be difficult. To judge from the birds of prey, the corpses have not yet been burned. As soon as the cave is finished, we will move out of this camp, which is now uncomfortable and too well known. I informed Alejandro that he should stay here with El Médico [Moro] and Joaquín (probably at Oso Camp). Rolando is also really exhausted.

I spoke with Urbano and Tuma; I could not even get Tuma to understand the basis of my criticism.

March 30

Calm has returned: Benigno and his compañeros turned up mid-morning. They had, in fact, gone through the Tiraboy ravine, but all they encountered were two people's footprints. They reached their destination, but some peasants saw them, so they came back. They report that it takes about four hours to get to Pirirenda, and that apparently there is no danger. Aircraft are constantly strafing the small house.

I sent Antonio with two others to explore upstream and the report is that the guards are staying put, although there are tracks left by a scouting party along the river. They have dug trenches.

The mare we needed arrived, so in the worst-case scenario, we will have meat for four days. Tomorrow we will rest and the day after the vanguard will start out for the next two operations: to capture Gutiérrez and to set up an ambush along the road from Algarañaz's house to Lagunillas.

March 31

No major events. Guevara announced that the cave will be finished by tomorrow. Inti and Ricardo reported that the guards had returned to take over our little farm, following an offensive with artillery (mortars), aircraft, etc. This holds up our plans to go to Pirirenda for supplies; nevertheless, I instructed Manuel to advance with his troops toward the little house. If it is vacant, he should occupy it and send two men to let me know so we can mobilize the day after tomorrow. If it is occupied, and we cannot launch a surprise attack, he should return; then we will explore the possibility of flanking Algarañaz's place in order to set up an ambush between Pincal and Lagunillas. The radio continues its clamor, with commentaries on top of official combat reports. They have fixed our position with absolute precision between the Yaqui and the Ñacahuazú and I fear they will try to make a move to surround us. I spoke with Benigno about his mistake in not coming to find us, and I explained Marcos's situation; he took it well.

I spoke with Loro and Aniceto during the evening. The conversation went very badly; Loro went so far as to say we were falling apart, and when I asked him to explain, he told me to ask Marcos and Benigno; Aniceto took Loro's side on a few issues, but later confessed to Coco that he was complicit in stealing some canned food and told Inti that he did not agree with what Loro said about Benigno and Pombo or about the "general disintegration" of the guerrilla force.

Analysis of the month

This month was full of events, but the general panorama is characterized as follows:

- The phase of consolidation and purging of the guerrilla force—fully completed.
- The phase of slow development with the incorporation of some Cuban elements, who do not seem bad, and Guevara's people, who are generally low level (two deserters, one "talking" prisoner, three cowards, and two quitters.)
- The initial phase of the struggle, characterized by a precise and spectacular blow, but marked by gross indecision before and after the fact (the withdrawal of Marcos, Braulio's action).

The beginning of the enemy's counteroffensive, characterized to this point by:

a) a tendency to take measures to isolate us,
b) a clamor at a national and an international level,
c) total ineffectiveness, so far, and
d) mobilization of peasants.

Evidently, we will have to hit the road before I expected and move on, leaving a group to recover, saddled with the burden of four possible informers.

The situation is not good, but now begins a new testing phase for the guerrilla force that will be of great benefit once surpassed.

Composition

* Vanguard: Miguel (head), Benigno, Pacho, Loro, Aniceto, Camba, Coco, Darío, Julio, Pablo, Raúl.

* Rear guard: Joaquín (head), Braulio (second in command), Rubio, Marcos, Pedro, El Médico [Ernesto], Polo, Wálter, Víctor, (Pepe, Paco, Eusebio, and Chingolo).

* Center group: Me, Alejandro, Rolando, Inti, Pombo, Ñato, Tuma, Urbano, Moro, Negro, Ricardo, Arturo, Eustaquio, Guevara, Willy, Luis, Antonio, León. (Visitors: Tania, Pelado, Dantón, Chino.) (Refugee: Serapio.)

APRIL 1967

April 1

The vanguard set off at 7:00 after a considerable delay. Camba was still missing, not having returned from his trip with Ñato to hide the weapons in the cave at Oso Camp. At 10:00, Tuma came from the lookout to warn us that he had seen three or four soldiers in the small hunting ground. We took up positions; Wálter told me from the lookout he had seen three soldiers and a mule or donkey, and they were setting up something; he tried to show me but I could not see anything. At 16:00, I withdrew, deciding that in any case it was no longer necessary to stay if they were not going to attack us, and, apparently, it was all just Wálter's imagination.

I decided to evacuate everyone tomorrow and that Rolando will be in charge of the rear guard in Joaquín's absence. Ñato and Camba arrived at 21:00, after having stored everything away except for food for the six who will stay behind. They are Joaquín, Alejandro, Moro, Serapio, Eustaquio, and Polo. The three Cubans are staying under protest. The other mare was killed to leave some *charqui*[1] for the six men. At 11:00, Antonio showed up with a sack of corn and the news that everything had gone smoothly.

---

1. Sun-dried meat or jerked beef.

At four in the morning Rolando left, burdened with the four quitters (Chingolo, Eusebio, Paco, and Pepe). Pepe wanted to be given a weapon and to stay. Camba went with him.

At 5:00, Coco arrived with a new message that they had slaughtered a cow and were waiting for us. I told him that we would meet the day after tomorrow at noon by the creek that flowed downhill from the farm.

April 2

We have accumulated such an enormous quantity of things it took us all day to store them in their respective caves, only finishing the transfer at 17:00. Four sentries kept watch, but the day passed in a *calma chichi*; no planes flew over the area. The broadcasts on the radio speak of the "tightening encirclement" and that the guerrillas are preparing to defend the Ñacahuazú gully; they report that Don Remberto is in prison and explain how he sold the farm to Coco.

Due to the lateness of the hour, we decided not to leave today but at 3:00 in the morning, and gain time by heading straight for the Ñacahuazú, despite the fact that our meeting place is in the other direction. I talked to Moro, explaining that I had not placed him in the group of the best compañeros because he has a weakness concerning food and a tendency to exasperate others with his jokes. We discussed this for a while.

April 3

Our plan went ahead with no hitches: we set off at 3:30 and walked slowly until we passed the bend in the shortcut at 6:30 and made it to the border of the farm at 8:30. When we passed in front of the ambush site, nothing remained of the seven corpses but perfectly clean skeletons, on which the birds of prey had done a good job. I sent two men (Urbano and Ñato) to make contact with Rolando and in the afternoon, we moved on to the Tiraboy ravine where we slept after stuffing ourselves with beef and corn.

I talked to Dantón and Carlos, giving them three alternatives: to continue with us, to leave on their own, or to wait until we could take over Gutiérrez and then leave from there, taking a chance; they chose the third option. We will try our luck tomorrow.

April 4

Almost a total disaster. At 14:30, we reached a place where there were guard tracks and even a paratrooper's beret and remains of US [Army] individual food rations. I decided to take the first house by force [illegible in the original], which we did at 18:30. Guaraní[2] farmhands came out and told us that the army had about 150 men who had withdrawn yesterday, and that the owner of the house had left to take his livestock away. They were charged with making a meal of pork and yucca, while our men went to occupy the second house belonging to [illegible in the original]. Loro, Coco, Aniceto, and later Inti went to the second house accompanied by one of the peasants.

The couple was not there, but when they arrived, the young farmhand escaped in the confusion. In the end, we established that approximately one company of the Second Regiment (the Bolívar) had been there and had left this morning. They had instructions to go down through the Tiraboy ravine, but

---

2. This refers to descendants of those people who, divided in many groups, extend from the Amazon to the La Plata River. The word comes from the phrase *abá guarini*, meaning man of war.

they chose to leave by another route, so we never ran into them. There are no soldiers in Gutiérrez, but they will return tomorrow, so it is best not to hang around.

In the first house we found military gear, such as plates, canteens, even bullets and equipment; we appropriated everything. After eating well, but not excessively, the rear guard set off at 3:00 and we departed at 3:30. The vanguard should have left when they finished eating their last rations. We ourselves got lost and left farther down from the ambush site, which caused confusion until daylight.

April 5

It was a day of few events but with a certain tension. At 10:00, we were reunited, and a little later Miguel's group started out with their backpacks to occupy the approach to the ravine; their orders were to send the three men on sentry duty from the rear guard to return for their backpacks. To speed up the process, I gave Urbano, Ñato, and León the task of replacing the three men from the rear guard. At 3:30, I halted the center group to organize an ambush to block any forces that might come down the ravine, so the vanguard and the rear guard could defend both access routes at the mouth of the little creek. At 14:00, I sent Tuma to see what had happened with the three men, and he returned at 17:00 without learning anything; we moved to our previous campsite and I repeated the order. At 18:15, Rolando arrived; because the men had never shown up, they had had to carry the three backpacks between them. Braulio gave me an explanation that raises very serious doubts about Marcos's actual combat capability.

I had thought we could head downstream at dawn, but

soldiers were seen bathing about 300 meters from our position. We decided to cross the river without leaving any tracks and to walk on the other trail back to our creek.

April 6

A day of great tension. We crossed the Ñacahuazú River at 4:00 and waited until daybreak to continue; later Miguel set off to explore but had to return twice because of errors that brought us very close to the soldiers. Rolando informed us at 8:00 that a dozen soldiers were at the entrance to the ravine that we had just left. We went slowly, and by 11:00 we were out of danger, on a ridge. Rolando came with the news that there were more than 100 soldiers stationed in the ravine.

At night, before we reached the creek, we heard voices of cowherds by the river. We approached and captured four of them, along with a herd of Algarañaz's cows. They had a safe-conduct pass from the army to look for 12 head of cattle; some of the cows were already gone and could not be caught. We took two cows for ourselves and took them along the river to our creek. The four civilians turned out to be a contractor and his son, a peasant from Chuquisaca and another from Camiri, who was very receptive so we gave him our communiqué [No. 1 To the Bolivian People, see Appendices], and he promised to disseminate it. We detained them for a while and then set them free, asking that they say nothing — which they promised.

We spent the night eating.

April 7

We waded into the creek, taking the surviving cow to be slaughtered to make *charqui*. Rolando stayed at the ambush site by the river with orders to shoot whoever came along; there was nothing all day. Benigno and Camba followed the path that should lead to Pirirenda and they reported hearing something like a motor from a sawmill in a canyon near our creek.

I sent off Urbano and Julio with a message for Joaquín but they did not return all day.

April 8

Little happened today. Benigno went on with his work and returned without finishing it, declaring that it would not be finished tomorrow either. Miguel set out to look for a canyon that Benigno had seen from above and has not returned.

Urbano and Julio came back with Polo. The soldiers have occupied the camp and are scouting the hills; they passed the "elevator" on their way down. Joaquín reports on these and other problems in the attached document (D. XIX).

We had three cows and their calves, but one escaped, leaving four animals from which we will make *charqui* with the salt we have left.

April 9

Polo, Luis, and Willy went off with the mission to deliver a note to Joaquín and to help them locate another hiding place upstream, which Ñato and Guevara will select. According to Ñato, there are good spots just over an hour away from our current position, although they are rather close to the creek. Miguel came back, having found a canyon that leads to Pirirenda and we will need a day to get there with our backpacks; I therefore ordered Benigno to stop the work he was doing, which would take at least another day to complete.

April 10

Dawn broke and the morning passed without much happening as we prepared to leave the creek, removing all traces of our presence, and then crossing through Miguel's ravine toward Pirirenda-Gutiérrez. Negro arrived very agitated mid-morning to warn us that 15 soldiers were coming downstream. Inti had gone to notify Rolando at the ambush site. There was no other option but to wait and so that is what we did; I dispatched Tuma so he could report back to me. The first reports soon arrived, with unfortunate news. Rubio (Jesús Suárez Gayol) had been mortally wounded. His body was carried to our camp; he had been shot in the head.

This is what happened: The ambush was made up of eight men from the rear guard and a reinforcement of three from the vanguard; they were spread out on both sides of the river. When Inti went to inform them that 15 soldiers were coming, he passed Rubio and realized he was in a very bad position, being clearly visible from the river. The soldiers advanced taking few precautions, searching the riverbanks for tracks. They ran into Braulio or Pedro before falling into the ambush. The exchange lasted a few seconds, leaving one dead and three wounded, plus six prisoners. Later a low-ranking officer was hit and four others escaped. Next to another wounded man, they found Rubio dying. His Garand had jammed and a grenade was beside him with the pin released but without having exploded. The prisoner could not be interrogated because he was seriously wounded and died shortly afterward, as did the commanding officer.

From interrogating the prisoners, the following information was gained: These 15 men belong to the same company that was upriver at the Ñacahuazú; they had crossed through the canyon, collected the skeletons, and then had occupied the camp. According to the soldiers, they had not found anything, although the radio reports that photos and documents had been found there. The company consists of 100 men, of which 15 accompanied a group of journalists to our camp. This group had left to go on a scouting expedition and returned at 17:00. The largest forces are in Pincal, and there are about 30 soldiers in Lagunillas; the group that had gone along the Tiraboy had probably been withdrawn to Gutiérrez. They described their odyssey, being lost in the woods without water and how they had to be rescued. Expecting that more of them would come later, I resolved to keep the ambush in place, which Rolando had moved forward about 500 meters, but now it was reinforced by the entire vanguard. At first I had ordered them to withdraw, but then it seemed logical to leave it as it was. Around 17:00, came information that the army was advancing with a large number of troops. There was nothing to do but wait. I sent off Pombo to get a clear idea of the situation. Some isolated shots were heard for a short time and Pombo returned to say they had fallen into our ambush again and that several were killed and a major had been taken prisoner.[3]

This time, events unfolded like this: The soldiers had advanced along the river, but they were spread out and did not take any real precautions and we took them completely by surprise. This time there were seven dead, five wounded, and a total of 22 prisoners. The balance sheet is the following: (There are no totals due to a lack of information).

---

3. Refers to Bolivian Army Major Rubén Sánchez Valdivia.

April 11

We began the transfer of all our gear in the morning and we buried Rubio in a small, shallow grave, given our lack of materials. Inti stayed with the rear guard to accompany the prisoners and to set them free, as well as to look for more scattered weapons. The only result of the search was two new prisoners and their Garands. We gave two copies of [Communiqué: To the Bolivian People, see Appendices] No. 1 to the major, who promised to pass them on to the press. The casualties are now 10 dead, including two lieutenants; 30 prisoners (a major, some non-commissioned officers, and the rest privates); six wounded—one from the first attack and the others from the second.

They are under the command of the Fourth Division, but mixed with elements of several other regiments; there are Rangers, paratroopers, and soldiers from the local area who are just kids.

Not until the afternoon did we finish the transfer and find a cave in which to leave the gear, but it is still not properly prepared. During the last trip, two cows took fright and ran away, so now all we have left is a calf.

Just as we reached the new camp very early, we ran into Joaquín and Alejandro, who had come with all their people. From their information, we concluded that what the soldiers reported was only a figment of Eustaquio's imagination and that moving here was a waste of time.

The radio reported a "new and bloody encounter" and mentioned nine dead from the army and at least four "confirmed" dead on our side.

A Chilean journalist gave a detailed description of our camp and reported the discovery of a photo of me, without a beard and with a pipe. There will have to be an investigation into how this was obtained. There is no proof that the upper cave has been found, although there are some suggestions this might be the case.

April 12

I brought all the combatants together at 6:30, except for the four from the reject group, to hold a small memorial for Rubio where I noted that the first blood spilled was Cuban. I mentioned I had observed a tendency in the vanguard to depreciate the Cubans, a tendency that surfaced yesterday when Camba commented that he had less and less confidence in the Cubans, after an incident with Ricardo. I made a new call for unity as the only possible way to develop our army, pointing out we had increased our firepower and gained combat experience, but our number has not increased; to the contrary, it has decreased in the last few days.

After storing all our booty in a cave prepared well by Ñato, we left at 14:00 at a slow pace. We were so slow that we barely advanced and had to sleep by a small water hole, although we had just set out.

Now the army admits to 11 dead; either they found another corpse or someone died of their wounds. I began a little course on Debray's book.

Part of a message has been decoded, but it does not seem very important.

April 13

We divided the group into two to be able to walk faster, but despite this, we still went slowly, reaching the camp at 16:00 and the other group arriving at 18:30. Miguel had come back in the morning; the caves had not been discovered and nothing had been touched: the benches, the stoves, the oven, and the seedbeds are still intact.

Aniceto and Raúl went off exploring but did not do well; tomorrow they must try again to reach the Iquira River.

The announcement by the North Americans that they are sending advisers to Bolivia corresponds to an old plan and has nothing to do with the guerrillas. Perhaps we are witnessing the first episode of a new Vietnam.

April 14

A monotonous day. We brought some things from the infirmary, giving us enough food for five days. When we went to get the canned milk from the upper cave, we discovered that 23 cans were inexplicably missing; Moro had left 48, and it seems nobody had time to take them. Milk is a corrupting factor. A mortar and a machine gun were taken from the cave to reinforce our position until Joaquín gets here. It is not quite clear how to conduct the operation, but it seems to me that the best way would be for everyone to leave here, to operate for a short time from the Muyupampa area, and then to withdraw to the north. If it is possible, Dantón and Carlos should head to Sucre-Cochabamba, depending on the circumstances. Communiqué No. 2 was written for the Bolivian people (D. XXI) and Report No. 4 is for Manila, which the Frenchman should deliver.

April 15

Joaquín arrived with the rear guard and we decided to leave

tomorrow. He reported that planes had flown over the area and that artillery had been fired into the woods. The day went by without incident. The group is now completely armed; the .30 caliber machine gun is assigned to the rear guard (Marcos), who will have the reject group as his assistants.

At night I talked about the trip, and issued a severe warning about the problem of the disappearing canned milk.

We decoded part of a long message from Cuba, which, to summarize, states that Lechín knows about me and is going to declare his support; he will reenter the country clandestinely in 20 days.

I wrote a note to Fidel (No. 4) informing him of recent events. It is going out in code and invisible ink.

April 16

The vanguard set out at 6:15 and we left at 7:15, walking at a good pace to the Iquira River, but Tania and Alejandro fell behind. When their temperatures were taken, Tania's was over 39 degrees and Alejandro's was about 38. Moreover, the delay prevented us from progressing as we had planned. We left the two of them, along with Negro and Serapio, a kilometer up the Iquira and we proceed to occupy the hamlet called Bella Vista; to be more precise, a place where we bought potatoes, a pig, and corn from four peasants. The peasants are poor and are quite terrified by our presence here. We spent the night cooking and eating and not moving, in the hope that in the morning we can reach Ticucha without being seen.

April 17

The news kept changing and with it our plans; according to the peasants, going to Ticucha would be a waste of time because there is a direct route to Muyupampa (Vaca Guzmán) that is shorter and the last stretch is wide enough for vehicles; we resolved to go directly to Muyupampa, after much vacillation on my part. I sent for the four stragglers who will stay with Joaquín and ordered him to make their presence known so as to preempt excessive troop movement in the area; he should wait for us for three days. Until then, he should stay in the area but should avoid engaging in direct combat until we return. At night it was learned that a peasant's son had disappeared and that he might have gone to raise the alarm, but we decided to leave in spite of everything in order to get the Frenchman and Carlos out once and for all. Moisés must stay with the group of stragglers because of an acute gallbladder attack.

Here is a sketch of our situation:

By returning via the same route, we risk clashing with army units alerted in Lagunillas or with some column coming from

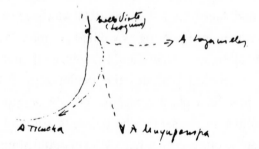

Ticucha, but we have to do this to avoid being separated from the rear guard.

We started out at 22:00, walking with breaks until 4:30, when we stopped for a nap. We had covered some 10 kilometers.

Of all the peasants we have encountered, there is one, Simón, who appears to want to cooperate, although he is scared, and another one, Vides, could be dangerous; he is the "rich man" of the area. Moreover, we have to consider that Carlos Rodas's son disappeared and might be an informer (under the influence of Vides, who is the economic boss of the area).

April 18

We walked until daybreak, napping for the last hour of night in considerably cold weather. In the morning, the vanguard went off to explore, finding a household of Guaranís, who offered very little information. Our sentries stopped a man on a horse who turned out to be Carlos Rodas's son (another one) traveling to Yakunday; we took him prisoner. It was a slow walk, and at 3:00 we reached Matagal, the house of A. Padilla, a poor brother of another peasant who lives a league from here and whose house we had passed. The man was terrified and tried to get rid of us by every possible means. To make matters worse, it began to rain and we had to take refuge in his house.

April 19

We stayed all day in the same place, detaining peasants coming from both directions, so we acquired an assortment of prisoners. At 13:00 the sentries brought us a Greek gift: an English journalist called Roth,[4] who had been brought by some kids from Lagunillas following our tracks. His documents were in order but there were some suspicious things: In his passport, the profession of student is crossed out and replaced

---

4. George Andrew Roth, British-Chilean photographer.

by journalist (he claims to be a photographer). He has a visa from Puerto Rico and when asked about an organizer's card from Buenos Aires, he confessed to have been a Spanish teacher for some Peace Corps students. He said he had been at the camp and had seen Braulio's diary that told of his experiences and trips. It is always the same old story: a lack of discipline and irresponsibility at every turn. The kids who brought the journalist told us they learned about us in Lagunillas our first night there, thanks to a report by someone. We pressured Rodas's son and he confessed that his brother and one of Vides's farmhands had gone to claim the reward of between $500 and $1,000. We confiscated his horse in reprisal and made this known to the other peasants we were detaining.

The Frenchman asked if he could discuss the problem with the Englishman, as a test of good faith, to see if he would help them get out. Carlos accepted this reluctantly and I washed my hands of the whole matter. We got to *[illegible in the original]* at 21:00 and continued on to Muyupampa, where, according to reports from the peasants, everything was calm. The Englishman accepted the conditions that Inti put to him, including a short account I had drafted. At 23:45, after shaking hands with those leaving us, the group set off to occupy the village; I stayed behind with Pombo, Tuma, and Urbano.

The cold was intense and we made a little bonfire. At 1:00 Ñato arrived to inform us that the village was in a state of alert, with about 20 army troops and self-defense patrols there; one of these patrols, with two M-3s and two revolvers, were surprised by our advance party, but surrendered without a fight. They asked for my instructions and I told them to withdraw due to the lateness of the hour, to release the English journalist, and let the Frenchman and Carlos make their own choices. At 4:00 we

Self-portrait taken by Che Guevara in the Hotel Copacabana, La Paz, Bolivia, where he was undercover before joining the other guerrillas.

All photographs copyright © Aleida March and the Che Guevara Studies Center, Havana.

Tuma and Che Guevara in disguise at Abapó, before leaving for Lagunillas.

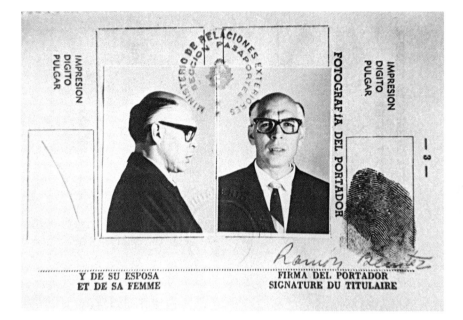

IMPRESION
DIGITO
PULGAR

IMPRESION
DIGITO
PULGAR

FOTOGRAFÍA DEL PORTADOR

MINISTERIO DE RELACIONES EXTERIORES
SECCIÓN PASAPORTES

— 3 —

Y DE SU ESPOSA
ET DE SA FEMME

FIRMA DEL PORTADOR
SIGNATURE DU TITULAIRE

False passport used by Che Guevara to enter Bolivia secretly in 1966.

FROM LEFT TO RIGHT: Arturo, Tuma, Che, Loro, and Pombo.

Chino and Che.

ABOVE: Che Guevara, Pombo, and Marcos.

BELOW: Mario Monje and Che Guevara meet, December 31, 1966.

Che Guevara and Loyola Guzmán.

Peasants of the area where the guerrillas were located. Photograph taken by one of the guerrilla fighters.

ABOVE: A guerrilla preparing his hammock.

BELOW, LEFT TO RIGHT: Rolando, Olo Pantoja, Pombo, and Marcos.

Tuma on guard duty in the observation post.

Che Guevara on guard duty in the observation post.

Che Guevara speaking with Régis Debray and Ciro Bustos.

Che Guevara.

Miguel (left) and Inti (right).

Che fixing a rifle on the banks of the Ñacahuazú River.

Coco Peredo and Tania.

FROM LEFT TO RIGHT: Inti, Pombo, Urbano, Rolando, Alejandro, Tuma, Arturo, and Moro.

FROM LEFT TO RIGHT: Coco, Loyola Guzmán, Inti, and Alejandro.

FROM LEFT TO RIGHT: Urbano, Miguel, Che, Marcos, Chino, Pachungo, Pombo, Inti, and Loro.

Guerrilla fighters resting.

Guerrilla fighter crossing a river.

Che Guevara reading in the observation post.

Olo Pantoja (left) and Moisés Guevara (right).

FROM LEFT TO RIGHT: Alejandro, Inti, Urbano, Rolando, Che, Tuma, Arturo, and Moro.

Tania.

Che Guevara on the banks of a river.

7 de noviembre   1

Hoy comienza una nueva etapa. Por la noche llegamos a la finca. El viaje fue bastante bueno. Luego de entrar, convenientemente disfrazados por Cochabamba, Pachungo y yo hicimos los contactos y viajamos en jeep, en dos días y dos vehículos. Al llegar cerca de la finca detuvimos las máquinas, y una sola llegó a ella para no atraer las sospechas de un propietario cercano, que murmura sobre la posibilidad de que nuestra empresa esté dedicada a la fabricación de cocaína. Como dato curioso, el inefable Tumaini es indicado como el químico del grupo. Al seguir hacia la finca, en el segundo viaje, Bigotes, que acababa de enterarse de mi identidad, casi se va por un barranco, dejando el jeep varado en el borde del precipicio. Caminamos algo así como 20 kilómetros, llegando a la finca, donde hay 3 trabajadores del partido, pasada la media noche.

Bigotes se mostró dispuesto a colaborar con nosotros,

Che Guevara's Bolivian Diary, first entry, November 7, 1966.

El punto negativo es la imposibilidad de hacer contacto con Joaquín, pese a nuestro peregrinar por las serranías. Hay indicios de que se ha movido hacia el norte.

Desde el punto de vista militar, tres nuevos combates, causándole bajas al Ejército e sin sufrir ninguna, además de las penetraciones en Pirirenda y Caraguatarenda indican el buen éxito. Los perros se han declarado incompetentes y son retirados de la circulación.

Las características más importantes son:

1º) Falta total de contacto con Manila, La Paz y Joaquín, lo que nos reduce a los 25 hombres que constituyen el grupo.

2º) Falta completa de incorporación campesina, aunque nos van perdiendo el miedo y se logra la admiración de los campesinos. Es una tarea lenta y paciente.

3º) El partido, a través de Kolle, ofrece su colaboración, al parecer, sin reservas.

4º) El clamoreo del caso Debray da a todo más beligerancia a nuestro movimiento que ... combates victoriosos.

5º) La guerrilla va adquiriendo una moral prepotente y segura que, bien administrada, es una garantía de éxito.

6º) El Ejército sigue sin organizarse y su técnica no mejora sustancialmente.

Noticia del mes es el apresamiento y fuga del Loro, que ahora deberá incorporarse o dirigirse a La Paz a hacer contacto.

El Ejército dio el parte de la detención de todos los campesinos que colaboraron con nosotros en la zona de Loicuri: ahora viene una etapa en la que el terror sobre los campesinos se ejercerá desde ambas partes, aunque con calidades diferentes; nuestro triunfo significará el cambio cualitativo necesario para un salto en el desarrollo.

"Analysis of the Month." A page from Che Guevara's Bolivian Diary.

Aelita = (4?)

Mittwoch

14

JUNI

S		4	11	18	25
M		5	12	19	26
D		6	13	20	27
M		7	14	21	28
D	1	8	15	22	29
F	2	9	16	23	30
S	3	10	17	24

Paramos el día en la aguada fría, al lado del fuego, esperando noticias de Miguel; Urbano que era la cocinadores. El plazo para moverse era hasta las

7 Uhr *pero Urbano llegó pasada esa hora a avisar que se había llegado a un arroyo y que se veían piquetes, por lo que creía que podría llegar al río*

8

9 *grande. Nos quedamos en el lugar, comiéndonos el último potaje; no falta más que una ración de maní y 3 de mote.*

10 *He llegado a los 39 y se acerca inexorablemente una edad que da que pensar sobre mi futuro guerrillero; por*

11 *ahora estoy "entero".*

h = 840

12

13

14

15

A page from Che Guevara's Bolivian Diary. His birthday, June 14, 1967, and the birthday of his daughter Celia.

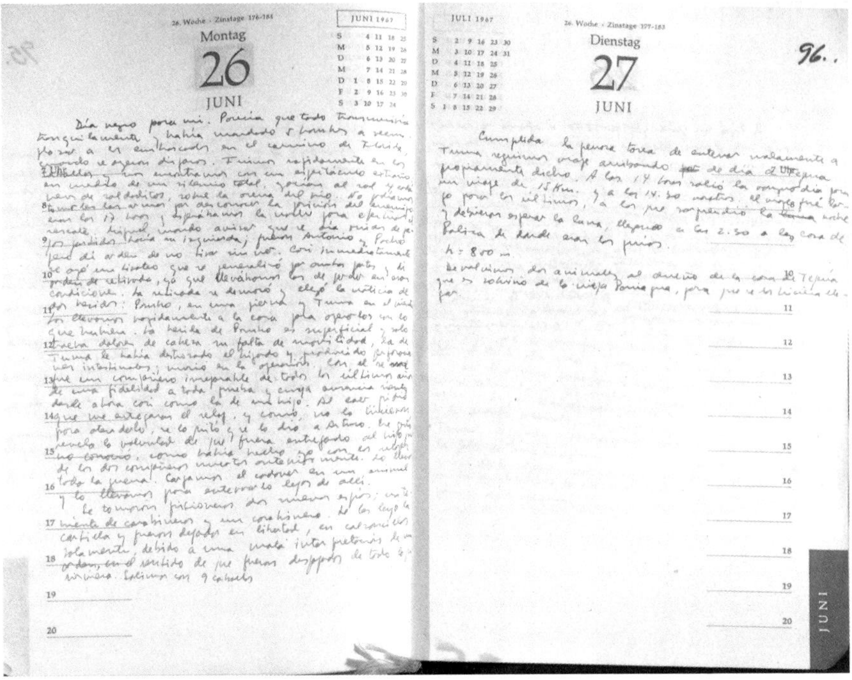

Che Guevara's Bolivian Diary.

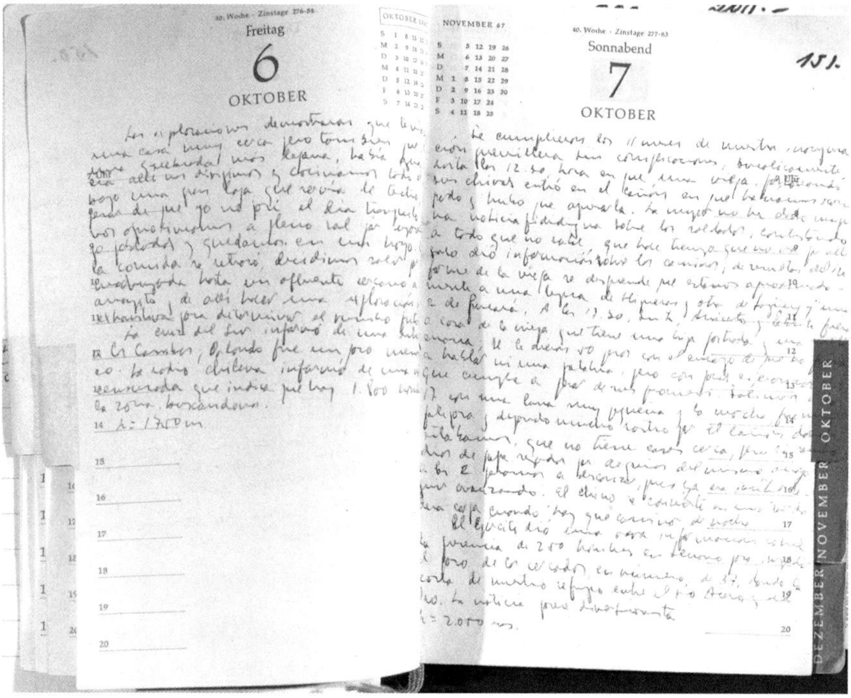

Che Guevara's Bolivian Diary, final entry, October 7, 1967.

Survivors of the guerrilla troop arriving in Chile.

began the retreat, without gaining our objective; Carlos decided to stay and the Frenchman followed him; this time he was the reluctant one.

April 20

At around 7:00, we reached the house of Nemesio Caraballo, whom we had met during the night and who had offered us coffee. The man had left, leaving the house locked, with some frightened servants still there. We prepared a meal there, buying some corn and *jocos*[5] (*zapallos*)[6] from the farmhands. At 13:00, a van showed up with a white flag, carrying a sub-prefect, the doctor, and the priest from Muyupampa; the priest was a German. Inti spoke with them. They had come in peace, but they wanted to be mediators for peace on the national level. Inti offered a truce for Muyupampa in exchange for a list of supplies to be brought to us before 18:30. They would not agree because, according to them, the army controlled the village, and they asked for an extension until 6:00 in the morning, but this was refused.

They brought two cartons of cigarettes as a sign of good will and told us that the three who left had been arrested in Muyupampa and that two of them are in trouble for having false documents. Bad news for Carlos, but Dantón should be all right.

At 17:30, three AT-6s aircraft came and dropped a few bombs on the house where we were cooking. One of them fell 15 meters away and Ricardo was slightly wounded by some shrapnel. That was the army's response. We have to make our

---

5. *Jocos* are a type of pumpkin with a hard shell.
6. *Zapallos* are pumpkin with a soft or smooth shell.

proclamations known so that the soldiers will be completely demoralized; judging by their envoy, they are already scared stiff.

We left at 22:30 with two horses, the confiscated one and the one belonging to the journalist. We headed straight to Ticucha until 1:30, where we stopped to sleep.

April 21

We walked a little way to the house of Rosa Carrasco, who looked after us very well, selling us whatever was necessary. At night we walked to the junction of the Muyupampa and Monteagudo road, a place called Taperillas. The idea was to stay at a water hole and explore the area to see where to set up our next ambush. Another reason to stay here is the news on the radio about the death of three mercenaries: a Frenchman, an Englishman, and an Argentine. There must be a response to this disinformation campaign so as to teach them a lesson.

Before dinner, we went to the house of old man Rodas, the stepfather of Vargas, who was killed at the Ñacahuazú; we explained what had happened and he seemed satisfied. The vanguard misunderstood their instructions and continued along the road, disturbing some dogs that barked excessively.

April 22

We began making mistakes in the morning; after we had withdrawn into the woods, Rolando, Miguel, and Antonio went to look for a site for an ambush; they surprised a small YPFB truck [Bolivian State Petroleum Reserves] that was checking out our footprints while a peasant was telling them about our presence here the night before; we decided to take everyone prisoner. This changed our plans, but we decided to position ourselves for an ambush during the day to capture any passing supply trucks and to ambush the army if it came this way. We seized a truck with some supplies and plenty of bananas, along with a considerable number of peasants; but another one was let go that was examining our tracks as were other small YPFB trucks. We were delayed, waiting for a meal that included the tempting offer of bread, but it never came.

My intention was to load up the small YPFB truck with food and to proceed with the vanguard to the junction of the road to Ticucha, four kilometers away. At nightfall, a little plane began to circle our position and the barking of dogs in neighboring houses became more persistent. At 20:00, we were ready to leave, despite the evidence that our presence had been detected. Just then, a brief clash occurred and then we heard voices calling on us to surrender; we were all hidden and had no idea what had happened, but fortunately, our belongings and the supplies were already on the small truck; after a while we got everything organized, only missing Loro, but all signs indicated that nothing had happened to him. It turned out that Ricardo was the one involved in the encounter, having surprised the soldier's guide as they were climbing the ridge to surround us; the guide might have been shot.

We left with the small truck and all the available horses, six in total; the people took turns walking and riding, but in the end everyone rode in the small truck, with six from the van-guard on horseback. We arrived in Ticucha at 3:30, and at El Mesón, the priest's property, at 6:30. The truck got stuck in a hole on the way.

The balance sheet of the action is negative; on the one hand, there was a lack of discipline and foresight, and on the other, the loss (temporary, I hope) of a man. In addition, we paid for goods but we failed to bring them with us. Finally, we lost a bundle of dollars that fell out of Pombo's bag. These are the results of the action. This is without considering the fact that we were surprised and forced to retreat by a group that must have been quite small. There is much to do to transform this group into combat unit, although morale is very high.

April 23

A day of rest was declared, and it passed uneventfully. At noon, the plane (AT-6) flew over the area; we reinforced the sentries but nothing happened. At night instructions for the next day were given: Benigno and Aniceto will go to find Joaquín — four days. Coco and Camba will explore the trail to the Río Grande and prepare it for use — four days. We will stay close to the cornfield, waiting to see if the army comes before Joaquín is able to join us. Joaquín is instructed to bring everyone, only leaving behind any mebers of the reject group, if they are sick.

The mystery still surrounds the fate of Dantón, Pelado, and the English journalist; the press is censored, and another clash has just been announced in which three to five prisoners were captured.

April 24

The explorers departed. We positioned ourselves one kilometer upstream on a small ridge; from our lookout, we could watch the last peasant's house, about 500 meters before the priest's farm. (We found marijuana in his fields.) The peasant showed up again and was inquisitive; in the afternoon, an AT-6 fired two machine-gun bursts at the little house. Pacho disappeared mysteriously; he was sick and had stayed behind; Antonio showed him the road and he started out in our direction. From where he was, he should have made it in five hours, but he never came back. Tomorrow we will search for him.

April 25

Bad day. At about 10:00 Pombo returned from the lookout warning us that 30 soldiers were advancing toward the little house. Antonio stayed at the observation post. While we were getting ready, Antonio arrived with the news that there were 60 soldiers and they were preparing to advance. The lookout proved to be inefficient in giving us sufficient warning. We decided to set up an improvised ambush along the access path to the camp; quickly, we chose a short stretch along the creek with a visibility of 50 meters. I positioned myself there with Urbano and Miguel, who had the automatic rifle. El Médico,[7] Arturo, and Raúl occupied a position on the right to impede anyone trying to flee or to advance that way. Rolando, Pombo, Antonio, Ricardo, Julio, Pablito, Darío, Willy, Luis, and León occupied the lateral position on the other side of the creek to completely cover the flank. Inti stayed at the river bed to attack anyone looking for refuge there. Ñato and Eustaquio went to the lookout with instructions to withdraw when the firing started. Chino remained behind, guarding the camp. My already meager troops were reduced by three men: Pacho, lost, with Tuma and Luis off looking for him.

In a while the army's advance guard appeared, which to our surprise included three German shepherds and their trainer.

---

7. From this point, references to "El Médico" refer to Moro, as the other two doctors (Negro and Ernesto) left with Joaquín's group.

The animals were restless, but it did not seem that they had detected us. However, they continued to advance and I shot at the first dog, but missed. When I aimed at the guide, the M-2 jammed. Miguel killed the other dog, from what we could see, but it was not confirmed. No one else entered the ambush. Intermittent gunfire commenced at the army's flank. When the shooting was over, I sent Urbano to order a retreat, but he came back with the news that Rolando was wounded. Shortly, they brought him back, but he was already dying; he died as we began to give him plasma. A bullet had split his femur and all the surrounding nerves and vessels; he bled to death before we could do anything. We have lost the best man of the guerrilla force, one of its pillars, my compañero since he was basically a child, when he became the messenger for Column 4 [during the Cuban revolutionary war], through the invasion, and now to this new revolutionary venture. Of his sorrowful death, only one thing can be said, for a hypothetical future yet to materialize: "Thy brave little captain's corpse has stretched to immensity in its metallic form."[8]

The rest of the day was spent on a slow withdrawal operation, collecting everything and the body of Rolando (Captain San Luis). Pacho joined us later: he had made a mistake and went to where Coco was, and it took him all night to return. At 3:00 we buried the body under a thin layer of earth. Benigno and Aniceto arrived at 16:00, reporting that they had fallen into an army ambush (or rather a skirmish), losing the backpacks but getting out unharmed. According to Benigno's calculations, this occurred as they had nearly reached the Ñacahuazú. Now we have the two natural exits blocked, so we will have to "head

---

8. From Pablo Neruda's *"Un Canto para Simón Bolívar."*

for the hills"; leaving along the Río Grande is not smart because it is predictable and would take us further from Joaquín, from whom we have had no news. At night we reached a crossroads: one leading to the Ñacahuazú and the other to the Río Grande, and we slept there; we will wait here for Coco and Camba to reunite our small troop. The balance sheet of the operation is extremely negative: Rolando was killed, but not only that—the losses we inflicted on the army cannot be more than two and a dog, even with everyone shooting, our position was not studied or prepared properly and those shooting could not see the enemy; and finally, the lookout system was very bad, failing to give us enough advance warning.

A helicopter landed twice at the priest's house; we do not know if it went to pick up the wounded, and aircraft bombed our previous positions, which indicates they have not advanced at all.

April 26

We walked for a few meters and I ordered Miguel to look for a place to camp while a search party went to find Coco and Camba, but he turned up at midday with both of them. They said they had cleared a path that would take us four hours to walk loaded with our supplies and that it is possible to climb the ridge. Nevertheless, I sent Benigno and Urbano to find a way up close to the canyon of the creek that flows into the Ñacahuazú, but they returned at dusk to say it is no good. We decided to continue on the trail cleared by Coco and to try to find another that leads to the Iquira.

We have a little mascot: Lolo, a baby *urina* [deer]. Let's see if it survives.

April 27

Coco's four hours turned out to be only two and a half. We thought we had reached a place on the map called Masico: an area with many bitter orange groves. Urbano and Benigno continued work on the path and cleared enough for one hour more. The cold is intense at night.

Bolivian radio transmitted military reports announcing the deaths of a civilian guide, a dog trainer, and the dog Rayo. Our losses are given as two dead: one presumed to be Cuban, nicknamed Rubio, and the other, a Bolivian. It is confirmed that Dantón is imprisoned near Camiri; it is certain the others are alive with him.

Altitude = 950 meters.

April 28

We made our way slowly until 15:00. By then, the creek had run dry and headed in another direction, so we stopped. It was already too late to explore, so we went back to where there was water to set up camp. We have just enough food for four days. Tomorrow we will try to reach the Ñacahuazú via the Iquira, and we will have to cut through the mountains.

April 29

We checked out some clearings that could be seen. The result was negative. At this point, at least, we are in a canyon with no easy way out. Coco thinks he saw a canyon that intersects with this one, but he did not explore it; tomorrow we will take the entire troop there.

After a long delay, we completely decoded Message No. 35,

which had a paragraph asking for me to add my signature to a call in support of Vietnam, organized by Bertrand Russell.

April 30

We began the attack on the hill. The supposed canyon ended at some cliffs, but we found a stretch we could climb; darkness took us by surprise close to the peak and we slept there; the chill was not too bad.

Lolo died, a victim of Urbano's impulsiveness when he threw his rifle at its head.

Radio Habana broadcast a report from Chilean journalists stating that the guerrillas are so strong that they can threaten cities and that they recently captured two military trucks full of supplies. The magazine *Siempre* interviewed Barrientos who, among other things, admitted that he had Yankee military advisers and that the guerrilla movement arose due to the social conditions in Bolivia.

Summary of the month

Things are developing normally, although we have to acknowledge two severe losses: Rubio and Rolando; the death of the latter is a severe blow because I was planning to give him command of an eventual second front. We have seen action four more times, all of them with generally positive results and one very good one—the ambush in which Rubio died.

On another level, we are totally cut off; illness has undermined the health of some compañeros, obliging us to divide our forces, which has greatly reduced our effectiveness; we have still not made contact with Joaquín; the peasant support base has yet to develop, although, it appears that the systematic terror they suffer will ensure the neutrality of most — support will come later. There has not been a single new recruit, and apart from the deaths, we have lost Loro, who disappeared after the action at Taperillas.

Of the points on military strategy noted above, we can emphasize:

a) The measures taken to control us have not been very effective to date, and while they bother us, they allow us some movement, given the army's weakness and lack of mobility; besides, after the last ambush against the dogs and the trainer, we can presume they will be more careful when entering the woods.

b) The clamor continues, but now from both sides; after the publication of my article in Havana, there can be no doubt about my presence here.

It seems certain that the North Americans will intervene heavily here, having already sent helicopters and apparently the Green Berets, although they have not been seen around here.

c) The army (at least one or two companies) has improved its technique; they surprised us at Taperillas and were not demoralized at El Mesón.

d) The mobilization of peasants is nonexistent, except as informers, which is somewhat troublesome; but they are neither quick nor efficient, and of no consequence.

Chino's status has changed and he will be a combatant until the second or third front is established. Dantón and Carlos were victims of their own haste, almost desperation, to leave and of my lack of energy to stop them; now communication with Cuba is cut off (Dantón) and the plan of action for Argentina (Carlos) is lost.

In summary: A month in which all has developed normally, considering the inevitable contingencies of a guerrilla force. Morale is good among all the combatants who have had their preliminary test as guerrilla fighters.

MAY 1967

May 1

We celebrated the date by clearing vegetation, but we walked very little; we have still not reached the point where the waters divide.

Almeida spoke in Havana, applauding the famous Bolivian guerrillas and me. The speech was rather long but good. We have sufficient food for three days. Ñato killed a small bird with a slingshot today; we now enter the era of the bird.

May 2

A day of slow progress and confusion about our geographical position. We effectively only walked for two hours, because the path was so difficult to clear. From a height we could locate a point close to the Ñacahuazú that suggests we are quite far north, but there is no sign of the Iquira. I ordered Miguel and Benigno to work on the path for the entire day in order to reach the Iquira or at least some water, because we have run out. There is enough food for five days but very meager.

Radio Habana continues its information offensive about Bolivia, with exaggerated reports.

Altitude = 1,760 meters reached; we slept at 1,730.

May 3

After a day of continuous slashing, which made it possible to walk for just over two hours, we reached a creek with plenty of water that seems to be flowing north. Tomorrow we will investigate to see if it changes direction, and at the same time we will continue clearing the way. We have enough food for only two days and it is rather skimpy. We are at 1,080 meters, 200 above the Ñacahuazú. In the distance is the sound of a motor, but we cannot identify which direction it comes from.

May 4

In the morning, the hike continued, while Coco and Aniceto scouted the creek. They returned around 13:00, confirming that the creek turns toward the southeast, so it is probably the Iquira. I gave the order to find the *macheteros* and to continue walking downstream. We set off at 13:30, and at 17:00 we stopped, certain that the creek's general direction was east-northeast, so it cannot be the Iquira unless it changes course. The *macheteros* reported that they had not found water and that they saw only ridges; it was decided to continue, under the impression that we were heading to the Río Grande. We caught a single *cacaré*[1] that was shared among the *macheteros*, given its small size; we have only light rations for two days.

The radio broadcast the news that Loro had been arrested and had a wounded leg; his statements have been good up to now. All signs indicate that he was not wounded at the house, but somewhere else, probably trying to escape.

Altitude = 980 meters.

---

1. Small mountain bird, so named because they announce the presence of a person or an animal with their crowing.

May 5

We walked for a good five hours, about 12 to 14 kilometers, to the camp Inti and Benigno had set up. We are at the Congrí Creek, which is not on the map, and much farther north than we had thought. This raises many questions: Where is the Iquira? Is this where Benigno and Aniceto were surprised? Could their attackers have been Joaquín's people? For the moment we are considering heading to Oso Camp, where there should be breakfast for two days, and from there to the old camp. Two large birds and a *cacaré* were killed today, so we can save some food. We still have rations for two days: packets of soup and canned meat. Inti, Coco, and El Médico are setting up hunting hide. There is news that Debray will face a military tribunal in Camiri as the supposed chief and organizer of the guerrillas; his mother arrives tomorrow and there is quite a ruckus about the matter. Nothing of Loro.

Altitude = 840 meters.

May 6

Our estimated arrival at Oso Camp turned out to be wrong because the distance to the little house from the creek was farther than we thought and the way was impassable, so we had to clear the trail. We reached the little house at 16:30 after passing through altitudes of 1,400 meters with the troops tired of walking. Our next to last meal was eaten, a meager one; only a partridge was caught and given to the *machetero* (Benigno) and to the two behind him on the march.

The news is focused on Debray's case.

Altitude = 1,100 meters.

May 7

We arrived early at Oso Camp, and there were eight cans of milk waiting for us, which made a fortifying breakfast. Some things were retrieved from the nearby cave, including a Mauser for Ñato, who will handle our bazooka with its five antitank missiles. He is feeling sick after a bout of vomiting. We had scarcely arrived at the camp when Benigno, Urbano, León, Aniceto, and Pablito left to scout the little farm. We ate the last of our soup and meat, but we have a provision of lard that was in the cave. There are footprints and other small signs that show soldiers have been here. At dawn, the explorers returned empty handed; the soldiers are at the farm and they have cut down the corn. (Today marks the six-month anniversary of the official establishment of the guerrilla force, upon my arrival.)

Altitude = 880 meters.

May 8

From early in the morning I insisted that we organize the cave, retrieve the other can of lard, and refill the bottles, because that is all we have left to eat. At about 10:30, a few isolated shots were heard coming from the ambush site; two unarmed soldiers had come up the Ñacahuazú. Thinking it was an advance party, Pacho wounded one in the leg and the other superficially in the stomach. He said he had fired because they had not stopped at his command, but they, of course, had heard nothing.

The ambush was poorly coordinated and Pacho's actions were not good; he was very nervous. The situation was improved by sending Antonio and some others to the right side. The soldiers stated they were based near the Iquira, but in reality they were lying. At 12:00, two soldiers were captured as they came rushing down the Ñacahuazú, saying they were in a hurry because they had gone hunting and were following the Iquira to get back, when they discovered that their company had disappeared, so they went to find them; they were lying too. In fact, they are camped at the hunting field and they went off to look for food at our farm because the helicopter had not come to bring them supplies. The two we had captured were loaded with toasted and raw corn, four cans of onions, plus sugar and coffee, so today's problem was resolved, with the help of the lard, and we all ate great quantities, making some people sick.

Later, the sentries reported that the soldiers were continually scouting the area, going back and forth to the edge of river. Everyone was tense until the soldiers arrived, apparently 27 of them. They had noticed something unusual and the group advanced under the command of Second Lieutenant Laredo,[2] who opened fire and fell dead on the spot, along with two recruits. Night had already fallen and our troops advanced, capturing six soldiers; the rest retreated.

The total result rashly speaking is three dead and 10 prisoners, two of them wounded; seven M-1s and four Mausers, personal gear, ammunition, and some food we consumed with the lard to mitigate our hunger. We slept there.

May 9

We got up at 4:00 (I never slept) and set the soldiers free, after giving them a lecture. We took their shoes, exchanged

---

2. Henry Laredo. Second lieutenant in the Bolivian Army whose wife had sent a letter asking him to bring home a guerrilla fighter's scalp to adorn their living room.

clothes with them, and sent the liars off in their underwear. They went toward the little farm, carrying their wounded. By 6:30 we completed our withdrawal toward Monos [Monkey] Creek along the path to the cave where we stored the captured goods.

The only food we have left is lard; I felt faint and had to sleep two hours to be able to continue at even this slow and hesitant pace; in general, the march has been that way. We ate soup made from the lard at the first water hole. The troops are sick and now many have edema. At night, the army reported on the action, naming its dead and wounded, but not its prisoners, and announcing major battles with heavy losses on our side.

May 10

We continued our slow progress. On arrival at the camp where Rubio's grave is, we found some *charqui* that we had left in a bad state, along with some fat; we gathered everything; there were no signs of soldiers. We took precautions crossing the Ñacahuazú and began the trek to Pirirenda through a ravine that Miguel had scouted, but the path had not been finished. We stopped at 17:00 and ate pieces of *charqui* and some fat.

May 11

The vanguard started out first; I stayed listening to the news. Urbano came in a while to tell me that Benigno had killed a peccary and wanted permission to start a fire and skin it; we decided to stay and eat the animal while Benigno, Urbano, and Miguel continued clearing the trail to the lagoon. At 14:00, we began the march again, setting up camp at 18:00. Miguel and the others went on ahead.

I need to speak seriously with Benigno and Urbano because the former ate a can of food the day of the battle and then denied it, and Urbano ate some of the *charqui* at Rubio's camp.

The news report stated that Colonel Roche,[3] head of the Fourth Division, which operates in this zone, will be relieved.

Altitude = 1,050 meters.

May 12

We went along slowly. Urbano and Benigno cleared the way. By 15:00, we could see the lagoon about five kilometers away and a little later we found an old trail. After an hour, we came across a giant cornfield with pumpkins, but there was no water. We prepared roasted and salted *jocos* with lard and corn kernels; we also made toasted corn. The scouts arrived with the news that they had stumbled across the house of Chicho,[4] the same one as last time. He is mentioned as a good friend in Lt. Henry Laredo's diary; he was not at home, but four farmhands were there along with a servant, whose husband came looking for her and was detained. We cooked a huge pig with rice and fritters, along with pumpkin. Pombo, Arturo, Willy, and Darío kept guard over the backpacks. The bad part is that we could not find water around the house.

We withdrew at 5:30 at a slow speed, with almost everyone sick. The owner of the house had still not shown up and we left him a note listing the damages and expenses; we paid $10 to each farmhand and the servant for their work.

Altitude = 950 meters.

---

3. Humberto Rocha Urquieta, colonel and head of the Fourth Division of the Bolivian Army, headquartered in Camiri.
4. Chicho Otero was the owner of one of the homes located in the area in which the guerrilla forces operated.

May 13

A day of burps, farts, vomiting, and diarrhea—a real concert from our organs. We remained completely immobile trying to digest the pig. We have two cans of water. I was feeling very bad until I vomited and then felt better. At night, we ate corn fritters and roast pumpkin, plus all the leftovers from the feast the day before—those who were in a condition to eat. All the radio stations are constantly covering news that some Cubans landing in Venezuela were intercepted. The Leoni[5] government presented two of the men with their names and ranks; I do not know them, but everything suggests that something has gone wrong.

May 14

We left early, with little enthusiasm, aiming to reach the lagoon at Pirirenda by a track that Benigno and Camba had found while exploring. Before setting out, I brought everyone together and gave them a blast about some problems we face, mainly concerning food; I criticized Benigno for eating a can of food and denying it, Urbano for eating some *charqui* on the sly, and Aniceto for his eagerness to assist in everything to do with food and his reluctance to do anything else. During the meeting we heard sounds of trucks approaching. We stashed about 50 *jocos* and two quintals [200 pounds] of corn kernels for future use in a hiding place nearby.

When we were off the path, busy gathering beans, we heard explosions nearby and shortly we saw aircraft "ferociously bombing us," about two or three kilometers from our position.

---

5. Raúl Leoni, president of Venezuela in 1967.

We continued down a hill and saw a lagoon, while the soldiers kept up their fire. At nightfall, we came to a recently abandoned house that was very well stocked and had water. We ate a delicious chicken fricassee with rice and stayed there until 4:00.

May 15

An uneventful day.

May 16

Just as we started out, I came down with intense abdominal pain, with vomiting and diarrhea. I got it under control with Demerol, but lost consciousness and had to be carried in a hammock. When I awoke I felt much better, but I was covered in shit like a newborn baby. I borrowed a pair of pants, but without water, the stench could be smelled for a league away. We spent the whole day there, with me dozing. Coco and Ñato scouted the area and found a path that runs due north. We followed it at night while the moon was out and then rested. We received Message No. 36, which illustrated just how completely isolated we are.

May 17

We continued the march until 13:00, when we came to a sawmill that seemed to have been abandoned for three days. There was sugar, corn, lard, flour, and water in barrels, all of which seem to have been transported some distance. We set up camp here, while scouting expeditions were conducted along the paths that lead to the woods. Raúl has an abscess on his knee and cannot walk because of the intense pain; he was given a strong antibiotic and tomorrow it will have to be lanced. We walked some 15 kilometers.

Altitude = 920 meters.

May 18

Roberto and Juan Martín.[6]

We spent all day in ambush, in case workers or soldiers came by, but nothing happened. Miguel left with Pablito and found water about two hours from the camp, using an intersecting path. Raúl's abscess was lanced and 50cc of purulent liquid was drained; he was given a general treatment to fight infection; he can barely take a step. I performed my first tooth extraction for this guerrilla campaign; the fortunate victim: Camba—everything went well. We ate bread baked in a little oven and at night had an incredible stew that filled me to bursting.

May 19

The vanguard set off early to occupy ambush positions at the crossroads; we left afterwards, replacing a section of the vanguard while they returned to get Raúl and carry him to the crossroads. The other part of the center group continued on to the water hole to leave their backpacks and then return to get Raúl, who is slowly recovering. Antonio scouted a little downstream and found a camp abandoned by the soldiers where there were also some leftover dry rations. The Ñacahuazú cannot be too far away and I estimate that we should come out below the Congrí Creek. It rained all night, surprising the experts.

---

6. Birthday of his two brothers, Roberto and Juan Martín Guevara de la Serna.

We have food for 10 days and in the immediate area there are pumpkins and corn.

Altitude = 780 meters.

May 20

Camilo.[7]

A day without moving. In the morning the center group set up the ambush and was relieved by the vanguard in the afternoon; Pombo was in charge the whole time, but expressed his view that the site chosen by Miguel is very poor. Miguel explored downstream, finding the Ñacahuazú to be a two-hour walk away, without backpacks. A shot was clearly heard, but we do not know who fired it; on the banks of the Ñacahuazú there are signs of another military camp with a couple of platoons. There was an incident with Luis who was complaining too much and he was excluded from the ambush as a form of punishment, but he seems to have taken it well.

At a press conference, Barrientos rejected Debray's status as a journalist and announced that he would ask Congress to reinstate the death penalty. Almost all the journalists, and all the foreigners, asked him about Debray; he defended himself extremely inarticulately. He is the most incompetent person imaginable.

May 21

Sunday. No movement. We are maintaining the ambush, replacing 10 men with 10 others at noon. Raúl is slowly improving; his abscess was lanced again and another 40cc of

---

7. Birthday of his son Camilo Guevara March.

purulent liquid was drained. He no longer has a fever, but he is in pain and can barely walk; he is my current concern. At night, we ate sumptuously: stew, corn flour, shredded *charqui*, and pumpkin topped with *mote*.

May 22

As expected, at noon the supervisor of the sawmill, Guzmán Robles,[8] showed up with a driver and his son in a beat-up jeep. At first we thought it was an army maneuver to see what was happening, but he opened up to us and agreed to go to Gutiérrez at night, leaving his son[9] as a hostage; he should be back tomorrow. The vanguard will stay in ambush position overnight and tomorrow we will wait until 15:00. After that, it will be necessary to withdraw because the situation could get dangerous. The man gives me the impression that he will not betray us, but we cannot be sure he will be able to buy things for us without raising suspicion. We paid him for everything we had consumed at the mill. He informed us of the situation in Tatarenda, Limón, and Ipitá — no soldiers are in these places, except for a lieutenant at Ipitá. He had not been to Tatarenda, but told us what he had heard.

May 23

A day of tension. The supervisor did not come back all day, and although there was no activity, we decided to withdraw at night with the hostage, a big 17-year-old lad. We walked an

---

8. Guzmán Robles, a Bolivian peasant, who was detained by the army when he returned from buying food for the guerrillas.
9. Moisés Robles, a young Bolivian peasant, 17 years old, who served as a guide for the guerrilla detachment.

hour on the trail in the moonlight, sleeping on the road. We left with enough food for about 10 days.

May 24

In two hours we made it to the Ñacahuazú, which was clear of soldiers. After another four-hour hike downstream, we came out at the Congrí Creek. We walked slowly to match Ricardo's sluggish pace, and Moro's as well. We reached the camp that we had used the first day hiking on our first expedition. We left no tracks, nor did we see any recent ones. The radio broadcast the news that the habeas corpus petition for Debray had been denied. I estimate that we are one or two hours from the Saladillo; when we get to the summit, we will decide what to do.

May 25

In an hour and a half we made it to the Saladillo, without leaving any tracks. We followed the creek for about two hours until reaching its source. We ate there and continued on at 15:30, walking for a few more hours until 18:00, when we made camp at 1,100 meters, still not having reached the top of the ridge. According to the boy, we are a few leagues away from his grandfather's *chaco*;[10] according to Benigno, it is also a full day's hike to Vargas's house by the Río Grande. Tomorrow we will decide where to go.

May 26

After two hours of walking, passing the peak at 1,200 meters,

---

10. Land used for cultivating smaller fruits.

we arrived at the farm belonging to the boy's great-uncle.[11] Two farmhands were working there and had to be apprehended when they came in our direction; they turned out to be brothers-in-law of the old man, who is married to a sister of theirs. They are 16 and 20 years old. They informed us that the boy's father had purchased the food but he was detained and confessed everything. There are 30 soldiers in Ipitá patrolling the village. We ate fried pork with pumpkin and lard stew, but there was no water in the area and it has to be transported from Ipitá in barrels. At night we headed for the farm that belongs to the boys, eight kilometers away, four toward Ipitá and four to the west. We arrived at dawn.

Altitude = 1,100 meters.

May 27

A day of idleness and a little despair: Of all the promised wonders, there was only a bit of old sugar cane and the sugar mill was useless. As expected, the old man who owned the farm showed up at noon with his cart full of water for the pigs; he saw something strange on his way past where the rear guard was in ambush position and was apprehended along with a farmhand; they were held until 18:00, when we released them together with the youngest of the brothers; they were instructed to stay there until Monday and to say nothing.

We walked for two hours and slept in a cornfield; now we are on the road that goes to Caraguatarenda.

---

11. Previously mentioned as Moisés Robles's grandfather.

May 28

Sunday. We rose early and began the march; in an hour and a half we hit the outskirts of the farms at Caraguatarenda. Benigno and Coco were sent to explore, but were seen by a peasant and they took him prisoner. In a short time we had a colony of prisoners who were not particularly scared, until an old woman began to scream along with her children when she was ordered to halt. Neither Pacho nor Pablo felt like stopping her and she fled toward the village. We occupied the village at 14:00, posting sentries at both sides. A little later we took over a YPFB oil company jeep; we captured a total of two jeeps and two trucks—half were privately owned and half belonged to the YPFB. We ate something, had coffee, and after 50 arguments, at 19:30 we headed off to Ipitacito; there we broke into a store and took $500 worth of supplies; we left the money with two peasants, ceremoniously handing them a receipt. We continued our pilgrimage, reaching Itai where we were received very well in a house, which happened to belong to the schoolteacher who owned the store at Ipitacito, so we went over the prices with her. I joined in the conversation, and apparently they recognized me; they had cheese and a little bread, which they gave us along with some coffee; but I detected a false note in their reception. We continued on to Espino, following the railroad tracks to Santa Cruz, but then the truck, a Ford that had the front-wheel drive removed, stalled; we were still three leagues away from Espino when morning came. The vehicle broke down completely two leagues out of town. The vanguard took over the settlement and the jeep had to make four trips to get us all there.

Altitude = 880 meters.

May 29

The settlement at Espino is relatively new because the old one was swept away by a flood in 1958. It is a Guaraní community whose members are very shy and who speak, or pretend to speak, very little Spanish. There were oil company workers nearby and so we inherited another truck in which we could fit everything, but the opportunity was lost when Ricardo got it stuck and we could not pull it out.

It was so peaceful there, like another world. Coco was put in charge of gathering information about the roads, but what he brought back was inadequate and contradictory. As a result, we were about to make a rather dangerous trip that would bring us close to the Río Grande; at the last moment we changed our plans and decided to go to Muchiri, a place where there is water. With all these organizational problems, we set out at 15:30, the vanguard group taking the jeep (six people, seven with Coco) and the rest on foot.

The radio brought us the news that Loro had escaped from where he was being held in Camiri.[12]

May 30

During the day we came to the railroad tracks, finding that the road to Muchiri did not exist. Searching around, we found a straight road used by the oil company workers, only 500 meters from the crossroads, so the vanguard went that way in the jeep. As Antonio was leaving, a little boy with a shotgun and a dog came along the tracks, fleeing when we told him to stop. In light

---

12. The news from the radio was false. It is known that Jorge Vázquez Viaña, after being tortured, was dropped into the woods from a helicopter.

of this, I left Antonio in ambush position at the entrance to the road and we moved back about 500 meters. Miguel appeared at 11:45 saying he had walked 12 kilometers east without finding any houses or water, only a road heading north. I gave him the order to take three men in the jeep on this road for 10 kilometers to the north and to return before nightfall. At 15:00, when I was sleeping peacefully, I was woken by the sound of gunfire at the ambush site. We soon learned that the army had advanced and had fallen into the ambush; the casualties are apparently three dead and one wounded. The participants: Antonio, Arturo, Ñato, Luis, Willy, and Raúl—the latter was weak. We withdrew on foot, walking the 12 kilometers to the junction without finding Miguel; we received news that the jeep was spluttering for lack of water. We found it about three kilometers on; after we all urinated in it and added a canteen of water, we made it to the farthest point we had reached, where Julio and Pablo were waiting. By 2:00 everyone was gathered together around a fire where we roasted three turkeys and fried some pork. We are saving one animal so it can drink out of the water holes, just in case.

We are descending from 750 meters; we are now at 650 meters.

May 31

The jeep bravely kept going with its urine and canteen water. Two events changed our pace: the road heading north ended, so Miguel halted the march; then one of the security groups detained a peasant called Gregorio Vargas, who had come along a side road on his bicycle to set some traps, which is his trade. The attitude of the man was not clear, but he gave us valuable information about water holes. One of these was behind us, so

I sent a group to fetch water and to cook. With the peasant as their guide, on reaching the spot, they saw two army trucks and hurriedly set up an ambush, apparently hitting two men. Ñato, missed at first with a blank from his grenade launcher; then he put in a real bullet, and it blew up in his face; the barrel was destroyed, but he was not hurt. We continued our withdrawal, without harassment from aircraft, walking about 15 kilometers before finding the second water hole after dark. The jeep gave its last gasp due a to lack of gas and overheating. We spent the night eating. The army issued a statement acknowledging the death of a second lieutenant and a soldier yesterday, and attributing to us deaths that were "witnessed." Tomorrow, I intend to cross the railroad tracks to get to the mountains.

Altitude = 620 meters.

Summary of the month

The negative point is the impossibility of making contact with Joaquín, in spite of our pilgrimage on the mountain range. There are indications he has moved to the north.

From a military viewpoint, we had three new battles with losses for the army and none for us. This, along with our forays into Pirirenda and Caraguatarenda, indicate success. The dogs have been declared ineffective and have been withdrawn from circulation.

The most important features are:

1) A total loss of contact with Manila, La Paz, and Joaquín, which reduces the number of our group to 25.
2) A complete failure to recruit peasants, although they are losing their fear of us and we are gaining their admiration. It is a slow and patient task.

3) The party, through Kolle, offers its collaboration, apparently without reservation.

4) The clamor surrounding Debray's case has given more momentum to our movement than 10 victories in battle could have.

5) The morale of the guerrilla movement is growing stronger and, if handled well, will certainly guarantee success.

6) The army remains disorganized and its technique has not significantly improved.

News of the month: The arrest and escape of Loro, who now should be rejoining us or heading to La Paz to make contact.

The army reported the arrest of all the peasants who collaborated with us in the Masicuri area; now comes the stage in which the peasants will be afraid of both sides, although in different ways; our triumph will signify the qualitative change necessary for their leap in development.

JUNE 1967

June 1

I sent the vanguard to position themselves along the road and to explore up to the junction with the oil company's road, about three kilometers away. Aircraft began to move over this area; according to information on the radio, bad weather had made activity over the previous days difficult, but now flights have been resumed. There was an odd report about two dead and three wounded, but it is not clear whether this is new or old news. After eating, we left at 17:00, heading for the railroad tracks, covering seven or eight kilometers without incident, then walked one and a half kilometers along the railroad tracks and took an abandoned, narrow road that should lead to a farm seven kilometers away, but everyone was tired, so we slept halfway there. On the entire journey, we only heard a single shot in the distance.

Altitude = 800 meters.

June 2

Altitude = 800 meters.

We covered the seven kilometers that Gregorio[1] had

---

1. Gregorio Vargas, a peasant who was a guide for the guerrilla force.

estimated and reached the farm where we caught and killed a robust pig and killed it; at that moment, however, Braulio Robles's cowherd, his son, and two farmhands showed up. One of the farmhands turned out to be the *achacao*[2] of the owner, Symuní. Using their horses, we transported the pig, now chopped in pieces, three kilometers to the creek where we detained them while we hid Gregorio, whose disappearance was known. Just as the center group arrived, an army truck went by with two young soldiers and some barrels, an easy target; but this was a day for revelry and pork. We spent the night cooking and at 3:30 set the four peasants free, paying each one $10 for the day. At 4:30 Gregorio departed, after waiting for the meal and his reenlistment bonus; he was paid $100. The water from the creek is brackish.

June 3

We started out at 6:30 by the left bank of the creek and walked until 12:00; Benigno and Ricardo were then sent off to scout the road and found a good place for an ambush. At 13:00, we took our positions, Ricardo and I each with our own group in the middle, Pombo was at one end, and Miguel was with the entire vanguard at the best point. At 14:30, we let a truck loaded with pigs go by, and at 16:20, a small truck with empty bottles; at 17:00, we saw an army truck, the same one as yesterday, with two soldiers wrapped in blanket in the back of the vehicle. I did not have the heart to shoot them, and my brain did not react fast enough to figure out how to detain them, so we let them drive by. At 18:00 we lifted the ambush and continued down the road until we came to the creek again. We had barely arrived when

---

2. In Bolivia a woman's son is called the stepson of the man.

four trucks came by in a row and then three more, but they did not seem to be carrying soldiers.

June 4

We continued walking beside the creek planning to set up another ambush if the conditions were right, we struck another path leading to the west and went that way; then we followed a dry creek bed in a southerly direction. We halted at 14:45 to make some coffee and oatmeal, by a pool of muddy water, but we dawdled so long we camped there. A cold front blew in from the south in the evening, bringing a light rain that fell all night.

June 5

We left the path and continued cutting through the woods, under the constant drizzle of the cold front. We walked until 17:00, spending two and a quarter hours cutting through the thick undergrowth on the side of the highest peak in the area. Fire became the great god of the day. The day passed without food; we saved the brackish water in our canteens for breakfast tomorrow.

Altitude = 250 meters.

June 6

After a meager breakfast, Miguel, Benigno, and Pablito set off to make a trail and to scout the area. At approximately 14:00, Pablo returned saying he had come across an abandoned farm with livestock. We all got ready to march and, following the course of the creek, we crossed the farm and headed to the Río Grande. From there a scouting party was sent off with the mission to occupy a house if an isolated one was found close by; this was done and the first reports suggested we were three kilometers from Puerto Camacho, where there were about 50 soldiers, and that it is connected by a road. We spent the whole night cooking pork and *locro;*[3] the day had not brought the expected results and we set out tired as day was breaking.

June 7

We hiked slowly, avoiding old ranches, until the guide, one of the owner's sons, announced that we had passed the last one. We continued along the "beach"[4] until we found another farm, not mentioned before, that had squash, sugarcane, bananas, and some beans. We set up camp here. The lad who was our guide began to complain about severe abdominal pain, but it is hard to know if they are real.

Altitude = 560 meters.

June 8

We moved our camp about 300 meters to avoid being doubly exposed to both the riverbank and the farm, although later we learned that the owner never goes there; he always uses a barge. Benigno, Pablo, Urbano, and León went to try to cut a path through the rocky cliffs, but they came back in the afternoon saying this was impossible. I had to warn Urbano again about his rudeness. We agreed to make a raft tomorrow, close to the cliff.

---

3. Quechua soup made with rice, *charqui*, potatoes, and vegetables in the eastern region of Bolivia.
4. *Playa* refers to a broad open sandy area along the river.

There is news of a state of siege and threats from the miners, but nothing substantial yet.

June 9

We walked two hours to get to the cliff. Ñato was there making the raft with great effort, but it took a long time and was not a success; it has yet to be tested. I dispatched Miguel to try to find another exit route, but he failed. Benigno caught a large fish, a *dorado*.

Altitude = 590 meters.

June 10

As expected, the raft was unable to carry more than three backpacks and even that was pushing it. The swimmers threw themselves into the water, but could do nothing because of the cold; I decided to send a group to the prisoner's house to look for a barge; Coco, Pacho, Aniceto, and Ñato went. Shortly, mortar fire was heard and Ñato returned with the news that they had clashed with the army, which was on the other side of the river. According to all indications, our people had set off taking no precautions and were spotted. The soldiers began their usual ruckus, and Pombo and Coco began firing without rhyme or reason, alerting them. We resolved to stay put and tomorrow begin a trail to get out of here. The situation is quite uncomfortable if they decide to attack us in full force because, in the best case scenario, we would have to cut through the arid, wooded cliffs.

June 11

A day of total calm; we maintained the ambush but the army

never came; only one small plane flew over the area for a few minutes. They might be waiting for us at the Rosita. The path over the ridge goes almost to the crest of the hill. Tomorrow we will leave at any rate; we have enough food for five or six days.

June 12

We thought at first we could make it to the Rosita or at least the Río Grande again, so we started out. On reaching a small water hole, however, this seemed more difficult than we expected, so we stayed there waiting for news. At 15:00, word came that there was a larger water hole, but it was impossible to get to, so we decided to stay here. The day turned nasty and finally the cold front treated us to a night of cold and rain. The radio broadcast some interesting news: the newspaper *Presencia* announced one dead and one wounded for the army from Saturday's clash; this is great and almost certainly true, and means that we have maintained our pattern of clashes resulting in casualties. Another report announced three dead, among them Inti, one of the guerrilla leaders, and noted the foreign components of the guerrilla force: 17 Cubans, 14 Brazilians, four Argentines, and three Peruvians. The Cuban and the Peruvian count is true; we will have to find out where they got this information.

Altitude = 900 meters.

June 13

We walked only one hour up to the next water hole, because the slashers have not made it to the Rosita or the Río [Grande]. Very chilly. Possibly it can be done tomorrow. We have enough light rations for five days.

The political upheaval in this country is fascinating—the incredible number of pacts and counter-pacts that are in the air. Rarely has the potential for a guerrilla catalyst been so clear.

Altitude = 840 meters.

June 14

Celita: 4?[5]

We spent the day by the "Aguada Fría" [Icy Water Hole] beside a fire, waiting for news from Miguel and Urbano, who were slashing a trail. The time set for moving out was 15:00, but Urbano arrived after that time to tell us they had reached a creek and had seen fences, and thought it might lead to the Río Grande. We stayed put eating the last of the stew; nothing else is left except for one ration of peanuts and three of *mote*.

I turned 39 [today] and am inevitably approaching the age when I need to consider my future as a guerrilla, but for now I am still "in one piece."

Altitude = 840 meters.

June 15

We walked less than three hours to reach the banks of the Río Grande, an area we recognize and which I estimate to be two hours from the Rosita; Nicolás, the peasant, says it is three kilometers. We gave him 150 pesos and the opportunity to leave and he took off like a rocket. We will stay where we are; Aniceto scouted the area and believes that we can cross the river. We ate peanut soup and some *totai* fruit boiled and

5. Birthday of his youngest daughter Celia Guevara March.

cooked in lard; all we have left is *mote* for three days.

Altitude = 610 meters.

June 16

We had walked a kilometer when we saw the people from the vanguard on the riverbank across from us. Pacho had crossed while exploring and found the ford. We crossed in icy water up to our waists, against a strong current, without mishap. An hour later we reached the Rosita, where there are some old footprints, probably made by the army. We find the Rosita to be a larger waterway than expected, and there is no sign of the road that is marked on the map. We walked an hour in the icy water and decided to camp to take advantage of the *totai* fruit and to try to find the beehive that Miguel had found during an earlier expedition. We did not find the beehive and ended up eating only *mote* and palm hearts with lard. There is enough food for tomorrow and the day after (*mote*). We walked some three kilometers along the Rosita and another three along the Río Grande.

Altitude = 610 meters.

June 17

We walked about 15 kilometers along the Rosita in five and a half hours. During the trek we crossed four streams, even though the map shows only one, the Abapocito. We have found many recent tracks. Ricardo killed a *hochi*[6] and this, along with *mote*, was how we got through the day. There is enough *mote* for tomorrow, but presumably we will find another house.

---

6. Species of rodent common in eastern Bolivia.

June 18

Many of us burned our bridges, eating the rest of the *mote* for breakfast. At 11:00, after two and a half hours of walking, we came across a farm with corn, yucca, sugarcane, and a sugar mill to grind it, *jocos*, and rice. We prepared a protein-less meal and sent Benigno and Pablito off to explore. Two hours later Pablo returned with the news that he had run into a peasant whose plot was 500 meters from this one; he said that other peasants were headed this way and they were taken prisoner when they arrived. At night, we moved our camp, and slept at the boys' farm plot, next to the start of the road to Abapó, seven leagues from here. Their houses are 10 to 15 kilometers above where the Mosquera and the Oscura rivers meet, next to the latter.

Altitude = 680 meters.

June 19

We walked at a slow pace for about 12 kilometers until we reached the settlement, which consists of three houses and the same number of families. Two kilometers farther down lives the Gálvez family, where the Mosquera and the Oscura meet; we have to hunt down the residents to be able to speak with them because they are like little animals. In general, they received us very well, but, Calixto, who was appointed mayor by a military commission that passed through here a month ago, was reserved and reluctant to sell us a few little things. When night fell, three pig merchants arrived, carrying a revolver and a Mauser rifle; they had passed the vanguard's observation post. Inti, who interrogated them, did not take their weapons and Antonio, who was guarding them, did so very negligently.

Calixto assured us that they were merchants from Postrer Valle
and that he knew them.

Altitude = 680 meters.

There is another river called the Suspiro that flows into the
Rosita from the left; no one lives along it.

June 20

In the morning, Paulino,[7] one of the boys from the farm below,
told us that the three individuals were not merchants: one was
a lieutenant and the other two were in a different line of work.
He obtained this information from Calixto's daughter, who is
his girlfriend. Inti went with several men and gave the officer
until 9:00 to come out — otherwise they would all be shot. The
officer came out immediately, crying. He is a second lieutenant
in the police force who was sent here with a *carabinero* and a
teacher from Postrer Valle who had volunteered to come along.
A colonel who is stationed in that village with 60 men sent
them. Their mission included a long trip for which they were
given four days, passing points along the Oscura as well. We
thought about killing them, but then I decided to send them
back with a severe warning about the norms of warfare.

Investigating how they had been able to get through, it was
established that Aniceto abandoned his post to call Julio and
this was the moment they came; besides, Aniceto and Luis were
found sleeping at their posts. They were punished with seven
days' kitchen duty and one day without eating the stew or the

---

7. Paulino Baigorria, a 20-year-old peasant who served as a liaison for
   the guerrilla force and requested to join it. While completing a mission
   for Che, he was arrested in Comarapa, held incommunicado, and
   tortured.

roast and fried pork that was served to excess. All the prisoners' belongings were confiscated.

June 21

The old lady.[8]

After two days of profuse dental extractions, which made me famous as "Fernando Sacamuelas" [Tooth-puller] alias Chaco, I closed my clinic and we set off in the afternoon, walking just over an hour. For the first time in this war, I traveled on a mule. The three detained men were brought along for an hour on the path beside the Mosquera, confiscating all their belongings, including watches and sandals. We considered bringing Calixto, the mayor, as a guide as well as Paulino, but he was sick, or pretended to be, and so we left him with a serious warning, which will probably be in vain.

Paulino promised to take my message to Cochabamba.[9] We will give him a letter for Inti's wife, a coded message for Manila, and four communiqués. The fourth [see Appendices] outlines the composition of our guerrilla force and clears up the rumor about Inti's death; it is the *[blank in the original]*. We will see if we can now establish contact with the city. Paulino pretended to come with us as our prisoner.

Altitude = 750 meters.

June 22

We walked in effect some three hours, leaving the Oscura or Moroco River to find a water hole in a place called Pasiones.

---

8. Birthday of his mother, Celia de la Serna.
9. Paulino was on his way with the message for Cochabamba when he was intercepted and arrested.

We consulted the map and everything indicates that we are no more than six leagues from Florida or the nearest houses at Piray, where Paulino's brother-in-law lives, but he does not know the way there.

We thought of continuing, making use of the moonlight, but it is not worth it considering the distance.

Altitude = 950 meters.

June 23

We walked for only one hour and then lost the path, and looking for it held us up all morning and part of the afternoon; then the rest of the day was spent clearing the trail for tomorrow. The night of San Juan's Eve was not as cold as it is reputed to be.

Altitude = 1,050 meters.

Asthma is becoming a serious problem for me and there is very little medicine left.

June 24

We walked a total of 12 kilometers, taking four hours. For some stretches, the path is good and quite visible, but at other times we have to feel our way. We climbed down an incredible cliff, following the tracks of some cowherds and their cattle. We camped by a trickle of water on the slopes of Durán Hill. The radio brings news of struggle in the mines. My asthma is worsening.

Altitude = 1,200 meters.

June 25

We followed the path made by the cowherds, but did not catch up with them. At mid-morning we saw a ranch on fire and a plane flying over the area. We never learned whether there was a connection between the two events, as we continued on and by 16:00 reached Piray, where Paulino's sister lives. There are three houses here, one of which is abandoned, another has no one inside and the sister lives in the third house with four children; her husband had gone to Florida with Paniagua, the man from the other house. Everything seemed normal. Paniagua's daughter lives a kilometer away, and we opted to camp at her house, buying a calf that was immediately slaughtered. Coco, with Julio, Camba, and León were sent to Florida to buy some things, but they discovered the army was there: about 50 men who were waiting for more to bring the total to 120 or 130. The owner of the house is an old man called Fenelón Coca.

An Argentine radio station broadcast the news of 87 victims at the mining area of Siglo XX;[10] the Bolivian stations are silent about the number. My asthma continues to grow worse and now it will not let me sleep well.

Altitude = 780 meters.

June 26

A bad day for me. Everything seemed to be going smoothly, and I had sent five men to relieve those in the ambush along the road to Florida when shots were heard. We went there quickly on horseback and found a strange spectacle: amid total silence, the bodies of four young soldiers were lying in the sun on the sand by the river. We could not take their weapons because we did not know where the enemy was; it was 17:00

---

10. Mining region of Bolivia where a massacre by the Bolivian Army took place, killing 87 people, including women and children, on June 24, 1967. This became known as the Massacre of San Juan.

and we waited for nightfall to recover their weapons; Miguel sent word that he heard sounds of breaking branches to our left; Antonio and Pacho went to see, but I gave the order not to shoot if they saw nothing. Almost immediately shooting was heard all around and I ordered a retreat, as we were at a disadvantage under those conditions. The withdrawal was delayed and we got news of two wounded: Pombo in his leg and Tuma in his abdomen. We carried them quickly to the house to operate on them the best we could. Pombo's wound is superficial and will just cause headaches because of his lack of mobility. Tuma's wound destroyed his liver and produced intestinal perforations; he died during the operation. With his death, I have lost an inseparable compañero of recent years, one whose loyalty was unwavering and whose absence I feel now almost as if he were my own son. As he died, he asked that his watch be given to me, but this was not done immediately as they were busy tending to him; so he took it off himself and gave it to Arturo. The gesture revealed his wish that it be given to his son whom he had never met, as I had done before with the watches of fallen compañeros. I will wear it for the rest of the war. We loaded his body onto an animal and we will take it to be buried away from here.

We have taken prisoner two new spies: a *carabinero* lieutenant and a *carabinero*. They were lectured and set free wearing only their underwear, due to a misinterpretation of my orders, which were to take everything from them that we could use. We left with nine horses.

June 27

After carrying out the painful task of burying Tuma in a badly made grave, we traveled on, reaching the center of Tejería during the day. The vanguard set off at 14:00 on a 15-kilometer expedition and we left at 14:30. The trip took longer for those at the rear, who were caught by nightfall and had to wait for the moon; by 2:30 they made it to the house in Paliza, where the guides were from.

Altitude = 850 meters.

We left two animals with the owner of the house in Tejería, who is the nephew of the old woman Paniagua, so that he could return them to her.

June 28

We found a guide who for $40 offered to take us to the junction of the road that goes to Don Lucas's[11] house, but we stayed in a house that we came across first that had a water hole. We left late. The last ones to leave, Moro and Ricardo, took an outrageous amount of time to get started and I missed the news. We covered an average of one kilometer per hour. According to different military broadcasts, or some radio station acting on its own, there were three killed and two wounded in an encounter with guerrillas in the Mosquera area; this must be a reference to our battle, but we saw — with almost absolute certainty — four bodies, unless one played dead perfectly.

The house of a certain Zea was not occupied but had several cows whose calves were fenced in.

Altitude = 1,150 meters.

---

11. Don Lucas was a Bolivian peasant who cooperated with the guerrillas.

June 29

I had strong words with Moro and Ricardo about the delay, especially Ricardo. Coco and Darío from the vanguard, along with Moro, set off with their backpacks loaded onto the horses. Ñato carried his own because he was in charge of all the animals. My backpack and Pombo's were loaded on a mule. Pombo traveled fairly easily on a lowland mare. We put him up at Don Lucas's house on the summit at an altitude of 1,800 meters; he was there with his two daughters, one of whom has a goiter. There are two other houses: one belongs to a seasonal worker, who has almost nothing, and the other is well-stocked. The night was rainy and cold. Reports suggest that Barchelón is a half-day walk away, but according to the peasants who have come that way, the path is in very poor condition. The owner of the house disagrees and assures us that the trail can be cleared easily. Peasants who came to see the person at the other house were detained because they might be suspicious.

On the way, I had a talk with our troops, now consisting of 24 men. I added Chino to our list of exemplary men; I explained the significance of our losses, and the personal loss that the death of Tuma meant to me, as I had viewed him almost like a son. I criticized the lack of self-discipline and the slowness of the march and promised to give them some ideas so that in future ambushes we could avoid what had just happened—needless loss of life due to a failure to abide by norms.

June 30

The old man Lucas gave us some information about his neighbors, from which we gather that the army has already started preparations in this area. One of his neighbors, Andulfo

Díaz, is the general secretary of the peasants' union in this region — a union that is pro-Barrientos; the other is an old chatterbox whom we let go because he is paralyzed; another is a coward who might talk, according to his colleagues, to avoid complications. The old man promised to accompany us and to help us clear the way to Barchelón; the two peasants will follow us. We spent the day resting; anyway, it was rainy and unpleasant.

In the political arena, the most important development is the official announcement by Ovando[12] that I am here. Moreover, he said that the army is facing a perfectly trained guerrilla force that includes the Vietcong commanders who have defeated the best US regiments. His information is based on statements made by Debray who apparently talked more than was necessary, although we cannot tell what implications this has, or what the circumstances were under which he talked. It is also rumored that Loro was murdered. They attribute to me a plan for insurrection in the mines, to coincide with the one in Ñacahuazú. Things are turning out beautifully, so very shortly, I will no longer be "Fernando Sacamuelas" [Tooth-puller].

A message was received from Cuba reporting on the low level of development of the guerrilla movement in Peru, where they scarcely have any men or weapons, but have spent a fortune and are talking of a supposed guerrilla force involving Paz Estenssoro, a colonel Seoane, and a certain Rubén Julio, a very rich man belonging to the movement in the Panda region; this will take place in Guayaramerin. It is the *[illegible in the original]*.

---

12. Alfredo Ovando Candia, commander in chief of the Bolivian Armed Forces at that time.

Analysis of the month

The negative points are the impossibility of making contact with Joaquín and the gradual loss of men, each of which constitutes a serious defeat, although the army does not know this. We have had two skirmishes this month, causing the army four dead and three wounded, according to their own information.

The most important features are:

1) Continued total lack of contact, which reduces us now to 24 men, with Pombo wounded and with reduced mobility.

2) Continued lack of peasant recruitment. It is a vicious circle: to recruit we need to maintain constant activity in populated territory, and to do this we need more people.

3) The legend of the guerrilla force is growing like wildfire, now we are invincible superhumans.

4) The lack of contact extends to the party, although we have made an attempt through Paulino that could bring results.

5) Debray is still in the news but now he is linked with my case, and I have been identified the leader of the movement. We will see the result of this move by the government and if it is positive or negative for us.

6) The morale of the guerrilla fighters continues to be strong and their commitment to the struggle is increasing. All the Cubans are exemplary in combat and there are only two or three weak Bolivians.

7) The army continues to be useless in its military tactics, but is doing work among the peasants that we cannot ignore, transforming all members of the community into

informers, either through fear or by fooling them about our goals.

8) The massacre in the mines greatly improves our outlook; if we can get our statement circulated, it will be a great clarifying factor.

Our most urgent task is to reestablish contact with La Paz, to replenish our military and medical supplies, and to recruit 50 to 100 men from the city, even if the number of active combatants comes to only 10 or 25.

JULY 1967

July 1

Without waiting for the weather to clear up completely, we started out for Barchelón—Barcelona on the map. The old man Lucas gave us a hand in clearing the path, but, everything considered, it was still quite steep and slippery. The vanguard left in the morning and we set off at noon, spending the entire afternoon climbing up and down the ravine. We had to stop to sleep at the first farm we came to, separated from the vanguard, which went on ahead. There were three children with the last name of Yépez, extremely shy.

Barrientos held a press conference in which he acknowledged my presence, but predicted that in a few days I would be wiped out. He spoke his usual stream of nonsense, calling us rats and snakes and repeated his intention to punish Debray.

Altitude = 1,550 meters.

We detained a peasant named Andrés Coca, whom we ran into on the path, and we took another two along with us: Roque and his son Pedro.

July 2

In the morning we caught up with the vanguard, which had camped on the hill at the house of Don Nicomedes Arteaga, where there is an orange grove, and they sold us some cigarettes. The main house is down below, beside the Piojera River, and we went there and ate lavishly. The Piojera River runs through a narrow canyon, and travels along it to Angostura is only possible on foot; the exit is toward the Junction, another point on the same river, but one has to cross a rather steep hill to get there. The Junction is important because it is a crossroads. This place is only 950 meters in altitude and more temperate; here *mariguís* replace the ticks. The settlement consists of Arteaga's house and those of some of his children; they have a small coffee plantation where people from different neighboring areas come to sharecrop. Right now there are six farmhands from the San Juan area.

Pombo's leg is not improving fast enough, probably due to the interminable trips on horseback, but there are no complications, nor fear of any at this point.

July 3

We stayed there all day, trying to give Pombo's leg some rest. We are being sold goods at high prices — so the peasants' fear is obviously mixed with their desire for profit, and they are providing us with what we need. I took some photos that made me the center of attention: we will see how we can develop them, enlarge them, and get them back here — three problems. A plane flew overhead in the afternoon and at night someone referred to the danger of nocturnal bombings, so everyone ran outside into the night; when we caught up with them, we explained there was no danger. My asthma continues to wage war.

July 4

We walked the two leagues to the Junction slowly, arriving at 15:30. A peasant called Manuel Carrillo lives there and he received us somewhat panic-stricken. We ate sumptuously, as has become our custom in recent days, and we slept in an abandoned shack. Asthma punished me severely and for the first time would not let me sleep at all.

Altitude = 1,000 meters.

Two days ago seven soldiers from El Filo passed by headed toward Bermejo.

July 5

Throughout the entire area, families with their belongings are fleeing to escape the army's repression. We walked mingling with oxen, pigs, chickens, and people until we reached Lagunillas; where we left the Piojera River behind and followed its tributary, the Lagunillas, for a kilometer. Serving as our guide was an unhappy peasant called Ramón, whose family is stricken with the proverbial fear found in this area. We slept beside the road; along the way we met up with one of Sandoval Morón's uncles, who lives in San Luis and seems much more alert.

Altitude = 1,160 meters.

July 6

We set out early and headed for Peña Colorada, crossing a populated area where people received us in terror. We got to Alto de Palermo as it was getting dark (altitude 1,600 meters) and from there we descended to a little grocery store where we made some purchases, just in case. It was already night when we came to a road where there was only one small house, belonging to an old widow. The vanguard did a poor job of capturing the road due to their indecisiveness. The plan was to seize a vehicle coming from Samaipata, check on the prevailing conditions in the town, go there with the driver of the vehicle, occupy the DIC office,[1] make purchases in the pharmacy, raid the hospital, buy some canned food and candy, and then return.

We changed the plan because no vehicles came from Samaipata and we heard that vehicles going there were not being detained, that is, the barrier had been raised. Ricardo, Coco, Pacho, Aniceto, Julio, and Chino were assigned to this action. They stopped a truck that came from Santa Cruz, without incident, however, behind it came another one that stopped to see if help was needed and this had to be detained also; then the hard bargaining began with a woman traveling in the truck who refused to let her daughter get out. A third truck stopped to see what was happening and blocked the road completely; a fourth stopped, all because of the indecisiveness of our people. Everything was resolved and the four vehicles remained at the side of the road, one driver when asked, said he needed a break. Our troops set off in one of the trucks and got to Samaipata, where they captured two *carabineros* and Lieutenant Vacaflor, the head of the post; they made the lieutenant give the sergeant the password to enter the post, and once inside they were able to occupy it by subduing 10 soldiers in a lightning-fast action, after a brief exchange of fire when one of the soldiers resisted. They seized five Mausers and one BZ-30 and drove the

1. Department of Criminal Investigations (DIC), secret police.

10 prisoners a kilometer out of Samaipata and left them there without any clothes.

From the perspective of supplies, the action was a failure; Chino allowed himself to be overruled by Pacho and Julio, and did not buy anything useful; as for medicines, nothing that I needed was obtained, although they did get the most indispensable items for the guerrilla force. The action happened in front of all the townspeople and a crowd of travelers, so word will spread like wildfire. By 2:00 we were already walking back with the booty.

July 7

We hiked without stopping until we came to a sugarcane field where there was a man who had received us well the last time, one league from Ramón's house. Fear remains entrenched among the people; the man sold us a pig and was friendly, but warned us that there were 200 men in Los Ajos and that his brother had just returned from San Juan, where there were 100 soldiers. He should have had some of his teeth pulled but preferred not to. My asthma is getting worse.

July 8

We went from the house beside the sugarcane field to the Piojera River, taking precautions, but the coast was clear and there were not even rumors of soldiers, and people coming from San Juan denied that any soldiers were there. It seems to have been a trick the man used to get rid of us. We walked about two leagues along the river until reaching the Piray, and from there another league to the cave, which we reached as night was falling. We are close to El Filo.

I injected myself several times so I could continue, finally, using an eyewash solution containing 1/900 adrenaline. If Paulino has not accomplished his mission, we will have to return to Ñacahuazú to retrieve my asthma medication.

The army issued a statement on the action, acknowledging one dead, which must have resulted from the exchange of fire when Ricardo, Coco, and Pacho took the small military post.

July 9

As we started out, we lost the trail and spent the morning looking for it. At noon, we followed one that was not very clearly marked, which led to the highest point we have reached so far: 1,840 meters; a little later we found a shack where we spent the night. We are not sure about the path to El Filo. The radio broadcast news of a 14-point agreement between the workers at the Catavi and the Siglo XX mines and the Comibol Company, representing a total defeat for the workers.

July 10

We left late because a horse was missing, but it turned up later. We passed through our highest altitude, 1,900 meters, along a path that is rarely used. At 15:30, we came across a shack where we could stay overnight, but the unpleasant surprise was that the paths ended here. Some old, abandoned trails were explored but they lead nowhere. Ahead of us, we can see some farms that could be El Filo.

The radio broadcast the news that there was a clash with guerrillas in the El Dorado region, which is not on the map but is between Samaipata and the Río Grande; they admit to one wounded and claim two dead on our side.

On the other hand, the statements from Debray and Pelado are not good; on top of everything, they have admitted to the continental aims of the guerrilla movement, something they did not have to do.

July 11

Coming back on a rainy day in a thick fog, we lost our way and became completely separated from the vanguard, which made its way down by clearing an old trail. We killed a calf.

July 12

The entire day was spent waiting for news from Miguel, but only at night did Julio bring word that they had gone down to a creek that flowed in a southerly direction. We stayed put. I am having regular asthma attacks.

Now the radio is broadcasting another report, an important part of which seems true; it talks of a battle at the Iquira with a fatality on our side; the body has been taken to Lagunillas. The euphoria about the body indicates that there is some truth in this report.

July 13

In the morning, we descended a steep hill that was slippery due to bad weather and met up with Miguel at 11:30. He had sent Camba and Pacho to scout a trail that led away from the one that followed the course of the creek, and they returned an hour later saying they had seen farms and houses and had entered an abandoned one. We headed that way, following the course of the little creek, and made it to the first house, where we spent the night. The owner of the house showed up later and said the magistrate's mother had seen us and that she must have already informed the soldiers at the settlement in El Filo, a league from here. We kept watch all night.

July 14

There was constant drizzle throughout the night, which continued all day. We nevertheless left at 12:00, bringing along two guides, Pablo, the mayor's brother-in-law, and Aurelio Mancilla, the man from the first house. The women stayed behind, crying. We reached the point where the trails diverged — one led to Florida and Moroco, and the other to Pampa. The guides proposed going to Pampa, from where we could take a recently made short cut to Mosquera; we agreed, but we had gone only about 500 meters when we ran into a young soldier and a peasant with a load of flour on his horse. They had a message for the second lieutenant in El Filo from his colleague in Pampa, where there are 30 soldiers. We decided to change direction and took the path to Florida, setting up camp after a little while.

The PRA[2] and PSB[3] have withdrawn from the Revolutionary Front[4] and the peasants are warning Barrientos about an alliance with the Falange.[5] The government is disintegrating rapidly. Such a pity that we do not have 100 more men right now.

July 15

We hiked very little due to the bad state of the path, abandoned

---

2. Revolutionary Authentic Party, led by Wálter Guevara Arce.
3. Bolivian Social Democratic Party.
4. The Revolutionary Front was a coalition that supported Barrientos.
5. Bolivian Socialist Falange (FSB), a right-wing party.

many years ago. Taking Aurelio's advice, we killed one of the magistrate's cows, eating sumptuously. My asthma has abated a bit.

Barrientos announced Operation Cynthia, to wipe us out within a few hours.

July 16

We started out very slowly, due to the heavy work of slashing through the foliage and the animals suffered greatly because the track is so bad; by the end of the day we came to a deep canyon, impossible to cross with loaded horses. Miguel and four men from the vanguard went on ahead and slept apart from us.

There was no decent news of any importance on the radio. We passed an altitude of 1,600 meters close to Durán Hill, on our left.

July 17

We continued to walk slowly because we kept losing the path. We were hoping to reach an orange grove that our guide told us about, but when we got there, all the trees were bare. There was a little pond that we camped beside. We did not walk more than three hours in total. My asthma is much better. It seems we will end up on the same path we used to get to Piray.

We are beside Durán Hill.

Altitude = 1,560 meters.

July 18

After an hour's hike, our guide lost the way and claimed that he did not know where to go. We finally found an old trail and while it was being cleared, Miguel went ahead, cutting through the woods, and reached the junction of the road to Piray. Arriving at a little creek where we camped, we released the three peasants and the young soldier, after reading them our statement. Coco went off with Pablito and Pacho to see if Paulino left anything in the hole; they should return tomorrow night if everything goes as planned. The young soldier says that he is going to desert.

Altitude = 1,300 meters.

July 19

We made the short trip back to the old camp and stayed there; reinforcing our guard while we waited for Coco; he returned after 18:00, announcing that everything is still as it was; the rifle is in its place and there are no signs of Paulino. There are, however, many tracks from passing troops, and also signs of them on the stretch of the trail where we are.

The political news is of a tremendous crisis and no one knows how it will be resolved. For now, the agricultural unions in Cochabamba have formed a political party of "Christian inspiration" that is backing Barrientos, who is asking to be "allowed to govern for four years"; it is almost a plea. [Vice-President] Siles Salinas is threatening the opposition that our rise to power would cost everyone's head and is calling for national unity, declaring the country to be in a state of war. On the one hand, they seem to be pleading, and using demagogy, on the other; maybe they are planning a takeover.

July 20

We took precautions while walking until we made it to the first two little houses, where we found one of Paniagua's boys and the son-in-law of Paulino.[6] They knew nothing about Paulino, except that the army was looking for him for having been our guide. The tracks are those of a group of 100 men who passed by a week after we did and continued on to Florida. The army apparently suffered the loss of three dead and two wounded in the ambush. Coco, (with Camba, León, and Julio), was sent to check out Florida and to buy what they could there. They returned at 4:00 with some provisions and a certain Melgar, the owner of two of our horses, who offered his services and gave us detailed information (somewhat embellished) from which we gleaned the following: Four days after our departure, Tuma's body was found, eaten by animals; the army only advanced the day after the battle, when the lieutenant showed up without his clothes; the action at Samaipata is known in full detail—albeit exaggerated—it is a source of amusement among the peasants; Tuma's pipe was found along with some scattered belongings; a major by the name of Soperna seems to be half-sympathetic toward us or perhaps even an admirer; the army went to Coca's house, where Tuma died, and from there to Tejería, before returning to Florida. Coco thought about using the man to deliver a letter for us, but it seemed more prudent to test him out first by sending him to buy some medicines. This Melgar talked about a group that is headed this way, with a woman, something he learned from a letter written by the magistrate in Río Grande to the one here. Since the latter lives on the road to Florida, we sent Inti, Coco, and Julio to talk to him. He denied

6. There is an error in the diary. This person is earlier referred to as Paulino's brother-in-law.

any knowledge of the other group, but generally confirmed the rest of Melgar's information. We spent a bitch of a night because of rain.

The radio broadcast a report identifying the body of the dead guerrilla fighter as Moisés Guevara, but Ovando, at a press conference, was very cautious about this and handed over responsibility for the identification to the Ministry of the Interior. There is still a possibility that the supposed identification is a farce or an invention.

Altitude = 680 meters.

July 21

We spent the day in peace. The old man Coca was talked to about the cow he had sold us that was not his and then claimed he had not been paid for it. He emphatically denied the whole thing; we insisted that he pay for it.

At night we went to Tejería, purchasing a large pig and *chankaka*.[7] The people there received those who went very well: Inti, Benigno, and Aniceto.

July 22

We set off early, with heavy loads on our shoulders and on the animals, intending to throw everyone off our scent. We left the path that goes to Moroco and took the one to the lagoon, one or two kilometers to the south. Unfortunately, we had no idea about the rest of the way and had to send out scouts; meanwhile, Mancilla and Paniagua's lad showed up herding

---

7. Type of brown sugar loaf made from sugar cane juice.

livestock beside the lagoon. They were warned not to say anything, but now things are very different. We walked a few more hours and slept beside a creek that had a trail following its course to the southeast; there were other less marked trails to the south.

The radio reported that the wife of Bustos (Pelao) says that he saw me here but that he had come with other intentions.

Altitude = 640 meters.

July 23

We stayed on at the same camp while scouts were sent off along two other possible paths. One of them leads to Río Seco at the point where the Piray flows into it and before gets lost in the sand, that is, between the ambush site we set up and Florida; the other path leads to a shack two to three hours away by foot, and according to Miguel, who explored it, from there it is possible to get to the Rosita. Tomorrow we will take that path, which could be the one Melgar mentioned to Coco and Julio.

July 24

We walked some three hours, following the path that had already been explored, which took us through altitudes of 1,000 meters; we camped at 940 meters, on the bank of a creek. The trails end here and tomorrow we will spend the entire day searching for the best way out. There is a bunch of farms under cultivation here, which indicates its proximity to Florida; it could be the place called Canalones. We are trying to decode a long message from Manila. Raúl spoke at a graduation ceremony for officers at the Máximo Gómez School; among other things, he refuted criticisms the Czechs made about my article on Vietnam. Our friends are calling me a new Bakunin and are sorry about blood that has been spilled and blood that would be spilled if there were three or four Vietnams.

July 25

We spent the day at rest, sending three pairs of scouts in different directions, led by Coco, Benigno, and Miguel. Coco and Benigno emerged at the same place from which one can take the road to Moroco. Miguel reported that the creek definitely flows into the Rosita and that it is possible to go that way although a path needs to be cleared with machetes.

There is a report of two actions, one in Taperas and another in San Juan del Potrero, which could not have been carried out by the same group, raising doubt about whether they really happened or if the reports were truthful.

July 26

Benigno, Camba, and Urbano were assigned to clear a path along the creek, avoiding Moroco; the rest of the personnel stayed in the camp and the center group set up an ambush at the rear. No incidents.

News of the action at San Juan del Potrero was circulated by foreign radio stations in full detail: 15 soldiers and one colonel were captured, their belongings were taken, and they were set free: our practice. This spot is on the other side of the highway between Cochabamba and Santa Cruz. In the evening I gave a little talk about the significance of July 26, the rebellion against oligarchies and against revolutionary dogmas. Fidel made a brief mention of Bolivia.

July 27

We were all ready to leave and the troops at the ambush site had been ordered to depart automatically at 11:00 when Willy showed up a few minutes before the hour, announcing the army was here. Willy, Ricardo, Inti, Chino, León, and Eustaquio were sent into action along with Antonio, Arturo, and Chapaco. Events unfolded like this: Eight soldiers appeared on the crest, walking south down an old path, and then they returned, firing a few mortar rounds and making signals with a cloth. At some point, we heard them call for Melgar,[8] who could have been the same one from Florida. After resting for a while, the eight soldiers started marching toward the ambush site. Only four fell into it as the rest were a little behind; there are three dead for sure and probably a fourth, who is wounded at least. We withdrew without taking their weapons and gear because it would have been too difficult, and we headed off downstream. When we came across the opening of another small canyon, we set up a new ambush, while the horses were sent to the end of the road.

My asthma hit me hard and those measly few sedatives are just about gone.

Altitude = 800 meters.

July 28

Coco, Pacho, Raúl, and Aniceto were commanded to cover the mouth of the river that we think is the Suspiro. Little progress was made clearing a path through a canyon that is very narrow. We camped apart from the vanguard because Miguel had gone

---

8. Antonio Melgar turned out to be a courier for the Bolivian Army.

too far for the horses to keep up as they were either sinking in the sand or suffering on the rocks.

Altitude = 760 meters.

July 29

We continued through a canyon that descends to the south, with good cover on the sides and plenty of water. At about 16:00 we met up with Pablito, who told us that we were at the mouth of the Suspiro with no incidents. I thought for a moment the canyon could not be the Suspiro, because it headed south, but at the last turn, it veered to the west and flowed into the Rosita.

At about 16:30 the rear guard arrived and I decided to travel on to get away from the mouth of the river, but I did not feel like demanding the effort needed to go farther than Paulino's farm, so we set up camp beside the road, an hour from the mouth of the Suspiro. During the evening, I gave the floor to Chino so he could talk about his country's [Peru] independence day, July 28; later, I explained why this camp was badly situated, and gave the order to get up at 5:00 and to occupy Paulino's farm.

Radio Habana reported some army troops had fallen into an ambush and were later rescued by helicopter, but it was hard to hear.

July 30

I was really bothered by asthma and was awake all night. At 4:30, when Moro was making coffee, he warned us that he had seen a lantern coming across the river. Miguel, who was awake because of the sentry change, went off with Moro to detain the travelers. From the kitchen, I heard this exchange: "Hey, who goes there?"

"The Trinidad Detachment." Shooting broke out right away. Immediately, Miguel brought back an M-1 and a cartridge belt taken from a wounded soldier, along with the news that there were 21 men on the road to Abapó and in Moroco there were 150. More casualties were inflicted on the enemy, but we could not be sure of the number in the prevailing confusion. It took a long time to load the horses and the black one got lost, and with it an ax and a mortar that had been taken from the enemy. It was already close to 6:00 and we lost even more time because some of the loads fell off. The end result was that the last of us to cross came under fire from the young soldiers who were becoming bolder. Paulino's sister was at her farm and received us very calmly, reporting that all the men in Moroco had been arrested and were in La Paz.

I hurried our troops along and went with Pombo, under fire again, past the river canyon where the path ends to where we could organize the resistance. I sent Miguel with Coco and Julio to take the forward position while I spurred on the cavalry. Covering the retreat were seven men from the vanguard, four from the rear guard, and Ricardo, who stayed behind to reinforce the defense. Benigno, (with Darío, Pablo, and Camba), was on the right side; the rest came along the left.

I had just given the order to rest at the first suitable spot, when Camba arrived with the news that Ricardo and Aniceto had been hit while crossing the river; I dispatched Urbano with Ñato and León and two horses, and sent for Miguel and Julio, leaving Coco at the forward post. They went through without receiving my instructions and, in a while, Camba returned again reporting that they and Miguel and Julio had been surprised and that the soldiers had advanced farther along. Miguel had withdrawn and was awaiting instructions. I sent Camba back again with Eustaquio, which left only Inti, Pombo, Chino, and me. At 13:00, I sent for Miguel, leaving Julio at the forward post and I withdrew with the group of men and horses. When I reached Coco's post on the high ground, the news caught up with me that all the survivors were there, that Raúl was dead, and that Ricardo and Pacho were wounded. Things happened like this: Ricardo and Aniceto were imprudently crossing the clearing when Ricardo was wounded. Antonio organized a line of fire between Arturo, Aniceto, and Pacho, and they rescued him, but then Pacho was wounded and a bullet to the mouth killed Raúl.

The withdrawal was difficult, dragging the two wounded men and with little help from Willy and Chapaco, especially the latter. Later Urbano and his group with the horses and Benigno and his people joined them. This left the other flank unguarded, through which the soldiers advanced and surprised Miguel. After a painful march through the woods, they came to the river and joined us. Pacho came on horseback but Ricardo could not ride and they had to carry him in a hammock. I sent Miguel, with Pablito, Darío, Coco, and Aniceto, to occupy the mouth of the first creek to the right, while we tended the wounded. Pacho had a superficial wound that went through his buttocks and the skin of his testicles, but Ricardo was in critical condition and the last plasma had been lost in Willy's backpack. Ricardo died at 22:00 and we buried him near the river, in a well-hidden place so that the soldiers could not find him.

July 31

At 4:00 we set off along the river, and after taking a shortcut, headed downriver without leaving tracks; later in the morning we reached the creek where Miguel had set up the ambush, but he had misunderstood the order and had left tracks. We walked upstream some four kilometers and went deep into the woods, covering our tracks and camping close to one of the creek's tributaries. At night I went through the errors of the action:

1) bad location of the campsite;
2) poor use of time, which enabled them to shoot at us;
3) an excess of confidence, which caused the loss of Ricardo and then of Raúl during the rescue; and
4) lack of decisiveness in saving all the gear.

We lost 11 backpacks with medicines, binoculars, and some potentially damaging items, such as the tape recorder onto which we copied the messages from Manila, Debray's book with my notes in it, and a book by Trotsky; all this does not take into account the political value that this haul has for the government and the confidence it will give the soldiers. We estimate about two dead and up to five wounded on their side, but there are two contradictory news reports: one, from the army, acknowledges four dead and four wounded on the 28th, and another from Chile talks of six wounded and three dead on the 30th. The army later issued another statement announcing they had found a body and that the second lieutenant was out of danger. Of our dead, it is hard to say how to categorize Raúl, given his introspection; he was not much in combat or at work, but he was always interested in political problems, although he never asked any questions. Ricardo was the most undisciplined of the Cuban group and the least resolute facing daily sacrifices, but he was an extraordinary combatant and an old comrade in arms from the first failure of Segundo,[9] in the Congo, and now here. It is another tangible loss, due to his capabilities. We are now 22 men, with two wounded, (Pacho and Pombo), and me, with full-blown asthma.

Analysis of the month

We still have the same negative points as the previous month, namely: the impossibility of contact with Joaquín and the outside world, and the loss of men. Now we have 22 men, with three disabled (including me), which decreases our mobility. We have had three encounters, including the taking of Samaipata, causing the army about 7 dead and 10 wounded, approximate figures from conflicting reports. We have lost two men and have one wounded.

The most important features are:

1) Total loss of contact continues.
2) Continued sense of the lack of peasant recruitment, although there are some encouraging signs in the reception from peasants whom we have known for a while.
3) The legend of the guerrilla force is acquiring continental dimensions; Onganía[10] is closing the borders and Peru is taking precautions.
4) The attempt at contact through Paulino failed.
5) The morale and combat experience of the guerrilla fighters

9. Refers to the nom de guerre of Jorge Ricardo Masetti.
10. Juan Carlos Onganía, military man who overthrew President Arturo Illía in a coup d'état in Argentina in 1966.

is increasing with each battle; Camba and Chapaco remain the weak ones.

6) The army continues to be ineffective, but there are units that appear to be more combative.

7) The political crisis of the government is growing, but the United States is giving small loans, which are of great assistance in tempering the level of Bolivian discontent.

The most urgent tasks are: To reestablish contact, to recruit combatants, and to obtain medicines.

AUGUST 1967

August 1

A quiet day: Miguel and Camba began work on the trail but got no farther than one kilometer due to the difficulty of the terrain and the vegetation. We killed a wild colt, which should give us meat for five to six days. We dug small trenches to set up an ambush if the army should come by. If they come tomorrow or the next day and do not discover the camp, the idea is to let them pass first and then open fire.

Altitude = 650 meters.

August 2

The path seems to be going well, thanks to Benigno and Pablo, who are working on it. They took almost two hours to get back to the camp from the end of the trail. There was no more news about us on the radio, after an announcement that they had moved the body of an "antisocial." My asthma is hitting me very hard and I have used up my last anti-asthmatic injection; all I have left are tablets for about 10 days.

August 3

The trail has become a fiasco; it took Miguel and Urbano 57 minutes to return today; we are progressing very slowly. There is no news. Pacho is recuperating; on the other hand, I am not doing so well; I had a bad day and a bad night and I have no idea how a solution will be found in the short term. I tried an intravenous Novocain injection, to no avail.

August 4

The troops found a canyon that runs southwest and may drain into the creeks that flow into the Río Grande. Tomorrow, two pairs of slashers will go to clear paths and Miguel will climb up our path to explore what seem to be old farms. My asthma improved somewhat.

August 5

Benigno, Camba, Urbano, and León split into pairs to make more progress, but they ran into a creek that flows into the Rosita and had to continue cross-country. Miguel went to scout the farm but never found it. The horsemeat was finished off; tomorrow we will try to fish and the day after we will sacrifice some other poor beast. Tomorrow we will head to the new water hole. My asthma was implacable; in spite of my aversion to splitting up, I had to send a group on ahead; Benigno and Julio volunteered to go; it remains to be seen if Ñato is willing.

August 6

The camp was moved; unfortunately, it took us not three hours but only one to cover the trail, which means we still have a long way to go. Benigno, Urbano, Camba, and León continued on with machetes, while Miguel and Aniceto set out to find where the new creek merges with the Rosita. By nightfall they had not returned, so we took precautions, especially because

I had heard something that sounded like a mortar shell in the distance. Inti and Chapaco spoke, and then I said a few words about today being the anniversary of Bolivia's independence.

Altitude = 720 meters.

August 7

By 11:00 in the morning we had given up Miguel and Aniceto for lost; I gave Benigno the order to proceed carefully to the mouth of the Rosita and to investigate a little in the direction they went, if they had made it that far. Nevertheless, the lost ones appeared at 13:00, having simply encountered difficulties along the way and night fell before they reached the Rosita. Miguel had really put me through hell. We stayed at the same place but the slashers found another creek, so we will go that way tomorrow. Today the old horse Anselmo died and we only have one pack horse left; my asthma is unchanged, but the medicine is running out. Tomorrow I will make the decision about sending a group to the Ñacahuazú.

Today marks exactly nine months since I arrived and we established the guerrilla force. Of the initial six, two are dead, one has disappeared, two are wounded; and I am suffering from asthma with no idea how to overcome it.

August 8

We walked for something like an hour, but to me it seemed like two because of the exhaustion of the little mare; at one point, I slashed her neck, opening a deep wound. The new campsite is probably the last one with water until we reach the Rosita or the Río Grande; the *macheteros* are 40 minutes from here (two to three kilometers). I appointed a group of eight men for the following mission: They will leave from here tomorrow, and hike all day; the next day, Camba is to return and report; the day after, Pablito and Darío will return with the news from that day; the other five will proceed to Vargas's house and from there Coco and Aniceto will return to report on how things are going. Benigno, Julio, and Ñato will continue on to the Ñacahuazú to get the medicine for me. They should go very carefully to avoid ambushes; we will proceed and meet either at Vargas's house, depending on our speed, or farther up at the creek that runs in front of the cave on the Río Grande, the Masicuri (Honorato), or the Ñacahuazú. There is news from the army saying that an arms cache was discovered in one of our camps.

I gathered everyone together tonight to make the following speech: We are in a difficult situation; Pacho is recuperating, but I am a complete wreck and the incident with the little mare shows that at times I am beginning to lose control; this will be corrected, but we are all in this together and anyone who does not feel up to it should say so. This is one of those moments when great decisions have to be made; this type of struggle gives us the opportunity to become revolutionaries, the highest form of the human species, and it also allows us to emerge fully as men; those who are unable to achieve either of those two states should say so now and abandon the struggle. All the Cubans and some of the Bolivians committed themselves to stay until the end and so did Eustaquio, but he criticized Muganga for putting his backpack on the mule and for not carrying firewood, which provoked an angry response from Muganga. Julio lashed out at Moro and Pacho for similar reasons, which brought another angry response, this time from

Pacho. I closed the discussion saying we were debating two things of a very different nature: one was if they were willing to continue or not, and the other was about petty arguments and internal problems of the guerrilla force which detract from the magnitude of the more important decision. I did not like the comments made by Eustaquio and Julio, but neither did I like the response from Moro and Pacho. In short, we have to be more revolutionary and strive to set an example.

August 9

Altitude = 780 meters.

The eight scouts set out in the morning. The *macheteros* Miguel, Urbano, and León progressed another 50 minutes beyond the campsite. An abscess on my heel was lanced, allowing me to put weight on my foot, but it is still very painful and I am running a fever.

Pacho is fine.

August 10

Antonio and Chapaco left to go hunting behind our site and caught a *urina* (or *guaso*) and a turkey hen; they checked out the first camp, where nothing new had happened, and brought back a load of oranges. I ate two and immediately had an asthma attack, but only a mild one. At 13:30 Camba, one of the eight, came back with the following news: Yesterday they slept without water and today they carried on until 9:00 without finding any. Benigno recognized the place and will head for the Rosita to get water; Pablo and Darío will return if they find water.

Fidel made a long speech in which he attacks the traditional parties, especially, the Venezuelan party; it appears there was a big behind-the-scenes row. My foot was treated again. I am getting better, but I am not well yet. Nevertheless, tomorrow we must move our base closer to the *macheteros*, who only cleared 35 minutes of the trail during the day.

August 11

The slashers are advancing very slowly. Pablo and Darío arrived at 16:00 with a note from Benigno, who says he is close to the Rosita and estimates it is three more days to Vargas's house. At 8:15 Pablito left the water hole where they had spent the night and at about 15:00, ran into Miguel, which means there is a lot farther to go. Turkey seems to be bad for my asthma and I gave my small portion to Pacho. We moved our camp to a new creek that dries up at noon and starts running again at midnight. It rained, but was not cold; there are lots of *mariguís*.

Altitude = 740 meters.

August 12

A dreary day. The *macheteros* made little progress. There was nothing new and not much food; tomorrow we will slaughter another horse, which should last us six days. My asthma has remained at a manageable level. Barrientos announced the twilight of the guerrilla force and renewed his threat of an intervention in Cuba; he was just as stupid as always.

The radio announced a battle near Monteagudo with the result of one dead on our side: Antonio Fernández from Tarata. This is similar to the real name of Pedro from Tarata.

August 13

Miguel, Urbano, León, and Camba went off to camp by the water hole that Benigno had discovered, and they will proceed from there. They took food for three days, that is, pieces of Pacho's horse, which was slaughtered today. There are four animals left and everything suggests we will have to sacrifice another one before finding more food. If everything has gone well, Coco and Aniceto should be back tomorrow. Arturo caught two turkeys, which were allotted to me, as there is hardly any corn left. Chapaco is showing increasing signs of becoming unstable, Pacho is recovering at a good rate, and my asthma has been getting worse since yesterday; I am now taking three tablets a day. My foot is almost better.

August 14

A bad day. It was dreary as we carried out our daily activities without incident, but at night the news bulletin reported in precise detail that the cave where the men were sent had been discovered, so there can be no doubt. I am now condemned to suffer from asthma indefinitely. They also seized all kinds of documents and photographs. This is the worst blow they have delivered; someone must have talked. Who? That is the question.

August 15

I sent Pablito off early with a message for Miguel that he should send two men to search for Benigno, as Coco and Aniceto had not yet arrived, but he ran into them on the way and the three returned together. Miguel sent word that he would stay wherever they are at nightfall, and asked for some water to be sent. Darío was dispatched to tell him we would be leaving early tomorrow, no matter what, but he ran into León who had come to say that the path was finished.

A broadcast from Santa Cruz reported in passing that two prisoners[1] were captured by the army's Muyupampa group, and there is no doubt that they are part of Joaquín's group, which is being pursued relentlessly, and that those two prisoners talked. It was cold, but I did not have a bad night; another abscess on my same foot needs to be lanced. Pacho is back on his feet.

Another clash was reported in Chuhuayako, with no losses for the army.

August 16

We effectively walked for three hours and 40 minutes, with one hour's rest, along a reasonably good trail. The mule threw me clear out of the saddle when she was jabbed by a branch, but I was all right; my foot is improving. Miguel, Urbano, and Camba continued clearing the path and reached the Rosita. Today was the day Benigno and his compañeros should have arrived at the cave; planes flew over the area several times. This could be due to some tracks that they left near Vargas's place or it could be that some troops are coming down the Rosita or advancing along the Río Grande. During the evening I warned the men about the danger of crossing the river, and they will take great care tomorrow.

Altitude = 600 meters.

---

1. This refers to Eusebio Tapia Aruni (Eusebio) and Hugo Choque Silva (Chingolo), two deserters from Joaquín's group.

August 17

We started out early, making it to the Rosita by 9:00. There Coco thought he heard two shots and an ambush was set up, but nothing happened. The rest of the trip was slow because of losing the trail and miscommunication. We reached the Río Grande at 16:30 and camped there. I thought of continuing in the moonlight, but the troops seemed very tired. We have two days' rations of horsemeat and for me one day of *mote*. It looks like we will have to slaughter another animal. The radio announced that the documents and other evidence from the four caves at the Ñacahuazú will be presented, which suggests they have also found the one at the camp on Monos Creek. My asthma is treating me well enough, under the circumstances.

Altitude = 640 meters. (This does not make sense, considering that yesterday it was 600.)

August 18

We set off earlier than usual, but we had to cross four fords, and one of them was rather deep, and we also had to clear the trail in some places. We finally reached the creek at 14:00, and the men were dead tired. There was no more activity. There are clouds of *niborigüises* in the area and it is still cold at night. Inti told me that Camba wants to quit; according to him, his physical condition will not let him go on, and furthermore, he sees no prospects for the struggle. Naturally, it is a typical case of cowardice and it would purge our ranks to let him go; but, as he knows the route we are taking to meet up with Joaquín, he cannot leave. Tomorrow I will talk to him and Chapaco.

Altitude = 680 meters.

August 19

Miguel, Coco, Inti, and Aniceto went to try to find a better way to Vargas's house, where it seems there is a military detachment, but there is nothing new and it appears we must continue on the same old path. Arturo and Chapaco went hunting and caught a *urina*, and the very same Arturo, while on guard duty with Urbano, killed a tapir, which made the whole camp nervous, because it took seven shots. The animal will provide us with meat for four days, the *urina* for one day, plus the reserve of beans and sardines means there is food for a total of six days. It seems the white horse, the next on the list, is reprieved. I spoke with Camba, making it clear that he cannot leave until we reach our next stage, which is reuniting with Joaquín. Chapaco insisted he is not a coward, and therefore will not leave, but that he wants some hope of leaving within six months to a year; I gave him my word, and then he talked about a range of unconnected topics. He is not well.

The news is all about Debray, but no mention of the other accused. No news of Benigno; he should have been here by now.

August 20

The *macheteros*, (Miguel and Urbano), and my "public works department," (Willy and Darío), made little progress, so we decided to stay put for one more day. Coco and Inti caught nothing, but Chapaco caught a monkey and a *urina*. I ate *urina* and it gave me a severe asthma attack in the middle of the night. El Médico is apparently still suffering from lumbago, which is affecting his general health and turning him into an invalid. There is no news from Benigno and this is now a serious concern.

The radio reports the presence of guerrillas 85 kilometers from Sucre.

August 21

Another day in the same place and another day without news of Benigno and his compañeros. Five monkeys were caught: four by Eustaquio while he was out hunting and one by Moro when it passed close to him. Moro still suffers from lumbago and was given some meperidine. *Urina* disagrees with my asthma.

August 22

We finally moved on, but before we did, the alarm was sounded because a man was spotted, apparently on the run along the riverbank; it turned out to be Urbano, lost. I gave El Médico a local anesthetic so he could travel on the mare, although it was still painful; he seems to have improved slightly; Pacho made the trip on foot. We set up camp on the right bank and only a small section of the path to Vargas's house needs to be cleared by machete before it is ready. We still have tapir meat for tomorrow and the next day, but after tomorrow we will not be able to hunt. There is no news from Benigno, making it 10 days since they separated from Coco.

Altitude = 580 meters.

August 23

The day was very strenuous as we had to go around a very rocky cliff; the white horse refused to go on and we left him stuck in the mud, without even being able to take advantage of his bones. We found a little hunting cabin that looked like it had recently been inhabited; we set up an ambush and shortly two people fell into it. Their alibi is that they had set 10 traps and had gone to check them; according to them, the army is at Vargas's house, and in Tatarenda, Caraguatarenda, Ipitá, and Ñumao, and that a few days ago, there was a clash in Caraguatarenda in which one soldier was wounded. It could have been Benigno, driven by hunger or encirclement. The men told us that tomorrow the army would come to fish, in groups of 15 to 20 men. Tapir meat was shared, along with some fish that were caught with a cartridge bag; I ate rice, which suited me very well. El Médico is somewhat better. It was announced that Debray's trial has been postponed until September.

Altitude = 580 meters.

August 24

Reveille was sounded at 5:30 and we started out for the ravine that we thought we would follow. The vanguard led the way and had gone a few meters when three peasants appeared on the other side; Miguel was called back with his troops and everyone set up an ambush; eight soldiers arrived. The instructions were to let them cross the river by the ford in front and to shoot them when they got to the other side; but the soldiers did not cross and only went back and forth, right in front of our rifles, which we did not fire. Our civilian prisoners said that they were nothing but hunters. Miguel and Urbano, with Camba, Darío, and Hugo Guzmán, the hunter, were sent to follow a trail toward the west, but we do not know where it goes. We stayed in the ambush all day. At dusk the *macheteros* returned with their trapped prey: a condor and a rotten cat, all of it ending up inside us along with the last of the tapir; we have some beans left and whatever we can hunt. Camba has reached the lowest depth of moral degradation, trembling at the mere mention of soldiers. El Médico is still in pain and is giving himself Talamonal; I am fairly well, but ravenously hungry. The army issued a statement saying they had found another cave and that two soldiers were slightly wounded, with more "losses for the guerrillas." Radio Habana broadcast news of an unconfirmed battle in Taperillas with one wounded on the army's side.

August 25

The day passed without incident. Reveille sounded at 5:00 and the *macheteros* set off early; the army (seven men) came within a few paces of our position, but did not try to cross over. It seems their gunfire is a signal to the hunters; we will attack them tomorrow if the opportunity presents itself. Insufficient progress has been made on the trail because Miguel sent Urbano to consult with us about something, but Urbano misinterpreted it, by which time it was too late to do anything.

The radio announced a battle in Monte Dorado, which seems to be in Joaquín's jurisdiction, as well as the presence of guerrillas three kilometers from Camiri.

August 26

Everything went wrong: seven soldiers came along, but they split up: five went downstream and two went across. Antonio, who was in charge of the ambush, fired prematurely and missed, allowing the two men to escape and seek reinforcements; the other five raced away, with Inti and Coco in pursuit, but the soldiers found cover and held them off. While I was watching the chase, I saw that the bullets were landing nearby, coming from our side. I ran over and found Eustaquio still shooting because Antonio had not told him what was happening. I was so furious I lost control and roughed up Antonio.

We set out at a weary pace as El Médico could not make much of an effort, but meanwhile, the army recovered and advanced toward the island ahead of us with 20 to 30 men; it was not worth attacking them. They might suffer two wounded, maximum. Coco and Inti distinguished themselves with their decisiveness.

Everything went smoothly until El Médico became exhausted and began to hold up the march. We stopped at 18:30 without having caught up to Miguel, who was, nevertheless, barely a few meters away, and made contact with us. Moro stayed in a ravine, unable to climb the last stretch, and we slept split into three groups. There are no signs of the army pursuing us.

Altitude = 900 meters.

August 27

The day was spent in a desperate search for a way out, and the result is still unclear; we are close to the Río Grande and have already passed Ñumao, but there are no new fords, according to reports; we could get there along Miguel's cliff, but the mules would not make it. There is a possibility of crossing a small chain of mountains and then proceeding to the Río Grande-Masicuri, but we will not know if this is feasible until tomorrow. We have gone over 1,300 meters, which is about the maximum altitude in this region; we slept at an altitude of 1,240 meters, and it was very cold. I am quite ok, but El Médico is doing very poorly; we have run out of water, but are saving a little for him.

The good news, or the good development, was the return of Benigno, Ñato, and Julio. Theirs was a great odyssey because there are soldiers at Vargas's house and in Ñumao and they almost clashed with them; later they followed troops down the Saladillo and came back up the Ñacahuazú, and they discovered there were three trails by the Congrí Creek made by the soldiers. They reached the cave at Oso Camp on the 18th, but found it is now an antiguerrilla camp with 150 soldiers; they were almost surprised there but managed to return without being seen. They went to the grandfather's farm, where they got *jocos*, the only thing there, because it is abandoned, and they passed near the soldiers again, heard our shooting, and slept close by to follow our tracks until they caught up to us. According to Benigno, Ñato conducted himself very well, but Julio got lost twice and was somewhat afraid of the soldiers. Benigno thinks that some of Joaquín's people went through the area a few days ago.

August 28

A gray and somewhat distressing day. We quenched our thirst with *caracoré*,[2] which was just a way to fool our throats a little. Miguel sent Pablito by himself, with one of the hunters, to find water, moreover, with only a small revolver. He had not returned by 16:30, so I sent Coco and Aniceto to find him and they did not return all night. The rear guard stayed down below and could not hear the radio; it seems there is a new message.

---

2. Mass found in the center of a *caracoré*, a parasitic plant that holds water.

We finally sacrificed the little mare, after she had been with us for two painful months; I had done everything possible to save her, but our hunger was becoming severe, so at least now we are suffering only thirst. We will probably not reach water tomorrow either.

The radio broadcast news of a wounded soldier in the Tatarenda area. The unanswered question for me is this: If they are so scrupulous in reporting their own losses, why are they lying in other reports? And if they are not lying, who is causing those casualties in places so far apart as Caraguatarenda and Taperillas? It could be that Joaquín's group is divided in two or there are new, independent guerrilla groups.

Altitude = 1,200 meters.

August 29

A heavy and quite distressing day. The *macheteros* made very little progress and at one point went the wrong way, thinking they were going to the Masicuri. We set up camp at 1,600 meters, in a relatively humid place where a cane plant grows whose pulp quenches thirst. Some compañeros, Chapaco, Eustaquio, and Chino, are collapsing from lack of water. Tomorrow we have to head straight to wherever we can find water. The mules are holding up quite well.

There is no major news on the radio; the most important item is Debray's trial, which is being extended from one week to the next.

August 30

The situation is becoming distressing now; the *macheteros* are fainting, Miguel and Darío are drinking their own urine, as is Chino, with the disastrous result of diarrhea and cramps. Urbano, Benigno, and Julio went down into a canyon and found water. They told me that the mules would not make it, and I decided to stay with Ñato, but then Inti came up again with water and the three of us stayed here, eating the mare. The radio remained below, so there was no news.

Altitude = 1,200 meters.

August 31

In the morning, Aniceto and León left to scout the area below, coming back at 16:00 with the news that the mules could get down from the camp to where water was ahead. The hardest part to get through was the first part; I checked it out and the animals can make it through. I ordered Miguel to make a detour tomorrow at the last cliff and continue clearing the path ahead; we will bring the mules down. There is a message from Manila but we could not copy it.

Summary of the month

Without doubt, this was the worst month we have had in this war. The loss of all the caves with the documents and medicines was a heavy blow, psychologically above all else. The loss of two men at the end of last month and the subsequent march on only horsemeat demoralized the troops and sparked the first case of desertion (Camba), which would otherwise constitute a net gain, but not under these circumstances. The lack of contact with the outside and with Joaquín, and the fact that the prisoners taken from his group talked, also demoralized the troops somewhat. My illness sowed uncertainty among several others and all this was reflected in our only clash, one in which we should have inflicted several enemy casualties, but only succeeded in wounding one of them. Besides this, the difficult march through the hills without water exposed some negative traits among the troops.

The most important features are:

1) We continue without contact of any kind and have no reasonable hope of establishing it in the near future.
2) We continue being unable to recruit peasants, which is logical considering how few dealings we have had with them recently.
3) There is a decline in combat morale; temporary, I hope.
4) The army has not increased its effectiveness or its aggressiveness.

We are at a low point in our morale and in our revolutionary legend. The most urgent tasks are the same as last month, notably: to reestablish contact, to recruit combatants, and to obtain medicine and supplies.

It must be recognized that Inti and Coco are becoming more and more outstanding as revolutionary and military cadres.

SEPTEMBER 1967

September 1

We led the mules down early, with many adventures that included a spectacular fall by the male mule. El Médico has not recovered, but I have and I can walk perfectly leading the mule. The trail is longer than we thought, and we only realized at 18:15 that we had reached the creek by Honorato's house.[1] Miguel went full steam ahead but only made it to the main road, by which time it was already completely dark. Benigno and Urbano advanced cautiously and saw nothing unusual, so they occupied the house but discovered it was empty; the army had added several barracks, which were not being used. We found flour, lard, salt, and goats, two of which were killed and cooked with flour for a feast, although we had to wait all night for it to be ready. We withdrew at dawn, leaving guards posted at the little house and at the entrance to the road.

Altitude = 740 meters.

September 2

Early in the morning we withdrew to the farms, but left an ambush at the house, with Coco, Pablo, and Benigno, and

---

1. Honorato Rojas.

Miguel in charge. A sentry remained watching on the other side. At 8:00 Coco came to tell us that a herder had come looking for Honorato; there were four of them and I ordered Coco to let the other three pass. This took time because we were an hour away from the house. At 13:30, several shots were heard; we learned later that a peasant had come by with a soldier and a horse; Chino, who was on sentry duty with Pombo and Eustaquio, shouted, "a soldier," and raised his rifle. The soldier shot at him and fled; Pombo fired, killing the horse. I flew into a rage, as this was the height of incompetence; poor Chino was crushed. We released the four, who had gone past in the meantime, along with the two prisoners, and sent everyone off up the Masicuri.

We bought a young bull from the herder for $700 and gave Hugo $100 for his work and $50 for some things we had taken from him. The dead horse turned out to be one that was left at Honorato's house because it was lame. The herder said Honorato's wife had complained about the army because soldiers had beaten her husband and had eaten everything they had. When the herders passed through eight days ago, Honorato was in Vallegrande recovering from a wildcat bite. In any case, someone had been in the house because we saw a lit fire there when we arrived. Owing to Chino's error, I decided to leave that night in the same direction as the herders and to try to reach the first house, assuming there were only a few soldiers and that they had continued to withdraw. But we left very late and it was already 3:45 when we crossed the ford. We did not come across any house, so we slept on a cow path waiting for daylight.

The radio broadcast a nasty piece of news about the annihilation of a group of 10 people led by a Cuban named Joaquín in the Camiri area; nevertheless, the report came from the "Voice of America" and local stations have not said anything.

September 3

As is appropriate for a Sunday, there was a clash. At dawn we followed the Masicuri downstream to its mouth, and then followed the Río Grande for a while. At 13:00 Inti, Coco, Benigno, Pablito, Julio, and León set out to try to find the house and, if the army was not there, they were to buy some supplies that would make our lives more bearable. First, the group captured two farmhands who said the owner was not around and neither were soldiers, and that they could get plenty of supplies. Other information: Yesterday five soldiers galloped past without stopping at the house. Honorato passed by two days ago on his way home with two of his children.

On reaching the landowner's house, they encountered 40 soldiers who had just arrived there as well, resulting in a confused skirmish in which our people killed at least one soldier, the one who had a dog with him; the soldiers reacted and surrounded them, but later retreated in the face of our shouts; we failed to obtain even a grain of rice. A plane flew over the area and fired some small rockets, apparently beside the Ñacahuazú. Other information from the peasants: No guerrillas have been seen in this area and the first they heard anything was from the herders who came through yesterday.

Once again the "Voice of America" reported on battles with the army, this time naming José Carrillo as the only survivor of the group of 10 people. As Carrillo is Paco, from the reject group, and the fact that the annihilation took place in Masicuri, everything seems to indicate that this is one big trick.

Altitude = 650 meters.

September 4

A group of eight men under Miguel's command set up an ambush on the road from the Masicuri to Honorato's house, maintaining it until 13:00, without incident. Meanwhile, Ñato and León, through a strenuous effort, brought back a cow and later two magnificent oxen. Urbano and Camba walked upriver for about 10 kilometers; we have to cross four fords, one of which is quite deep. The young bull was killed and volunteers were requested to make an incursion in search of food and information. Inti, Coco, Julio, Aniceto, Chapaco, and Arturo were chosen, led by Inti; Pacho, Pombo, Antonio, and Eustaquio also volunteered. Inti's instructions are: Arrive at the house at dawn, observe any movement, stock up on supplies if there are no soldiers. If there are soldiers, surround the house, carry on and try to capture one; remember it is most essential to avoid any losses and to use the utmost caution.

The radio brings news of a death at a new clash at Vado del Yeso, near where the group of 10 was wiped out, which makes the news about Joaquín seem like a trick; but on the other hand, they gave a physical description of Negro, the Peruvian doctor, killed in Palmarito and his body was taken to Camiri; Pelado assisted with the identification.

This seems to be a real death; the others could be fictitious or members of the reject group. In any case, there is a strange tone to the reports that are now focusing on the areas of Masicuri and Camiri.

September 5

The day passed without incident, while we were waiting for news. At 4:30 the group returned with a mule and some supplies. In the house of the landowner, Morón, there were soldiers, who almost discovered our group because of their dogs; they apparently mobilize during the night. They surrounded the house and cut through the woods to Montaño's house, where no one was home but they took a quintal of the corn that was there. Around 12:00, they crossed the river and found two houses on the other side; everyone fled from one of the houses and so they requisitioned the mule; in the other house there was very little cooperation, so they had to resort to threats.

The information they received was that no guerrillas had been seen in the area until now, except for those who had been at Perez's house (us) before the carnival. They returned by day and waited for darkness to get past Morón's house. Everything went perfectly, but Arturo got lost and fell asleep on the path and two hours were lost looking for him; they left footprints that could be tracked if cattle do not go over them; moreover, they dropped some things along the way. The spirit of the troops changed immediately.

The radio broadcast that the dead guerrillas could not be identified, but any moment there might be more news. We decoded the entire report that stated that OLAS [Organization of Latin American Solidarity] was a triumph, but the Bolivian delegation was shit; Aldo Flores of the PCB [Bolivian Communist Party] pretended to represent the ELN [National Liberation Army] so they had to show he was lying. They have requested that one of Kolle's men come to discuss matters; Lozano's[2] house was raided and he is now underground; they

---

2. Dr. Hugo Lozano, Bolivian, a stomatologist and member of the urban network.

think that they can make an exchange for Debray. That is all; evidently they have not received our last message.

September 6

Benigno.

Benigno's birthday looked promising; at dawn we made cornmeal with what had been brought and had a little *mate* with sugar. Later Miguel, in command of eight men, went to set up an ambush while León found another young bull to take with us. As it was rather late, just after 10:00, and they had not returned, I sent Urbano to tell them to lift the ambush at 12:00. A few minutes later a shot was heard, then a short burst of fire, and then another shot sounded in our direction. As we took our positions, Urbano came racing up; there had been an encounter with a patrol that had dogs. With nine men on the other side, and not knowing their precise location, I was desperate: the path was cleared, but did not go as far as the riverbank, so I sent Moro, Pombo, and Camba, with Coco, that way. I thought we could move the backpacks and make contact with the rear guard, if possible, so they could rejoin the group; on the other hand, it was possible that they might fall into the ambush. Nevertheless, Miguel was able to rejoin us with all of his troops, cutting through the woods.

Explanation of what happened: Miguel advanced without posting a guard on our little path, and was busy looking for cattle; León heard a dog bark and Miguel decided to withdraw just in case; just then they heard shots and saw that a patrol had come along a path that lay between them and the woods. The soldiers were ahead of them, so they had to make it back through the woods.

We withdrew calmly, with three mules and three head of cattle. After crossing four fords, two of them difficult, we camped about seven kilometers from where we were before; we slaughtered a cow and ate sumptuously. The rear guard reported that sustained gunfire was heard coming from the direction of the camp, with a number of machine guns.

Altitude = 640 meters.

September 7

A short trip. Only one ford was crossed and then we ran into difficulties with a rocky cliff; Miguel decided to set up camp to wait for us. Tomorrow we will conduct some good scouting expeditions. This situation is this: Aircraft are not looking for us here, despite having found the camp and the radio reports that I am the leader of the group. The question is: Are they afraid? Not likely. Do they consider it impossible to climb to the top? Based on what we have already done, of which they are aware, I do not think so. Do they want to let us advance to wait for us at some strategic point? It is possible. Do they think that we will stay in the Masicuri area for supplies? This is also possible. El Médico is much better, but I had a relapse and spent a sleepless night.

The radio brings news of the valuable information supplied by José Carrillo (Paco). We should make an example of him.

Debray responded to the accusations Paco made against him, saying that he likes to hunt and that is why he might have been seen with a rifle. Radio Cruz del Sur announced the discovery of the body of Tania the guerrilla on the banks of the Río Grande; it is news that does not ring true, like the news of Negro did; her body was taken to Santa Cruz, according to this radio station—and only this one, not the Altiplano station.

Altitude = 720 meters.

I spoke with Julio; he is doing very well but he is worried about the lack of contact and recruitment.

September 8

A quiet day. We set up ambushes with eight men from morning to night, with Antonio and Pombo in charge. The animals are doing well, eating from the *chuchial*[3] and the mule is recovering from its injuries. Aniceto and Chapaco went to explore upriver and returned to say that the way was relatively good for the animals. Coco and Camba crossed the river with water up to their chests and climbed the hill in front of us, but they came back with little new information. I dispatched Miguel and Aniceto and the result of their more extensive exploration was that, according to Miguel, it would be very difficult for the animals to get through. Tomorrow we will stay on this side, because there is always the possibility that the animals can get across the water with no loads on them.

The radio brought information that Barrientos attended the interment of the remains of Tania the guerrilla, who was given a "Christian burial." Later he was in Puerto Mauricio, where Honorato's house is; he made a proposal to those deceived Bolivians, who had never received their promised salaries that they should present themselves with their hands on their heads at army posts and no action would be taken against them. A small plane bombed the area below Honorato's house, as if making a show for Barrientos.

---

3. A place with *chuchío*—a species of hollowed cane similar to the willow or bamboo.

A Budapest daily is criticizing Che Guevara, a pathetic and apparently irresponsible figure, and applauds the Marxist stand of the Chilean Party for taking a pragmatic position when faced with reality. How I would like to have power, for nothing more than to expose cowards and lackeys of all stripes and to rub their snouts in their own filth.

September 9

Miguel and Ñato went off exploring and returned with the news that we could get through, but the animals would have to swim over; the men can cross at the fords. There is a fairly large creek to the left where we can set up camp. The ambushes have been maintained with eight men, under the command of Antonio and Pombo, without incident. I spoke with Aniceto; he seems very steady, although he thinks there are several Bolivians who are weakening; he complained about the lack of political work by Coco and Inti. We finished off the cow, and all that remains are its four hooves for a broth tomorrow.

The only news on the radio is the postponement of Debray's trial to September 17, at the earliest.

September 10

A bad day. It began auspiciously but then the animals refused to go on a track that was very rough and, finally, the male mule refused to walk any farther and was left behind on the other bank. Coco made the decision due to the violent flooding of the river, but four weapons were left on the other side, among them Moro's and the three antitank shells for Benigno's gun. I swam across the river with the mule, but lost my shoes in the process so now I have only sandals, which does not amuse me at all. Ñato made a bundle out of his clothing, wrapped his weapons in an oilcloth, and jumped in where the torrent was the strongest, and lost everything. The other mule got stuck and then jumped in to go across by herself, but we had to bring her back because there was no way she would make it. León tried to take the mule across, but they both nearly drowned as the current had increased.

Finally, we made it to the creek that was our goal; El Médico was in a very bad way, complaining throughout the night of neuralgia in his extremities. From here, our plan was to make the animals swim back to the other side, but the rising water level interrupted this plan, at least until it goes down again. Furthermore, planes and helicopters have been flying over this area; I do not like helicopters at all because they could be setting up ambushes along the river. Tomorrow we will explore upstream and downstream, in order to determine exactly where we are.

Altitude = 780 meters. Walked = three to four kilometers.

I forgot to mark an event: Today, I took a bath, after more than six months. This constitutes a record that several others are already approaching.

September 11

A quiet day. Scouts went upriver and to the creek; those who explored the river returned at dusk with the news that most likely we could cross it when the river level drops further and said there were sandy areas where the beasts could walk. Benigno and Julio explored the creek, but only superficially and they were back by 12:00. With the assistance of the rear guard, Ñato and Coco went to find the things we left behind, passing the mule and leaving behind only a bag of machine-gun bullet casings.

There was an unpleasant incident: Chino came to tell me that Ñato had roasted and eaten a whole piece of meat in front of him; I was furious with Chino because it was his job to stop him, but after investigating further, things got complicated because it was hard to tell whether or not Chino had authorized the act. He asked to be replaced and I put Pombo in charge again, but this was a bitter pill for Chino.

In the morning, the radio reported that Barrientos claimed that I have been dead for some time; it was all propaganda, and at night it was reported that he was offering 50,000 pesos (US$4,200) for information leading to my capture, dead or alive. The armed forces apparently gave him a [illegible in the original]. Leaflets were distributed in the area, probably with my description. Requeterán[4] says that Barrientos's offer could be considered a psychological maneuver, since the tenacity of the guerrilla force is well known and they are preparing for a long war.

I talked at length with Pablito, who, like everyone else, is worried by the lack of contact and believes that our fundamental task is to reestablish links with the city. But he showed himself to be steady and determined, the "Homeland or death" type, wherever it leads.

September 12

The day began with a tragicomic episode: right on 6:00, the hour of reveille, Eustaquio came to warn us that people were advancing along the creek; he called for arms and everyone

---

4. Army Colonel Luis Reque Terán.

was mobilized; Antonio had seen them, and when I asked him how many there were, he responded holding up five fingers. In the end, it turned out to be a hallucination, dangerous for the morale of the troops, because immediately afterwards they began to talk of psychosis. Later on, I spoke with Antonio and clearly he is not himself; tears came to his eyes, but he denied that he was worried about anything, saying he was only affected by a lack of sleep as he has been on kitchen duty for six days for falling asleep at his post and then denying it. Chapaco disobeyed an order and was sanctioned with three days' kitchen duty. During the night he asked me to assign him to the vanguard because, according to him, he did not get along with Antonio. I refused. Inti, León, and Eustaquio went off to make a thorough exploration of the creek to determine whether we could get to the other side and make it to a large mountain chain that can be seen in the distance. Coco, Aniceto, and Julio went upstream to scout the fords and see how we could take the animals if we went that way.

Barrientos's offer has apparently caused quite a stir; in any case, one crazy journalist thinks that US$4,200 is too little money, considering what a menace I am. Radio Habana reported that OLAS has received a message of support from the ELN: a miracle of telepathy!

September 13

The explorers returned: Inti and his group climbed along the creek all day and slept at a high altitude, which was very cold; apparently, the creek begins in a mountain range ahead of us and flows west; the animals cannot get through there. Coco and his compañeros tried unsuccessfully to cross the river, clambering over 11 cliffs before reaching the canyon where the Pesca River should be located; they saw some signs of life there: farms cleared by fire and an ox. The animals will have to cross over to the other side, unless we can put everything on a raft, which is what we will try to do.

I spoke with Darío about the issue of his leaving, if that is what he wants to do. At first he argued that to leave would be very dangerous, but I warned him that this is not a refuge and if he decided to stay then it would be for once and for all. He agreed and said that he would correct his shortcomings. We will see.

The only news on the radio was that a shot was fired over the head of Debray's father and that all Debray's preparatory documents for his defense were confiscated under the pretext that they should not become political propaganda.

September 14

An exhausting day. Miguel set off at 7:00 with the vanguard and Ñato, with instructions to walk as far as possible on this side and to make a raft when it became difficult to continue. Antonio stayed with the rear guard in an ambush position. A couple of M-1s were left in a little cave that Ñato and Willy know about. At 15:30, after receiving no news, we started out.

I found it impossible to ride a mule and, sensing an asthma attack coming on, I had to leave the animal to León and continue on foot. The rear guard had orders to begin their march at 15:00, if there were no counter orders. At about this time, Pablito arrived to say that the ox had reached the place where the animals could cross and that the raft was being built a kilometer farther up. I waited for the animals to arrive, which did not happen until 18:15, after some men were sent to help them. The two mules then went across (the ox had done so earlier) and we continued at a weary pace until reaching the raft, where I discovered that 12 men were still on this side— only 10 had gone across. So thus split up, we spent the night, eating the last ration of ox, which was half-rotten.

Altitude = 720 meters. Walked = two to three kilometers.

September 15

A slightly longer stretch was covered: five to six kilometers, but we did not make it to the Pesca River because we had to take the animals across twice, and one of the mules refused to go. We still need to make one more crossing and to see if the mules can get through.

The radio broadcast news of Loyola's arrest; the photos must be at fault. Our remaining bull died—at the hands of the executioner, naturally.

Altitude = 780 meters.

September 16

The day was spent constructing the raft and crossing the river, hiking only 500 meters to a camp where there was a little spring. The crossing went without incident in a good raft that was pulled by ropes from both sides of the river. When finally left alone, Antonio and Chapaco had another row and Antonio gave Chapaco six days punishment for insulting him; I respected his decision, but I am not sure it is fair. During the evening there was another incident when Eustaquio complained that Ñato had eaten an extra meal, which turned out to be some pieces of fatty bull hide. Another difficult situation over food. El Médico raised another little problem with me concerning his illness and what the others thought about it, based on some comments made by Julio; it all seems trivial.

Altitude = 820 meters.

September 17

Pablito.

A day of stomatology; I extracted teeth from Arturo and Chapaco, while Miguel explored up to the river and Benigno to the road; the news is that the mules can get up, but first have to swim, crossing and recrossing the river. In Pablito's honor we made some rice: he is 22 years old, the youngest of the guerrillas.

The only radio report is about the postponement of the trial and a protest over the arrest of Loyola Guzmán.

September 18

We started out at 7:00, but Miguel soon brought news that they had seen three peasants around a bend, but did not know if they had seen us; the order was issued to detain them. True to form, Chapaco sparked off another dispute, accusing Arturo of having stolen 15 bullets from his magazine; this bodes ill and the only good thing is that, although his rows are with Cubans, no Bolivian pays him any attention. The mules made the whole journey without having to swim, but when crossing a gully, the black mule fell and hurt itself, falling down about 50 meters. Four peasants and their little donkeys were seized, while traveling to Piraypani, a river located a league upstream from this one; they told us that Aladino Gutiérrez and his troops were hunting and fishing on the banks of the Río Grande.

Benigno was thoroughly reckless by letting himself be seen, and then releasing the man, the woman, and the other peasant. When I found out about this, I blew my top, describing it an act of treason, which reduced Benigno to tears. All the peasants have been warned that they will be coming with us to Zitano tomorrow, the settlement where they live, six to eight leagues from here. Aladino and his wife are a bit shifty and it took a lot of effort to convince them to sell us food. The radio is now reporting two suicide attempts by Loyola "for fear of guerrilla reprisals," as well as the arrest of several teachers who, if they are not involved, are at least sympathetic to us. Apparently a lot of things were taken from Loyola's house, but it would not be strange if everything stemmed from the photos in the cave.

At dusk a small plane and a Mustang aircraft flew over the area in a suspicious way.

Altitude = 800 meters.

September 19

We did not leave particularly early because the peasants could not find their animals. Finally, after really giving them a mouthful, we set off with a caravan of prisoners. Moro was walking slowly and when we reached the river we learned that three more prisoners had been taken and that the vanguard had just gone to find a sugarcane plantation two leagues away. These leagues seemed long, as long as the first two had been. Around 9:00 we got to the plantation, which was only a cane field; the rear guard arrived later.

I had a conversation with Inti about some of his weaknesses concerning food and he became very upset, agreeing with what I had said and saying he would make a public self-criticism when the group was alone again, but he denied some of the accusations. We passed through altitudes of 1,440 meters and are now at 1,000; from here to Lusitano is a three-hour hike — maybe four, the pessimists say. Finally, we ate pork and those with a sweet tooth filled up on *chankaka*.

The radio is going on about the Loyola case and the teachers are out on strike; the students of the secondary school where Higueras worked — one of those arrested — are on a hunger strike; and the oil company workers are about to strike because of the creation of an oil company.

A sign of the times: I have run out of ink.

September 20

I decided to leave at 15:00 to get to the Lusitano settlement by nightfall, as they said it would only take three good hours to get there, but various mishaps delayed us until 17:00 and total darkness caught us on a hill. Despite lighting a lamp, we only reached Aladino Gutiérrez's house at 23:00, and he had few supplies, although we did get some cigarettes and other trifles, but no clothing. We slept a little before heading off at 3:00 straight to Alto Seco, which is said to be four leagues away. We seized the magistrate's telephone, but it does not work — has not worked for years — and besides, the line is down. The magistrate's name is Vargas and he has only been in the post a short time.

The radio reports nothing important; we passed altitudes of 1,800 meters and Lusitano is at 1,400 meters.

We walked some two leagues to the settlement.

September 21

We left at 3:00 under bright moonlight along a trail we had checked out beforehand and walked until about 9:00 without seeing anyone and crossing altitudes of 2,040 meters, the highest we have reached so far. At this time, we ran into a couple of herders who gave us directions to Alto Seco, two leagues away. We had barely covered two leagues during part of the night and the morning. When we came to the first houses at the bottom of the hill, we bought some supplies and went to the mayor's house to cook some food; later we passed a corn mill run by hydraulic power on the banks of the Piraymiri (1,400 meters altitude.) People here are quite afraid and try to avoid us; we have lost a lot of time due to poor mobility. To cover the two leagues to Alto Seco took from 12:35 to 5:00.

September 22

When our center group reached Alto Seco, we learned that the magistrate had apparently left yesterday to raise the alarm that we were in the area; in retaliation, we seized everything in his store. Alto Seco is a village of 50 houses, located at an altitude of 1,900 meters, and we were received with a well-seasoned mixture of fear and curiosity. The provisioning machine was set in motion and we soon had a respectable amount of food at our camp, which was an abandoned house next to a water hole. The little truck that was supposed to come from Vallegrande never showed up, confirming the theory that the magistrate went to sound an alert. Nevertheless, I had to bear his wife's tears, who, in the name of God and her children, asked for payment, something I did not accede to. During the evening, Inti gave a talk at the local school (for first and second grades) to a group of 15 amazed and silent peasants, explaining the scope of our revolution. The teacher was the only person to speak, asking if we were fighting in the towns. He is a mix of the cunning peasant, educated, but with a childlike naivety; he asked a bunch of questions about socialism. An older boy offered to serve as our guide and warned us about the teacher, whom they describe as a bit of a fox. We left at 1:30, heading for Santa Elena, where we arrived at 10:00.

Altitude = 1,300 meters.

Barrientos and Ovando gave a press conference in which they went over all the information in the documents and said that Joaquín's group had been wiped out.

September 23

The place was a lovely orange grove that still had a good amount of fruit. We spent the day resting and sleeping but kept a careful watch. At 1:00 we got up and at 2:00 left in the direction of Loma Larga, which we reached at dawn, passing altitudes of 1,800 meters. The men are heavily loaded with supplies and the march is slow. Benigno's cooking upset my stomach.

September 24

By the time we reached the settlement called Loma Larga, I had pains in my liver and was vomiting; the troops are exhausted from these unproductive hikes. I decided to spend the night at the junction of the road to Pujío; we killed a pig sold to us by the only peasant still left in his house (Sóstenos Vargas), the others fled as soon as they saw us coming.

Altitude = 1,400 meters.

September 25

We got to Pujío early, but there were people who had seen us down below the day before, which means Radio Bemba[5] is preceding us. Pujío is a small settlement on a hill; the people fled when they saw us, but later approached us and treated us well. A *carabinero* had left early in the morning, having come from Serrano in Chuquisaca state to arrest a debtor; we are at the point where the three states converge. Traveling with mules is now dangerous, but we are trying to make it as easy as possible for El Médico who is becoming very weak. The peasants say they know nothing about the army being in this area. We walked in short stretches until we reached Tranca Mayo, where we slept beside the road because Miguel did not take the precautions I had demanded. The magistrate of La Higuera is in the area and the sentries were ordered to detain him.

Altitude = 1,800 meters.

Inti and I talked with Camba and he will stay with us until we are within sight of La Higuera, the point located close to Pucará, from where he will try to get to Santa Cruz.

September 26

Defeat. At the crack of dawn we came to Picacho where everyone was involved in a fiesta; this is the highest point we have reached: 2,280 meters; the peasants treated us very well and we carried on without too many fears, despite Ovando having made assurances of my capture any moment now.

On reaching La Higuera, everything changed; the men had

---

5. Cuban expression meaning "word of mouth" or "grapevine."

disappeared and only a few women remained. Coco went to the telegraph operator's house, where there is a telephone, and brought back a cable dated the 22nd, from which we learned that a sub-prefect of Vallegrande told the magistrate that if he had news of a guerrilla presence in the area, that information should be communicated to Vallegrande, which will cover the costs; the man had fled, but his wife assured us that he had not spoken to anyone today because everyone was off celebrating in the next town, Jagüey.

The vanguard set out at 13:00 to try to reach Jagüey and make a decision there about the mules and about El Médico; a little later I was talking to the only man left in town, who was very scared, when a coca merchant turned up, saying he had come from Vallegrande and Pucará and had seen nothing. He also was very nervous, which I attributed to our presence and let both of them go, in spite of the lies they told us. As I was going up to the crest of the hill, at approximately 13:30, shots coming from along the ridge indicated our men had fallen into an ambush. I organized the defense in the little village, to wait for the survivors, and set up an exit on the road that leads to the Río Grande. A few moments later, Benigno arrived, wounded, followed by Aniceto and Pablito, with a foot in a bad way. Miguel, Coco, and Julio had been killed and Camba had disappeared, leaving behind his backpack. The rear guard advanced quickly along the road and I followed them, bringing the two mules. Those in the rear were under fire and fell behind and Inti lost contact. After waiting for him for half an hour in an ambush position, with more gunfire coming from the hill, we decided to get out; but he caught up with us shortly. By this time we realized León had disappeared, and Inti said that he had seen his backpack by the gorge he came through; we saw a man who was walking fast along a canyon and concluded it was him. To try to throw them off our trail, we let the mules go in the canyon below and we proceeded along a small gorge that farther up had brackish water; we slept at 12:00 as it was impossible to go on.

September 27

At 4:00 we started out again, trying to find a way up, which we found at 7:00, but it was on the opposite side from where we had wanted to be. Ahead there was a barren hill, which seemed harmless. We climbed a little higher to find a refuge from the aircraft, in a sparsely wooded spot; there we discovered that the hill had a path, although no one had used it all day. At dusk a peasant and a soldier climbed halfway up the hill and were there for a while, without seeing us. Aniceto was just returning from scouting the area, when he saw a large group of soldiers in a nearby house, so the easiest route for us was now blocked off. In the morning we saw a column of soldiers going up a nearby hill, with their equipment shining in the sun; later, at noon, isolated shots were heard together with some bursts of machine-gun fire; then shouts were heard of "there he is," "come out of there," and "are you coming or not?" accompanied by shooting. We had no idea of the fate of the man, whom we presume to be Camba. We set out at dusk to try to get down to the water along the other side, halting in some vegetation that was a little thicker than before; we have to seek water in the same canyon because we could not get past the cliff.

The radio broadcast the news that we had clashed with the Galindo company, leaving three dead, whose bodies were being

taken to Vallegrande for identification. Apparently they have
not caught Camba or León. Our losses have been very great
this time; the deepest loss is that of Coco, but Miguel and Julio
were magnificent fighters and the human value of the three is
incalculable. León had a lot of promise.

Altitude = 1,400 meters.

September 28

Day of anguish, and for a moment it seemed it would be our
last.

Water was fetched at dawn and Inti and Willy left right
away to explore another possible way into the canyon, but they
returned immediately because a track runs across the hill ahead
of us and a peasant on a horse was traveling along it. At 10:00,
46 soldiers went past in front of us, carrying backpacks, and it
seemed like centuries for them to move on. At 12:00, another
group made its appearance, this time with 77 men; to top it off,
a shot was heard at that moment, and the soldiers took their
positions; the officer gave the order to go down into the ravine
that seemed to be where we were, but after communicating by
radio, he seemed satisfied to resume the march.

Our refuge has no defense against an attack from above
and the possibilities of escaping are remote if they discover us.
Later a lagging soldier passed by dragging an exhausted dog,
trying to get it to walk. Later on, a peasant came along, guiding
a soldier who had fallen behind; the peasant returned after
a while, and although nothing happened the anguish at the
moment the shot was fired was considerable. All the soldiers
carried their backpacks, which gives the impression that they
are withdrawing, and we did not see any fires at the little house

during the evening, nor did we hear the shots they usually fire as a night salute. Tomorrow we will spend all day exploring the settlement. A light rain soaked us but was probably insufficient to erase our tracks.

The radio announced the identification of Coco, and gave a confused report about Julio; Miguel was mixed up with Antonio, describing his responsibilities in Manila. At first they ran a news item about my death; later this was retracted.

September 29

Another tense day. The scouts, Inti and Aniceto, went off early to watch the house all day. From early on there was activity on the road, and by mid-morning, there were soldiers without backpacks going in both directions, while more came up from below leading donkeys. The donkeys had no loads but returned with them. Inti arrived at 18:15 reporting that 16 soldiers who had gone down the hill were at the farm and could no longer be seen; the donkeys are apparently being loaded down there.

In view of this, it was difficult to make a decision about taking that route, the easiest and most logical option, but it was also easy for the soldiers to ambush us, and besides, the dogs in the house might give us away. Tomorrow we will conduct two more scouting expeditions: one will go to the same place and the other will try to get as far as possible along the ridge to see if there is a way out, probably by taking the same road used by the soldiers.

The radio broadcast no news.

September 30

Another day of tension. In the morning, Radio Balmaseda

of Chile announced that highly placed sources in the army announced Che Guevara is cornered in a canyon in the jungle. The local stations are silent; this could be a betrayal and they are convinced about our presence in the area. In a while, the soldiers began moving back and forth. At 12:00, 40 soldiers went past in separate columns with their weapons at the ready, on their way to the little house where they set up camp and established a lookout with nervous guards.

Aniceto and Pacho reported this. Inti and Willy returned with the news that the Río Grande was about two kilometers away, as the crow flies, and that there are three houses above the canyon, and that there are places to camp where we would be hidden from every side. We went to find water, and at 22:00 began an exhausting night march, slowed down by Chino who walks very badly in the dark. Benigno is fine, but El Médico has not fully recovered.

Summary of the month

It should have been a month of recuperation, and almost was, but the ambush in which Miguel, Coco, and Julio were killed ruined everything, and left us in a perilous position, losing León as well; losing Camba is a net gain.

We have had several small skirmishes: one in which we killed a horse; another in which we killed one soldier and wounded another; one where Urbano had a shoot-out with a patrol; and the disastrous ambush at La Higuera. Now we have abandoned the mules and I believe it will be a long time before we have animals like that again, unless I fall into another bad state of asthma.

On the other hand, there may be truth to the various reports about fatalities in the other [Joaquín's] group, so we must consider them wiped out, although it is still possible there is a small group wandering around, avoiding contact with the army, because the news of the death of seven people at once might well be false, or at least, exaggerated.

The features are the same as last month, except that now the army is demonstrating more effectiveness in action and the peasant masses are not helping us with anything and are becoming informers.

The most important task is to escape and seek more favorable areas; then focus on contacts, despite the fact that our urban network in La Paz is in a shambles, where we have also been hit hard. The morale of the rest of the troops has remained fairly high, and I only have doubts about Willy, who might take advantage of some commotion to escape, if he is not spoken to first.

OCTOBER 1967

October 1

This first day of the month passed without incident.

At daybreak we came to some sparse little woods where we camped, posting sentries at different points of approach. The 40 men, firing a few shots, moved on to a canyon where we were planning to go; we heard the last shots at 14:00; there seems to be no one in the little houses, although Urbano saw five soldiers go down there, not following any path. I decided to stay here one more day because this is a good spot with a guaranteed exit, and, moreover, we can see almost all the enemy troops' movements. Pacho, with Ñato, Darío, and Eustaquio, went to look for water and returned at 21:00. Chapaco cooked fritters and we had a little bit of *charqui* to ease our hunger.

There was no news.

October 2

Antonio.[1]

The day went by with no sign of any soldiers, but some little goats driven by sheepdogs passed by our position and the dogs

---

1. A reference to the birthday of Antonio (Orlando Pantoja Tamajo), one of the guerrilla fighters.

barked. We decided to try to leave by flanking the farm closest to the canyon and began our descent at 18:00, leaving plenty of time to get there and to cook before making the crossing; Ñato became lost, but still insisted we go ahead. When we decided to go back, we got lost again and spent the night on high ground, without being able to cook and terribly thirsty. The radio explained the deployment of soldiers on the 30th, stating that according to a Cruz del Sur broadcast the army had reported a clash at Abra del Quiñol with a small group of us, resulting in no losses on either side, although they said that they had found traces of blood after we escaped.

The group was made up of six individuals, according to the same report.

October 3

A long and unnecessarily intense day: While we were preparing to go back to our base camp, Urbano came to tell us that while we were walking, he had heard some passing peasants say, "Those are the people who were talking last night." It is pretty clear the report was inaccurate, but I decided to act as if it were perfectly true, and so without quenching our thirst, we again climbed up to the ridge that overlooks the road used by the soldiers. The rest of the day remained absolutely calm, and at dusk we went down and made some coffee, which tasted heavenly, despite the brackish water and the greasy pan it was made in. Afterwards, we made cornmeal to eat there and rice with tapir meat to take with us. At 3:00 we began the march, after scouting the area, successfully avoiding the farm and ending up at the ravine we had chosen; there was no water but there were soldiers' tracks made by a scouting party.

The radio brought news of two prisoners: Antonio Domín-guez Flores (León) and Orlando Jiménez Bazán (Camba), the latter admits fighting against the army, and the former says that he had turned himself in, trusting the president to keep his word. They both gave plenty of information about Fernando [Che], his illness, and lots more, not to mention what else might have been said but not made public. Here ends the story of two heroic guerrillas.

Altitude = 1,360 meters.

We heard an interview with Debray, who was very cour-ageous when confronted by a student acting as an agent provocateur.

October 4

After resting in the ravine, we went farther down for half an hour until reaching another adjoining one, which we climbed, resting until 15:00 to escape the sun. At that time we resumed the march for just over half an hour and caught up with the scouts, who had gone to the end of the small canyons without finding any water. At 18:00, we left the ravine and followed a cow path until 19:30, by which time we could not see a thing, so we halted until 3:00.

The radio reported that the general command of the Fourth Division had transferred its forward post from Lagunillas to Padilla to better monitor the Serrano area, where it is presumed the guerrillas might try to escape. The commentary also said if I were captured by the Fourth [Division], I would be tried in Camiri, and if the Eighth got me, in Santa Cruz.

Altitude = 1,650 meters.

October 5

We started out again, walking with difficulty until 5:15, when we left the cow path and buried ourselves in some sparse woods, with vegetation high enough to give us cover from prying eyes. Benigno and Pacho made various expeditions looking for water, thoroughly searching around the nearby house but did not find any; there might be a little well off to the side. As they finished scouting, six soldiers were spotted at the house, apparently just passing through. We set off at nightfall with the troops exhausted due to lack of water, Eustaquio making a spectacle of himself, crying for a mouthful of water. After an awful hike, with too much stopping and starting, by dawn we reached a little woods where we could hear the barking of nearby dogs. A high barren ridge can be seen quite close.

We took care of Benigno, whose wound was oozing a bit, and I gave El Médico an injection. As a result of the treatment, Benigno complained of pain during the night.

The radio reported that our two *Cambas* were taken to Camiri to act as witnesses in Debray's trial.

Altitude = 2,000 meters.

October 6

The scouting expeditions revealed that there was a house quite close to us, and also that there was water in a ravine farther away. We headed off and spent the whole day cooking under a big rock slab that served as a roof, but in spite of this, I did not have a restful day as we had passed close to populated areas in full daylight, and were now in a hole. Because preparing the food took so long, we decided to leave at dawn and make our way to a tributary near this little creek, and from there scout the area more exhaustively to determine our future route.

Radio Cruz del Sur reported an interview with the *Cambas*; Orlando was a little less of a rogue. A Chilean radio station reported some censored news that indicates there are 1,800 men in the area looking for us.

Altitude = 1,750 meters.

October 7

The 11-month anniversary of our establishment as a guerrilla force passed in a bucolic mood, with no complications, until 12:30 when an old woman tending her goats entered the canyon where we had camped and we had to take her prisoner. The woman gave us no reliable information about the soldiers, saying that she knew nothing because it had been a while since she had been over there. She only gave us information about trails, from which we conclude we are approximately one league from La Higuera, another from Jagüey, and about two more from Pucará. At 17:30, Inti, Aniceto, and Pablito went to the old woman's house; she has one daughter who is bedridden and the other is almost a dwarf. They gave her 50 pesos with instructions to not say a word, but we have little hope she will stick to her promise.[2]

The 17 of us set out under a sliver of a moon; the march was exhausting and we left tracks in the canyon we walked through; there were no nearby houses, but there were potato seedbeds irrigated by ditches from the same creek. We stopped to rest at 2:00 because it was futile to continue. Chino becomes a real burden when we have to walk at night.

---

2. The old woman (Epifania Cabrera) herding goats never was an informer: she never spoke to the military, and did not denounce Che.

The army issued an odd report about the presence of 250 men in Serrano to block the escape of the 37 [guerrillas] that are said to be surrounded. Our refuge is supposedly between the Acero and Oro rivers.

The report seems to be diversionary.

Altitude = 2,000 meters.

16

Siguiendo una norma del ~~nuestras fuerzas~~ E.L.N
escenarios, curamos los heridos con nuestros escasos medios y pusimos en libertad a todos los prisioneros, previa explicación de ~~nuestra~~ los objetivos de nuestra lucha revolucionaria.

Las pérdidas del ejército enemigo se resumen así: 10 muertos, entre ellos dos tenientes, y 30 prisioneros, incluyendo al mayor Sánchez Castro, de los cuales 6 resultaron heridos. El botín de guerra es proporcional a las bajas enemigas, incluyendo...

Appendices

una baja, ~~~~ comprensible si se tiene en cuenta que en todos los combates hemos elegido el momento y lugar de desencadenarlo y que el ejército boliviano está enviando soldados bisoños, casi niños, al matadero, mientras ellos inventan partes en la Paz y luego se dan golpes de pecho en funerales de mayoppios, culpando al...

Hacemos un llamado a los nuevos reclutas para que sigan las siguientes instrucciones: al iniciarse el fuego combate tiren el arma a un lado y llevarse las manos a la cabeza permaneciendo quietos en el punto donde el fuego los sorprendiera; nunca avanzar al frente de la columna en marchas de aproximación a zonas de combate, obliguen a los oficiales que los incitan a combatir a que ocupen esta porción de extremo peligro contra la vanguardia de la columna, tírenlos, siempre a mata por mucho que nos duela se corre la sangre, etc.

Ejército de Liberación Nacional de Bolivia

Appendices

INSTRUCTIONS TO URBAN CADRES[1]

Document III

January 22, 1967

A support network of the character we want to create should be guided by a series of norms, which are summarized below.

Activity will be primarily clandestine in nature, but it will be necessary, at times, to establish contact with certain individuals or organizations, requiring some cadres to surface. This necessitates a very strict compartmentalization, keeping each area of work quite separate from the other.

Cadres should strictly adhere to the general line of conduct established by our army's[2] general command and transmitted through leadership bodies, while at the same time, they will have full freedom in the practical implementation of this line.

To accomplish the difficult tasks assigned, as well as to ensure survival, cadres functioning underground will need to develop to a high degree the qualities of discipline, secrecy,

---

1. This document was written by Che and given to Loyola Guzmán when she visited the guerrilla camp on January 26, 1967.
2. Established in March 1967 as the National Liberation Army of Bolivia (ELN).

dissimulation, self-control, and coolness under pressure; moreover, they will need to develop methods of work that will protect them in all eventualities.

All comrades carrying out tasks of a semipublic nature, will operate under the direction of a higher body that will be underground, and which will be responsible for passing on instructions and overseeing their work.

As far as possible, both the leader of the network and those assigned to head up different tasks will have a single function, and contact between different work areas will be made through the head of the network. The following are the minimum areas of responsibility for a network that has already been organized:

The head of the network, under whom are individuals with the following responsibilities:

1. Supplies
2. Transport
3. Information
4. Finances
5. Urban actions
6. Contacts with sympathizers

As the network develops, someone will need to be in charge of communications, in most cases working directly under the head of the network.

The head of the network will receive instructions from the leadership of the army, and will put these into effect through those in charge of the different work areas. The head of the network should be known only by this small leadership nucleus, to avoid endangering the entire network in the event of their capture. If those in charge of work areas know each other, then their work will also be known to each other, and changes in assignment need not be communicated.

In the event of the arrest of a key member of the network, the head of the network and all those known by the arrested person will take steps to change their residences or methods of contact.

The person in charge of supplies will be responsible for provisioning the army; this task is an organizational one. Starting from the center, secondary support networks will be created, extending all the way to ELN territory. In some cases, this could be organized exclusively through peasants; in other cases, it will include the aid of merchants or other individuals and organizations that offer their assistance.

The person in charge of transport will be responsible for transferring supplies from storage centers to points where the secondary networks will pick them up, or, in some cases, for bringing them directly to the liberated territory.

These comrades should carry out their work under a rock-solid cover; for example, they can organize small commercial enterprises that will shield them from suspicion by the repressive authorities when the scope and aims of the movement become public.

The person in charge of information will centralize all military and political information received through appropriate contacts. (Contact work is conducted partially in the open, gathering information from sympathizers in the army or government, which makes the task particularly dangerous.) All information gathered will be transmitted to our army's chief of information. The person in charge of information for the network will function under dual lines of authority, being responsible both to the head of the network and to our intelligence service.

The person in charge of finances should oversee the organization's expenses. It is important for this comrade to have a clear view of the importance of this responsibility, because while it is true that cadres working under conditions of clandestinity are subject to many dangers and run the risk of an obscure and unheralded death, as a result of living in the city they suffer none of the physical hardships that the guerrilla fighter does. It is therefore possible for them to get used to a certain negligence in handling supplies and money that pass through their hands. There is also a risk that their revolutionary firmness will grow lax in the face of constant exposure to sources of temptation. The person in charge of finances must keep account of every last peso spent, preventing a single centavo from being dispensed without just cause. In addition, this person will be responsible for organizing the collection and administration of money from funds or dues.

The person in charge of finances will function directly under the head of the network, but will also audit the latter's expenses. For all these reasons, the person responsible for finances must be extremely steady politically.

The task of the comrade in charge of urban actions extends to all forms of armed action in the cities: elimination of an informer or some notorious torturer or government official; kidnapping of individuals for ransom; sabotage of centers of economic activity in the country, etc. All such actions are to be conducted under the orders of the head of the network. The comrade in charge of urban actions is not to act on their own initiative, except in cases of extreme urgency.

The comrade responsible for sympathizers will have to function in public more than anyone else in the network. This person will be in contact with individuals who are not particularly firm, who clear their consciences by handing over sums of money or extending support while not fully committing themselves. Although these are people who can be worked with, it must never be forgotten that their support will be conditioned by the risks involved. Therefore, it is necessary, over time, to try to convert them into active militants, urging them to make substantial contributions to the movement, not only in money but also in medical supplies, safe houses, information, etc.

In this type of network some individuals will need to work very closely with each other; for example, the person in charge of transport has an organic connection with the comrade responsible for supplies, who will be his or her immediate superior. The person in charge of sympathizers will work with the head of finances. Those responsible for actions and for information will work in direct contact with the head of the network.

The networks will be subject to inspection by cadres, sent directly by our army, who will have no executive function but will simply verify whether instructions and norms are being complied with.

In making contact with the army, the networks should follow the following "route": The high command will give orders to the head of the network, who will be responsible, in turn, for organizing the task in the important cities. Routes will then lead from the cities to the towns, and from there to the villages or peasant houses, which will be the point of contact with our army, the site of the physical delivery of supplies, money, or information. As our army's zone of influence grows, the points of contact will get closer and closer to the cities, and the area of our army's direct control will grow proportionately. This is a long process that will have its ups and downs; and, as in any war like this, its progress will be measured in years.

The central command of the network will be based in the capital; from there other cities will be organized. For the time being, the most important cities for us are: Cochabamba, Santa Cruz, Sucre, and Camiri, forming a rectangle surrounding our zone of operations. Those heading up work in these four cities should, as far as possible, be experienced cadres. They will be put in charge of organizations similar to those in the capital, but simplified: supplies and transport will be headed by a single individual; finances and sympathizers by another one; a third person will coordinate urban actions; it is possible to dispense with the assignment of information, as this can be left to the head of the network. The coordination of urban actions will increasingly be linked to our army as its territory grows nearer to the city in question. At a certain point, those involved in urban actions will become semi-urban guerrillas, operating directly under the army's general command.

At the same time, it is important not to neglect the development of networks in cities that are today outside our field of action. In these places we should seek to win support among the population and prepare ourselves for future actions. Oruro and Potosí are the most important cities in this category.

Particular attention must be paid to areas along the borders. Villazón and Tarija are important for making contacts and receiving supplies from Argentina; Santa Cruz is important for Brazil; Huaqui [Guaqui] or some other location along the border with Peru; and some point along the frontier with Chile.

In organizing the supply network, it would be desirable to assign reliable militants who have previously earned a living in activities similar to what we are now asking them to do. For example, the owner of a grocery store could organize supplies or participate in this aspect of the network; the owner of a trucking company could organize transport, etc.

Where this is not possible, the job of developing the apparatus must be done patiently, not rushing things. By doing so we can avoid setting up a forward position that is not sufficiently protected—causing us to lose it, while at the same time putting other ones at risk.

The following shops or enterprises should be organized: grocery stores (La Paz, Cochabamba, Santa Cruz, Camiri); trucking firms (La Paz-Santa Cruz; Santa Cruz-Camiri; La Paz-Sucre; Sucre-Camiri); shoemakers (La Paz, Santa Cruz, Camiri, Cochabamba); clothing shops (the same); machine shops (La Paz, Santa Cruz); and farms (Chapare-Caranavi).

The first two will enable us to store and transport supplies without attracting attention, including military equipment. The shoemaking and clothing shops could carry out the twin tasks of making purchases without attracting attention and doing our own manufacturing. The machine shop would do the same with weapons and ammunition, and the farms would serve as bases of support in the eventual relocation of our forces, and would enable those working on the farms to begin carrying out propaganda among the peasants.

It should be stressed once again that all this requires political firmness and comrades who take from the revolutionary movement only what is strictly essential to their needs, who are ready to devote all their time — as well as their liberty or their lives, if it comes to that. Only in this way can we effectively forge the network necessary to accomplish our ambitious plans: the total liberation of Bolivia.

COMMUNIQUÉ NO. 1
TO THE BOLIVIAN PEOPLE
Document XVII

Revolutionary Truth against Reactionary Lies

March 27, 1967

The military brutes who have usurped power, after killing workers and laying the groundwork for the total handover of our resources to US imperialism, are now mocking the people with a comic farce. Even as the hour of truth arrived and the masses took up arms, responding to the armed usurpers with armed struggle, they tried to continue with their lies.

On the morning of March 23, troops from the Fourth Division, quartered in Camiri, about 35-strong and led by Major Hernán Plata Ríos, penetrated guerrilla territory along the Ñacahuazú River. The entire group fell into an ambush set up by our forces. As a result of the action, we confiscated 25 weapons of all kinds, including three 60-mm mortars with a supply of shells and other ammunition and equipment.

Enemy casualties consisted of seven dead, including a lieutenant, 14 prisoners, five of them wounded in the clash and cared for by our medics to the best of our capabilities. All the prisoners were freed after explaining the aims of our movement.

The list of enemy casualties is as follows:

Dead: Pedro Romero, Rubén Amezaga, Juan Alvarado, Cecilio Márquez, Amador Almasán, Santiago Gallardo, and an army informer and guide whose last name was Vargas.

Prisoners: Major Hernán Plata Ríos, Captain Eugenio Silva, soldiers Edgar Torrico Panoso, Lido Machicado Toledo, Gabriel Durán Escobar, Armando Martínez Sánchez, Felipe Bravo Siles, Juan Ramón Martínez, Leoncio Espinosa Posada, Miguel Rivero, Eleuterio Sánchez, Adalberto Martínez, Eduardo Rivera, and Guido Terceros. The last five were wounded.

In publicly announcing the first battle of the war, we are establishing what will be our norm: revolutionary truth. Our actions have demonstrated the integrity of our words. We regret the shedding of innocent blood by those who died; but peace cannot be built with mortars and machine guns, as those clowns in braided uniforms would have us believe. They try to portray us as common murderers. But there never has been, and there will not be, a single peasant who has any cause to complain of our treatment or our manner of obtaining supplies, except those who, as traitors to their class, served as guides or informers.

Hostilities have begun. In future communiqués we will set forth our revolutionary positions clearly. Today we make an appeal to workers, peasants, intellectuals, to everyone who feels the time has come to confront violence with violence and rescue a country being sold off in great slabs to Yankee monopolies, and raise the standard of living of our people, who grow hungrier every day.

National Liberation Army of Bolivia

COMMUNIQUÉ NO. 2
TO THE BOLIVIAN PEOPLE

Document XXI

Revolutionary Truth against Reactionary Lies

April 14, 1967

On the morning of April 10, 1967, there was an ambush of an enemy patrol led by Lieutenant Luis Saavedra Arombal and made up mostly of soldiers from the Center of Instruction for Special Troops. In the encounter, the above lieutenant was killed as well as soldiers Ángel Flores and Zenón Prada Mendieta, and the guide Ignacio Husarima from the Boquerón Regiment was wounded and taken prisoner, along with another five soldiers and a lower level officer.

Four soldiers escaped and managed to warn Major Sánchez Castro at headquarters so he was able to send as reinforcements 60 men from a neighboring unit. They, too, fell into another ambush, which cost the lives of Lieutenant Hugo Ayala, non-commissioned officer Raúl Camejo, and soldiers José Vijabriel, Marcelo Maldonado, Jaime Sanabria, and two unidentified others.

In this action the wounded soldiers included Armando Quiroga, Alberto Carvajal, Fredy Alove, Justo Cervantes, and Bernabé Mandejara, who were taken prisoner with the Unit Commander, Major Rubén Sánchez Castro, and 16 more soldiers.

In line with the norms of the ELN, we tended to the wounded as best as we could and set the prisoners free after explaining our revolutionary objectives.

Enemy losses amount to 10 killed, including two lieutenants, and 30 prisoners, including Major Sánchez Castro, six of whom were wounded. The spoils of war were proportional to enemy casualties and include a 60-mm mortar, machine guns, rifles, M-1 carbines, and submachine guns, all with ammunition.

There was one casualty [Rubio] on our side that should be recorded with regret. The disparity in losses is understandable if one considers that it is we who have chosen the time and place of every combat. Moreover, the Bolivian Army is sending off green soldiers, practically children, to be slaughtered.

Meanwhile, back in La Paz, the chiefs invent strategies and pound their chests in fake grief at demagogic funeral services, hiding the fact that they bear the guilt for the bloodshed in Bolivia.

They are now removing their masks and starting to call in US "advisers," just as occurred in the beginning of war in Vietnam, which has drained the blood from that heroic people and put world peace in jeopardy. We do not know how many "advisers" will be sent against us (although we will know how to confront them), but we warn the people of the dangers of this action by the military sell-outs.

We appeal to all young [Bolivian Army] recruits with the following instructions: when the battle begins, throw your weapons to the ground and put your hands on your head.

Remain still in spite of the gunfire, and never go to the front of the column when marching near combat zones. Make the officers who are inciting the conflict take those extremely dangerous positions. We will always shoot to kill the front line, and, as much as it hurts to see the blood of innocent recruits flow, this is one of the imperious requirements of war.

National Liberation Army of Bolivia

COMMUNIQUÉ NO. 3
TO THE BOLIVIAN PEOPLE
Document XXII

Revolutionary Truth against Reactionary Lies

May 1967

On May 8, in the guerrilla-held zone of Ñacahuazú, there was an ambush of troops from a mixed company led by second lieutenant Henry Laredo. The above officer and students Román Arroyo Flores and Luis Peláez were killed, and the following prisoners were taken: José Camacho Rojas, Bolívar Regiment; Néstor Cuentas, Bolívar Regiment; Waldo Veizaga, noncommissioned officers school; Hugo Soto Lora, noncommissioned officers school; Max Torres León, noncommissioned officers school; Roger Rojas Toledo, Braun Regiment; Javier Mayan Corella, Braun Regiment; Néstor Sánchez Cuéllar, Braun Regiment—the last two were wounded after they failed to halt when intercepted. As always, prisoners were set free after our goals were explained. Seven M-1 carbines and four Mauser rifles were captured, and our troops escaped injury.

The repressive army has been issuing frequent communiqués announcing guerrilla casualties, mixing truth and fantasy. Desperate because of their impotence, they lie or vent their fury on journalists, who due to their ideological makeup are natural adversaries of the regime, attributing to them all the problems they face.

We want it to be understood that the ELN of Bolivia is the only responsible party for the armed struggle, which its people lead, and which will not stop short until final victory is achieved. We will know how to punish all the crimes that have been committed in this war, independently of any reprisals our military command judges opportune to counter acts of vandalism by the repressive forces.

National Liberation Army of Bolivia

COMMUNIQUÉ NO. 4
TO THE BOLIVIAN PEOPLE
Document XXIV

Revolutionary Truth against Reactionary Lies

June 1967

Recently, the [Bolivian] Army has acknowledged some of its casualties, suffered in clashes with reconnaissance missions and claiming, as usual, that they inflicted greater losses than they achieved in fact. Although we lack some reports from some patrols, we can state with assurance that our casualties are quite minimal and we have not suffered from any of the recent actions announced by the army.

Inti Peredo is a member of our army's general command and occupies the post of political commissar, and recent actions have taken place under his command. He enjoys good health and remains untouched by enemy bullets. The announcement of his death is a palpable example of the absurd lies being spread by the army in its impotence against our forces.

Regarding announcements of the supposed presence of combatants from other countries in the Americas, for secret military reasons and in light of our philosophy, that of revolutionary truth, we will not give figures. We can simply state that any citizen who accepts our minimum program, the liberation of

Bolivia, is accepted into the revolutionary ranks with equal rights and duties as the Bolivian combatants, who naturally constitute the vast majority of our movement. Every person who engages in armed struggle for the liberty of our homeland deserves, and will receive, the honorable title of Bolivian, independently of where they might have been born. That is how we interpret genuine revolutionary internationalism.

National Liberation Army of Bolivia

COMMUNIQUÉ NO. 5
TO THE BOLIVIAN MINERS
Document XXV

Revolutionary Truth against Reactionary Lies

June 1967

Comrades:

Proletarian blood is running once more in our mines. Over centuries, the blood of enslaved miners has been alternately sucked dry and then spilled, unleashing protest after protest.

In recent times the pattern has been temporarily broken and the insurgent workers were the main factor in the triumph of April 9.[1] This event brought hope of a new dawn, and that finally workers would become masters of their own destiny. But the mechanisms of the imperialist world have been exposed — for those who are able to see clearly: that when social revolution is posed there can be no half measures. Either power is seized or advances are lost, along with so much sacrifice and blood.

---

1. On April 9, 1952, miners led a popular uprising in Bolivia that overthrew the military dictatorship and installed the MNR government.

The armed militias of the mining proletariat were the only serious force at the beginning. They were then joined by militias made up of declassed sectors and the peasants. But these groups failed to recognize their essential community of interests and instead fell into conflict, a situation that was then manipulated by anti-plebeian demagogy. In the end, the professional army could reappear dressed in lambskin concealing its wolf's claws.

That army, small and easy to discount at first, was transformed into the armed instrument wielded against the proletariat and became imperialism's most reliable accomplice. That is why imperialism gave the go-ahead for the military coup d'état [by General Barrientos in 1964].

Now we are recovering from a defeat provoked by the repetition of tactical errors by the working class, but also patiently preparing the country for a profound revolution that will transform the system from its roots.

False tactics must be avoided at all costs: heroic, yes, but not futile tactics that lead the proletariat into a bloodbath that depletes its ranks and neutralizes its most combative elements.

Over long months of struggle, the guerrillas have shaken the country, producing many casualties and demoralizing the Bolivian Army while scarcely suffering any losses ourselves. After one encounter lasting several hours, in which they emerged victorious, this same army strutted around like a turkey over the proletarian bodies on the battlefield. The difference between victory and defeat depends on the choice of correct or erroneous tactics.

Comrade miner: don't listen again to the false apostles

of mass struggle who interpret this as the people marching forward, in compact formation, against the armed oppressors.

Learn from reality!

Heroic chests are of no avail against machine guns, and even well-built barricades cannot resist modern weapons of mass destruction. The struggle of the masses in underdeveloped countries, with a large rural base and extensive territories, must be carried out by a small and mobile vanguard, guerrillas who are well integrated among the people. This guerrilla force will gain its strength at the expense of the enemy army and catalyze the revolutionary fervor of the masses to the point where a revolutionary situation is created and state power can be overthrown in one single, well-aimed, opportune strike.

Let it be understood that we are not calling for total inactivity, rather that effort not be wasted on actions where success cannot be guaranteed. Pressure, however, must be continuously wrought by the working classes against the government, because that is what class struggle is about, with no limits. Wherever they may find themselves, a worker has the obligation to struggle with all their strength against the common enemy.

Comrade miner, the guerrillas of the National Liberation Army of Bolivia wait for you with open arms and invite you to join workers of the underground already fighting alongside us. Here we are reconstructing the worker-peasant alliance that was broken by anti-plebeian demagogy. Here we are converting defeat into triumph so that the lament of proletarian widows becomes a hymn of victory.

We await you.

National Liberation Army of Bolivia

Siguiendo una norma del ~~nuestras fuerzas revolu-~~ E.L.N
~~cionarios~~, curamos los heridos con nuestros escasos medios y pusimos en libertad a todos los prisioneros, previa explicación
de ~~nuestra~~ los objetivos de nuestra lucha revolucionaria.

Las pérdidas del ejército ^enemigo se resumen así: 10 muertos, entre
ellos, dos tenientes, y 30 prisioneros, incluyendo al mayor
Sánchez Castro, de los cuales 6 resultaron heridos. El botín
de guerra es proporcional a las bajas enemigas, incluyendo

Glossary

en todos los combates hemos elegido el momento y
lugar de desencadenarlo y que el ejército boliviano está enviando soldados bisoños, casi niños, al matadero, mientras
ellos inventan partes en la Paz y luego se dan golpes de pecho en
~~~~ que son los verdaderos culpables de lo que se rompe en Bolivia. ①
Hacemos un llamado a los jóvenes reclutas para que
sigan las siguientes instrucciones: al iniciarse el fuego tiren
el arma ~~lejos~~ a un lado y llevarse las manos a la cabeza
permaneciendo quietos en el punto donde ~~sea~~ el fuego los sorprendiera;
nunca avancen al ~~la cabeza~~ frente de la columna en marchas de
aproximación a zonas de combate obliguen a los oficiales que
los incitan a ~~~~ combatir a que ocupen esta posición de extremo peligro.
Contra la cabeza de la columna ~~~~ tiraremos siempre a matar
por mucho que nos duela ver correr la sangre de estos inocentes,
es una ~~~~ de la guerra. Ejército de Liberación Nacional de Bolivia

GLOSSARY

ACUÑA NÚÑEZ, JUAN VITALIO (Joaquín or Vilo). Born in the Sierra Maestra, Cuba, in 1925. He was one of the first peasants recruited by the Rebel Army, which he joined in April 1957. Due to his role in the revolutionary war, he attained the rank of major. A member of the central committee of the Communist Party of Cuba, he arrived at the Ñacahuazú farm at the end of November 1966. He commanded the rearguard detachment, soon after it left for Muyupampa to facilitate the withdrawal of Ciro Bustos and Régis Debray. Before he was able to meet up with Che, he was killed along with his entire group on August 31, 1967, in the ambush at Puerto Mauricio, on the Río Grande River. Vado del Yeso, the name under which this action has passed into history, is on the Masicuri River, a tributary of the Río Grande.

ADRIAZOLA VEIZAGA, DAVID (Darío). Born in Oruro, Bolivia, in 1939. He joined the guerrilla movement with Moisés Guevara's group and was part of the vanguard detachment. He survived the battle of Quebrada del Yuro (October 8, 1967) and left the guerrilla area in the group led by Inti. Later, together with Inti, he participated in the underground reorganization of the ELN. He was gunned down by police in La Paz on December 31, 1969.

ALARCÓN RAMÍREZ, DARIEL (Benigno). Born in Manzanillo, Cuba, in 1939. A veteran of the Sierra Maestra, he achieved the rank of captain in the Rebel Army. He arrived at the Ñacahuazú farm on December 11, 1966, and was part of the vanguard detachment. He survived the battle of Quebrada del Yuro, leaving Bolivia through Chile, together with Urbano and Pombo, arriving in Cuba on March 6, 1968. In 1995, he published a book *Los sobrevivientes*. He left Cuba in 1996.

Alejandro. See MACHÍN HOED DE BECHE, GUSTAVO (Alejandro).

ALVARADO MARÍN, CARLOS CONRADO DE JESÚS (Merci). A Guatemalan internationalist combatant who later proved his honesty and loyalty to the revolutionary cause.

Aniceto. See REINAGA GORDILLO, ANICETO (Aniceto).

Antonio. See DOMÍNGUEZ FLORES, ANTONIO (León or Antonio).

Antonio. See PANTOJA TAMAYO, ORLANDO (Antonio or Olo).

Apolinar or Apolinario. See AQUINO QUISPE, APOLINAR (Apolinar, Apolinario, or Polo).

AQUINO QUISPE, APOLINAR (Apolinar, Apolinario, or Polo). A Bolivian, born in Viacha, Ingavi province, state of La Paz, in 1935. He was a trade union leader at the Figliozzi factory in La Paz and a member of the PCB. He joined the guerrilla struggle as a combatant in December 1966 after he had been working for several months as an unskilled laborer at the Ñacahuazú farm, purchased by Coco Peredo. He was killed in the ambush at Vado del Yeso on August 31, 1967.

AQUINO TUDELA, SERAPIO (Serapio or **Serafín).** A Bolivian, born in Viacha in 1951. He was a nephew of Apolinar. Like his uncle, he initially joined the guerrilla force as an unskilled laborer at the farm, which is why Che — in his analysis of the month of March — still described him as a "refugee" and a noncombatant. Subsequently, he joined the rear guard. He was killed in combat in the Iquira River canyon on July 9, 1967, when alerting his compañeros to the presence of the military.

ARANA CAMPERO, JAIME (Chapaco or **Luis).** Born in Tarija, Bolivia, on October 31, 1938. He was a member of the youth organization of the National Revolutionary Movement (MNR). He was studying in Cuba when he decided to join the guerrilla struggle. He arrived at the Ñacahuazú farm in March 1967 and was part of the center group. In the battle of Quebrada del Yuro, he was able to break through the encirclement. The group of survivors advanced to Cajones, where they were gunned down on October 14, 1967.

ARANCIBIA AYALA, WÁLTER (Wálter). Born in Macha, state of Potosí, Bolivia, on January 21, 1941. He was one of the founders of the local "Lincoln-Murillo-Castro" youth movement in solidarity with Cuba. He was active in the JCB and a member of its national committee. He arrived at the Ñacahuazú farm on January 21, 1967, and was assigned to the rear guard. He was killed in the Vado del Yeso ambush on August 31, 1967.

Arturo. See MARTÍNEZ TAMAYO, RENÉ (Arturo).

BAIGORRIA, PAULINO. A peasant, about 20 years of age, who served as a liaison for the guerrilla force and asked to join their ranks. While fulfilling the mission assigned by Che, he was detained in Comarapa, held incommunicado, and tortured.

BARRERA QUINTANA, PASTOR (Daniel). A Bolivian who joined the guerrilla forces with the group led by Moisés Guevara. He deserted within a few days, before the start of armed actions in March 1967. He was acquitted in the Camiri trial.

BARRIENTOS ORTUÑO, General RENÉ. Born in Tarata, Cochabamba, Bolivia, in 1919. An air force career officer, Barrientos imposed his candidacy for vice-president on the MNR, and seized office in a coup against MNR President Víctor Paz Estenssoro in 1964. He was the constitutional president of Bolivia from August 6, 1966, until his death in a helicopter accident on April 27, 1969, which was never completely explained. As president, Barrientos was known for his authoritarian tendencies, his special relations with the rural sector through what was known as the Military Peasant Pact, and his pro-US position.

BÉJAR RIVERA, HÉCTOR. In 1963, Héctor Béjar Rivera was the key leader of the National Liberation Army (ELN) of Peru. In 1966, he was arrested and jailed in that country's San Quintín prison.

Benigno. See ALARCÓN RAMÍREZ, DARIEL (Benigno).

Benjamín. See CORONADO CÓRDOBA, BENJAMÍN (Benjamín).

Bigotes. See VÁZQUEZ VIAÑA, JORGE (Bigotes, Loro, or Jorge).

Braulio. See REYES ZAYAS, ISRAEL (Braulio).

BRAVO, DOUGLAS. An activist in the Communist Party of Venezuela and a member of its central committee. Bravo took up arms in the struggle against the dictatorship of Marcos Pérez

Jiménez and was commander-in-chief of the Armed Forces of National Liberation (FALN) of Venezuela. He opposed the Communist Party's decision to suspend the armed struggle and was expelled from that organization.

BUNKE BIDER, HAYDÉE TAMARA (Tania). Born in Argentina in 1937, the daughter of German parents. In 1961, Tania traveled to Cuba as a translator. She went to Bolivia in 1964 as an underground combatant, with the mission of infiltrating the higher echelons of the Bolivian government. She made considerable progress, but had to join the guerrilla unit after she was identified, having contacted Debray and Bustos. Assigned to the rear guard, she was killed in the Vado del Yeso ambush on August 31, 1967.

BUSTOS, CIRO (Mauricio, Pelao, Pelado, or Carlos). Ciro Bustos was an Argentine to whom Che entrusted the task of exploring northern Argentina and sending combatants to be trained in guerrilla warfare. He was captured, together with Debray and the photographer Andrew Roth, in Muyupampa in April 1967, and received a 30-year prison sentence by the military tribunal based in Camiri. He was freed by the government of Juan José Torres in 1970.

CABALLERO, EVARISTO. Mayor of Arenales in 1967.

CABRERA FLORES, RESTITUTO JOSÉ (El Médico or Negro). Born in Callao, Peru, in 1931. He was a member of the Peruvian ELN and joined the guerrillas in Bolivia in the first half of March 1967, together with Chino and Eustaquio, in the rearguard detachment. On August 31, during the ambush at Vado del Yeso, he attempted to escape along the river, but was captured and brutally murdered on September 3 on the Palmarito River.

Camba. See JIMÉNEZ BAZÁN, ORLANDO (Camba).

Carlos. See BUSTOS, CIRO (Mauricio, Pelao, Pelado, or Carlos).

Carlos. See VACA MARCHETTI, LORGIO (Carlos).

CASTILLO CHÁVEZ, JOSÉ (Paco). A Bolivian member of the PCB, until the organization split in 1965. He joined the guerrilla movement as part of Moisés Guevara's group and was captured in the ambush at Vado del Yeso. He was used by the Bolivian Army to identify the bodies of the guerrillas, to provide information, and to offer testimony in the Camiri trial; he remained in prison until 1970.

CHANG NAVARRO LÉVANO, JUAN PABLO (Chino). Juan Pablo Chang Navarro Lévano was a leader of the Peruvian ELN. He met with Che in December 1966, and returned with Eustaquio and Negro in March 1967. Events forced him to remain with the guerrilla movement in Bolivia. He survived the battle at Quebrada del Yuro, but was reported to have been captured alive (he was almost blind), taken to La Higuera and killed along with Willy and Che.

Chapaco. See ARANA CAMPERO, JAIME (Chapaco or Luis).

CHÁVEZ, MARIO (The Lagunillero). A Bolivian member of the PCB, he is also identified as the scout, Mario Chávez. He was recruited by Coco Peredo, with the mission of establishing a small hostel in Lagunillas, a place from where he was to gather information for the guerrilla movement.

Che. See GUEVARA DE LA SERNA, ERNESTO (Che, Mongo, Ramón, or Fernando).

Chinchu. See MARTÍNEZ TAMAYO, JOSÉ MARÍA (Papi, Ricardo, Chinchu, Mbili or Taco).

Chingolo. See CHOQUE SILVA, HUGO (Chingolo).

Chino. See CHANG NAVARRO LÉVANO, JUAN PABLO (Chino).

CHOQUE CHOQUE, SALUSTIO (Salustio). A Bolivian who joined the guerrilla forces as part of Moisés Guevara's group and was detained on March 17, 1967. His case was dismissed in the Camiri trial, but authorities detained him for a considerable period of time.

CHOQUE SILVA, HUGO (Chingolo). A Bolivian who joined the guerrilla movement as part of Moisés Guevara's group and deserted in July 1967, together with Eusebio. He apparently led the Bolivian Army to the guerrilla's caves, where weapons, medicines, documents, and food were stored.

COCA, FENELÓN. Bolivian peasant farmer who collaborated with the guerrilla force. Tuma was operated on in his home.

Coco. See PEREDO LEIGUE, ROBERTO (Coco).

CODOVILA, VICTORIO. First secretary of the Argentine Communist Party.

COELLO, CARLOS (Tuma or Tumaini). Born near the city of Manzanillo, Cuba, in 1940. The son of a peasant, he joined the guerrilla movement in the Sierra Maestra before he was 17 years old but still almost illiterate. He became Che's inseparable companion from that moment on and was a member of Che's personal bodyguard. He also fought in the Congo with Che and rose to the rank of lieutenant. He arrived in La Paz in July 1966 and traveled to the Ñacahuazú farm, prior to Che's arrival. He died in combat on June 26, 1967, in Piray in the province of Florida, in the state of Santa Cruz. "With his death, I have lost an inseparable compañero of recent years, one whose loyalty was unwavering and whose absence I feel now almost as if he were my own son," Che wrote in his diary.

CONDORI VARGAS COCHI, CASILDO (Víctor). A Bolivian, born in Corocoro, Pacajes province, in the state of La Paz, on April 9, 1941. He joined the guerrilla movement as part of Moisés Guevara's group. He was part of the rearguard detachment and was killed in an ambush in the Bella Vista area on June 2, 1967, together with Antonio Sánchez Díaz (Marcos).

CORONADO CÓRDOBA, BENJAMÍN (Benjamín). Born in the city of Potosí, Bolivia, on January 30, 1941. He was a member of the PCB and joined the guerrilla movement on January 21, 1967. He was assigned to the vanguard detachment and participated in scouting parties. He drowned while crossing the Río Grande on February 26, 1967.

CUBA SANABRIA, SIMEÓN (Willy, Willi, Wily, or Wyly). Born in Cochabamba, Itapaya, Bolivia, on January 5, 1935. He was a miner at Huanuni and a compañero of Moisés Guevara, with whom he joined the guerrilla force in March 1967. Willy was assigned to the center group. He was captured in Quebrada del Yuro on October 8, attempting to save Che, who was wounded in the leg and whose weapon was disabled. He was executed on October 9, 1967, in the school at La Higuera, along with Che and Chino.

DAGNINO PACHECO, JULIO. A Peruvian journalist who resided in La Paz as a liaison for Peru's National Liberation Army (ELN).

Daniel. See BARRERA QUINTANA, PASTOR (Daniel).

Dantón. See DEBRAY, JULES RÉGIS (The Frenchman, Dantón, or Debray).

Darío. See ADRIAZOLA VEIZAGA, DAVID (Darío).

DE LA CONCEPCIÓN DE LA PEDRAJA, OCTAVIO (Moro, Morogoro, Muganga, El Médico, or Tavito). Born in Havana, Cuba, in 1935. He fought on the Second Eastern Front in the Sierra Maestra, and attained the rank of lieutenant. He arrived at the Ñacahuazú farm on December 11, 1966, as a doctor and combatant. In the final period of the guerrilla struggle he became seriously ill. For that reason, Che assigned him, together with Eustaquio and Chapaco, to Pablito's care when the battle of Quebrada del Yuro began. The group made it to Cajones, at the junction of the Río Grande and Mizque rivers, where they were killed on October 14, 1967.

DEBRAY, JULES RÉGIS (The Frenchman, Dantón, Debré or Debray). Jules Régis Debray was a French left-wing intellectual who participated in the preparations for guerrilla warfare in Bolivia. He met with Che in March 1967, who entrusted him with several overseas missions. Debray was captured on April 20, 1967, in Muyupampa, together with Bustos and Roth, and sentenced to 30 years in prison by the military tribunal that deliberated in Camiri. He was later freed by the government of Juan José Torres in 1970.

DIC Department of Criminal Investigations (DIC) in Bolivia.

DOMÍNGUEZ FLORES, ANTONIO (León or Antonio). A Bolivian of rural origin, Domínguez was a member of the PCB. He initially worked as an unskilled laborer at the Ñacahuazú farm and later became a combatant. He deserted on September 26, 1967, at La Higuera, surrendering to the authorities and offering information on the guerrillas. Domínguez testified against Régis Debray and Ciro Bustos at the trial in Camiri, but was not released. He was eventually freed in 1970 by the government of Juan José Torres.

EGP (Ejército Guerrillero del Pueblo). People's Guerrilla Army (Argentina).

ELN (Ejército de Liberación Nacional de Bolivia). National Liberation Army of Bolivia.

ELN. National Liberation Army of Peru.

Ernesto. See MAYMURA HURTADO, FREDDY (Ernesto or El Médico).

Estanislao. See MONJE MOLINA, MARIO (Estanislao, Monje, Mario or Negro).

Eusebio. See TAPIA ARUN, EUSEBIO (Eusebio).

Eustaquio. See GALVÁN HIDALGO, LUCIO EDILBERTO (Eustaquio).

Falange. Bolivian Socialist Falange (FSB), an ultra-right party.

Félix. See SUÁREZ GAYOL, JESÚS (Félix or Rubio).

FERNÁNDEZ MONTES DE OCA, ALBERTO (Pacho or Pachungo). A Cuban, born near Santiago de Cuba in 1935. When the Sierra Maestra campaign ended, he had achieved the rank of captain in the Rebel Army. He occupied different posts in the Cuban government, including director of mines in the Ministry of Industry. He arrived in La Paz on September 3, 1966, with instructions from Che to transfer operations to the Alto Beni agricultural region. He returned to Bolivia on November 3, 1966, and with Che traveled to the Ñacahuazú farm, guided by Loro, Tuma, and Pombo. He died on October 9 of wounds received in the battle of Quebrada del Yuro.

Fernando. See GUEVARA DE LA SERNA, ERNESTO (Che, Mongo, Ramón, or Fernando).

Frenchman, The. See DEBRAY, JULES RÉGIS (the Frenchman, Dantón, or Debray).

GALVÁN HIDALGO, LUCIO EDILBERTO (Eustaquio). Born in the city of Huancayo, Peru, in 1937. He was a member of the Peruvian ELN and joined the guerrilla forces, together with Negro and Chino, in March 1967. He was killed in combat in Cajones, at the fork of the Río Grande and Mizque rivers on October 14, 1967.

GELMAN, JUAN. Argentine revolutionary and member of the Communist Party of Argentina.

GUEVARA DE LA SERNA, ERNESTO (Che, Mongo, Ramón, or Fernando). Born in Rosario, Argentina, on June 14, 1928. After graduating with a degree in medicine, Guevara traveled to Bolivia in 1953, undertaking his second trip around Latin America. He subsequently participated in the revolutionary struggle in Guatemala. After the Guatemalan government was crushed in 1954, he left for Mexico and while there signed up for the November 1956 expedition on the *Granma* to launch the guerrilla struggle against the dictatorship of Fulgencio Batista. From the first moments of the struggle in the Sierra Maestra, Che stood out as a military and political leader and later held key posts in the Cuban revolution, which triumphed on January 1, 1959. In 1965, he surrendered all his official positions within the Cuban government, and left secretly for the Congo, at the head of a Cuban contingent, to support the anticolonial struggle in Africa. Subsequently, in November 1966, Che went to Bolivia, where he led the guerrilla movement up to October 8, 1967, when he was captured and wounded by the Bolivian Army at Quebrada del Yuro. He was murdered the following day, at a school in the town of La Higuera, close to Vallegrande. His remains, located after a long search, were returned to Cuba in July 1997.

GUEVARA RODRÍGUEZ, MOISÉS (Moisés or Guevara). A Bolivian, born in Cataricagua on December 25, 1939. He worked in the Huanuni mines and in 1965 was fired as a result of the repression waged by General Barrientos's government. He was a member of the PCB and later joined the Communist Party (Marxist-Leninist), from which he was expelled due to his differences with party leader Oscar Zamora Medinacelli. He joined the guerrilla force in March 1967, following an initial meeting with Che in January, in which he agreed to recruit a group of combatants. He belonged to the center group, but due to health problems, remained in the rear guard, led by Joaquín. He was killed in the ambush at Vado del Yeso on August 31, 1967.

Guevara. See GUEVARA RODRÍGUEZ, MOISÉS (Moisés or Guevara).

GUTIÉRREZ ARDAYA, MARIO (Julio). A Bolivian, born in Sachojere, near the city of Trinidad, in the state of Beni, on May 22, 1939. A member of the PCB, he graduated as a doctor in Cuba and joined the guerrilla movement in March 1967. He was killed, together with Coco and Miguel, in the ambush at Quebrada del Batán, near La Higuera, on September 26, 1967.

GUZMÁN LARA, LOYOLA. A Bolivian woman member of the national executive committee of the Bolivian Communist Youth until February 1967. In January 1967, she met with Che, who assigned her the task of handling the finances of the movement's urban network. She was detained in September 1967, following the discovery of photographs found in the Ñacahuazú farm caves, but freed in 1970, in exchange for the German hostages captured by the guerrilla force at Teoponte. Guzmán rejoined the ELN's clandestine struggle during the

Hugo Bánzer dictatorship and was again detained in 1972 when she entered Chile clandestinely with her husband who was subsequently disappeared.

GUZMÁN LARA, VICENTA. Sister of Loyola Guzmán.

GUZMÁN, ROBLES. Bolivian peasant who was detained by the Bolivian Army when he returned from purchasing food for the guerrillas.

HERNÁNDEZ OSORIO, MANUEL (Miguel or Manuel). Born in the Santa Rita neighborhood, Granma province, Cuba, in 1931. A veteran of the Sierra Maestra, he attained the rank of captain in the Rebel Army, under Che's command. He joined the guerrilla forces at the end of November 1966 and was designated chief of the vanguard detachment, replacing Marcos. He was killed at Quebrada del Batán, close to La Higuera, on September 26, 1967.

HUANCA FLORES, FRANCISCO (Pablo or Pablito). Born in Bolivia in 1945, either in the state of Oruro, or the village of Laja. He joined Moisés Guevara's group and was assigned to the vanguard detachment. He was the youngest among the guerrillas. Surviving the Quebrada del Yuro action, he went with the group of survivors to the fork of the Mizque and Río Grande rivers, where he was killed on October 14, 1967.

Humberto. See VÁZQUEZ VIAÑA, HUMBERTO (Humberto).

Inti. See PEREDO LEIGUE, GUIDO (Inti).

Iván. See MONTERO, IVÁN (Renán or Iván).

JCB. Bolivian Communist Youth.

JIMÉNEZ BAZÁN, ORLANDO (Camba). Born in Riberalta, state of Beni, Bolivia, on June 27, 1934. A Bolivian peasant leader and member of the PCB, he initially worked as an unskilled laborer on the farm at Alto Beni, an area where it was initially planned to launch the guerrilla campaign. In December 1966, he was transferred to the Ñacahuazú farm and assigned to the vanguard detachment. He had asked to be discharged from the guerrilla force, and after he deserted he was captured on September 27, 1967, near La Higuera. He was taken to the military tribunal in Camiri, and was a prosecution witness against Debray and Bustos. After being freed in 1970, he obtained political asylum in Sweden, where he died in 1994.

JIMÉNEZ TARDÍO, ANTONIO (Pan Divino or Pedro). Born in Tarata, Cochabamba, Bolivia, on May 3, 1941. An activist in the Bolivian Communist Youth, he was a member of its national executive committee until February 1967. He joined the guerrilla struggle at the end of 1966 and was assigned to the rear guard. He died fighting in the Iñaó mountains on August 9, 1967.

Joaquín. See ACUÑA NÚÑEZ, JUAN VITALIO (Joaquín or Vilo).

Jorge. See VÁZQUEZ VIAÑA, JORGE (Bigotes, Loro, or Jorge).

JOZAMI, EDUARDO. Former member of the Argentine Communist Party. Journalist and lawyer.

Julio. See GUTIÉRREZ ARDAYA, MARIO (Julio).

KOLLE CUETO, JORGE (Kolle). Organizational secretary of the Bolivian Communist Party.

Lagunillero, The. See CHÁVEZ, MARIO (the Lagunillero).

LECHÍN OQUENDO, JUAN. Key leader of the Bolivian Workers' Confederation (COB).

LEONI, RAÚL. President of Venezuela in 1967.

Loro. See VÁZQUEZ VIAÑA, JORGE (Bigotes, Loro, or Jorge).

Loyola. See GUZMÁN LARA, LOYOLA.

LOZANO, Dr. HUGO. Bolivian stomatologist, member of the guerrilla movement's urban network in La Paz.

LUCAS, Don. Peasant farmer who collaborated with the guerrillas.

Luis. See ARANA CAMPERO, JAIME (Chapaco or Luis).

MACHÍN HOED DE BECHE, GUSTAVO (Alejandro). Born in Havana, Cuba, in 1937. He participated in the struggle against Batista, in the ranks of the Revolutionary Directorate, reaching the rank of major. He was Vice-Minister of Industry in the Cuban revolutionary government and a top military official in Matanzas province. He joined the guerrilla force in November 1966 and was appointed by Che as chief of operations. He belonged to the center group, but due to health problems, remained in the rear guard. He was killed at Vado del Yeso on August 31, 1967.

Manila. Code for Cuba.

Manuel. See HERNÁNDEZ OSORIO, MANUEL (Miguel or Manuel).

Marcos. See SÁNCHEZ DÍAZ, ANTONIO (Marcos or Pinares).

Mario. See MONJE MOLINA, MARIO (Estanislao, Monje, Mario or Negro).

MARTÍNEZ TAMAYO, JOSÉ MARÍA (Papi, Ricardo, Chinchu, Mbili or Taco). Born in Mayarí, Holguín province, Cuba, in 1937. He participated in the clandestine struggle of the July 26 Movement and then joined the Rebel Army to fight on the Second Eastern Front during the war against Batista. By the end of the revolutionary war, he had attained the rank of sergeant, commanding a tank. He was among the founders of the Ministry of the Interior and attained the rank of captain in the Revolutionary Armed Forces. He completed several internationalist missions and arrived in Bolivia for the first time in July 1963, to coordinate, together with the Bolivian Communist Party, support for the People's Guerrilla Army (EGP) that was operating in northern Argentina under the leadership of Ricardo Masetti. He fought in the Congo with Che and returned to La Paz in March 1966 to prepare for Che's arrival. He belonged to the center group. He was seriously wounded on July 30, 1967, and died shortly afterwards while being cared for by his compañeros.

MARTÍNEZ TAMAYO, RENÉ (Arturo). Born in Mayarí, Holguín province, Cuba, in 1941. A combatant in the Sierra Maestra, after the revolution he worked in the Ministry of the Interior and in the research department of the Rebel Army. He arrived at the Ñacahuazú farm in December 1966 and joined the center group, and was put in charge of radio communications. He was killed in the battle of Quebrada del Yuro on October 8, 1967.

MASETTI, JORGE RICARDO (Segundo). An Argentine, Jorge Ricardo Masetti was the first Latin American journalist to interview Fidel Castro and Che and others, in the Sierra Maestra in 1958. After the revolution, he was the founder and first director of the Prensa Latina news agency. Later, as a leader of the People's Guerrilla Army (EGP) Masetti (known as Comandante Segundo) was killed in combat on April 21, 1964, in the Salta mountains of northern Argentina.

Mauricio. See BUSTOS, CIRO (Mauricio, Pelao, Pelado, or Carlos).

MAYMURA HURTADO, FREDDY (Ernesto or El Médico). A Bolivian, born in Trinidad, state of Beni, on October 18, 1941. A member of the PCB, he graduated as a doctor in Cuba, and joined the guerrilla forces in November 1966. He was captured alive in the ambush at Vado del Yeso, but because he refused to collaborate, he was killed by his captors on August 31, 1967.

Médico, El. See CABRERA FLORES, RESTITUTO JOSÉ (El Médico or Negro).

Médico, El. See DE LA CONCEPCIÓN DE LA PEDRAJA, OCTAVIO (Moro, Morogoro, Muganga, El Médico, or Tavito).

Médico, El. See MAYMURA HURTADO, FREDDY (Ernesto or El Médico).

MELGAR, ANTONIO. Courier for the Bolivian Army, killed in combat.

MÉNDEZ KORNE, JULIO (Ñato). A Bolivian, born in Trinidad, state of Beni on February 23, 1937. He was a member of the PCB. Before arriving at the Ñacahuazú farm, he was in charge of the farm at Alto Beni, which was considered by Che and the Cuban officials as an alternative site for launching the guerrilla campaign. He functioned as head of supplies and weapons. He survived the battle at Quebrada del Yuro, but after the encirclement had been broken, was killed in the final military action on November 15, 1967.

Merci. See ALVARADO MARÍN, CARLOS CONRADO DE JESÚS (Merci).

Miguel. See HERNÁNDEZ OSORIO, MANUEL (Miguel or Manuel).

MNR. National Revolutionary Movement (Movimiento Nacionalista Revolución) came to power in the 1952 revolution in Bolivia.

Moisés. See GUEVARA RODRÍGUEZ, MOISÉS (Moisés or Guevara).

Mongo. See GUEVARA DE LA SERNA, ERNESTO (Che, Mongo, Ramón, or Fernando).

MONJE MOLINA, MARIO (Estanislao, Monje, Mario or Negro). A Bolivian teacher by profession, from a very young age Monje was active in political work and became the first secretary of the Bolivian Communist Party, a position he occupied until his resignation in January 1968. On December 31, 1966, Monje met with Che at the Ñacahuazú farm, and argued that the political direction of the struggle belonged to the PCB leadership as long as the revolution took place on Bolivian soil, an argument not accepted by Che. From that moment, a split occurred between the PCB and the guerrilla force.

MONTERO, IVÁN (Renán or Iván). A Cuban, who was one of the contacts of the urban network in Bolivia. His identity was not revealed for almost 30 years. He functioned as the liaison between La Paz and Havana, until just before the guerrilla campaign was launched. He participated in the armed struggle in Nicaragua and worked in the Sandinista government's security apparatus between 1979 and 1990.

Moro. See DE LA CONCEPCIÓN DE LA PEDRAJA, OCTAVIO (Moro, Morogoro, Muganga, El Médico, or Tavito).

Muganga. See DE LA CONCEPCIÓN DE LA PEDRAJA, OCTAVIO (Moro, Morogoro, Muganga, El Médico, or Tavito).

MURILLO, PEDRO DOMINGO. Bolivian patriot who led the first struggle for independence of a Spanish colony in the Americas in 1809.

Negro. See CABRERA FLORES, RESTITUTO JOSÉ (El Médico or Negro).

Negro. See MONJE MOLINA, MARIO (Estanislao, Monje, Mario or Negro).

Ñato. See MÉNDEZ KORNE, JULIO (Ñato).

Olo. See PANTOJA TAMAYO, ORLANDO (Antonio or Olo).

ONGANÍA, JUAN CARLOS. A military man who overthrew President Arturo Illía in a coup d'état in Argentina in 1966.

Orlando. See ROCABADO TERRAZAS, VICENTE (Orlando).

OTERO, CHICHO. Owner of one of the homes located in the area in which the guerrilla forces operated.

OVANDO CANDIA, ALFREDO. In 1967, Ovando was commander-in-chief of the Bolivian Armed Forces and a leader of the 1964 coup. He actively participated in waging the counterinsurgency campaign. He was president of Bolivia 1965-66 and again after he overthrew Luis Adolfo Siles Salinas, in September 1969.

Pablo or **Pablito.** See HUANCA FLORES, FRANCISCO (Pablo or Pablito).

Pacho. See FERNÁNDEZ MONTES DE OCA, ALBERTO (Pacho or Pachungo).

Pachungo. FERNÁNDEZ MONTES DE OCA, ALBERTO (Pacho or Pachungo).

Paco. See CASTILLO CHÁVEZ, JOSÉ (Paco).

Pan Divino. See JIMÉNEZ TARDÍO, ANTONIO (Pan Divino or Pedro).

PANIAGUA, BENJAMÍN. Bolivian peasant farmer.

PANTOJA TAMAYO, ORLANDO (Antonio or Olo). Born in Maffo, Santiago de Cuba, Cuba, in 1933. He fought in the July 26 Movement underground, and subsequently joined the struggle in the Sierra Maestra. He achieved the rank of captain in the Cuban armed forces. He arrived at the Ñacahuazú farm on December 19, 1966, and was part of the center group. He was killed at Quebrada del Yuro on October 8, 1967.

Papi. See MARTÍNEZ TAMAYO, JOSÉ MARÍA (Papi, Ricardo, Chinchu, Mbili or Taco).

Paulino. See BAIGORRIA, PAULINO.

PCB. Communist Party of Bolivia.

PCC. Communist Party of Cuba.

PCML. Communist Party (Marxist-Leninist) of Bolivia.

Pedro. See JIMÉNEZ TARDÍO, ANTONIO (Pan Divino or Pedro).

Pelado or **Pelao.** See BUSTOS, CIRO (Mauricio, Pelao, Pelado, or Carlos).

Pepe. See VELAZCO MONTAÑO, JULIO (Pepe).

PEREDO LEIGUE, GUIDO (Inti). Born in the city of Cochabamba, Bolivia, on April 30, 1938. He was a member of PCB from a very young age and was distinguished as one of the party's most dedicated and brave cadres. Peredo was first secretary of the PCB regional committee of La Paz and member of the central committee of the party, elected at its second national congress in 1964. Like his brother Coco, he participated in support efforts for the Peruvian guerrilla fighters of the ELN and the organization of the EGP of Argentina. He was one of the most outstanding guerrillas, operating as a political commissar and military officer. After Quebrada del Yuro, he escaped the tenacious military encirclement, and, along with the other survivors was saved by local peasants. With the Cuban Urbano, Inti reached the city of Santa Cruz and then went by air to Cochabamba, where through his father-in-law, the writer Jesús Lara, he made contact with the PCB, which assisted in the rescue of the three remaining guerrillas. Functioning clandestinely in the city, he reorganized the ELN, but while preparing his return to the mountains, he was killed by the repressive forces in La Paz on September 9, 1969.

PEREDO LEIGUE, ROBERTO (Coco). Inti's brother, born in Cochabamba, Bolivia, on May 23, 1939. He was one of the four members of the PCB assigned by Mario Monje to work with the Cuban liaisons. He was involved in all the preparations of the guerrilla organization from its beginnings and posed as the owner of the Ñacahuazú farm. He was part of the vanguard detachment and was killed in the September 26, 1967, ambush at Quebrada del Batán, near La Higuera, together with Miguel and Julio. Che wrote in his diary: "The deepest loss is that of Coco, but Miguel and Julio were magnificent fighters and the human value of the three is incalculable."

Pinares. See SÁNCHEZ DÍAZ, ANTONIO (Marcos or Pinares).

PLATA RÍOS, HERNÁN. A major in the Bolivian Army, one of the officers captured by the guerrillas during the March 23, 1967, ambush. Plata gave false testimony in the trial of the captured guerrilla fighters.

Polo. See AQUINO QUISPE, APOLINAR (Apolinar, Apolinario or Polo).

Pombo. See VILLEGAS TAMAYO, HARRY (Pombo).

PRA. Authentic Revolutionary Party, led by Wálter Guevara Arce in Bolivia.

PSB. Bolivian Social Democratic Party.

Quebrada del Yuro (El Yuro ravine). Site of Che Guevara's last battle on October 8, 1967.

QUISPAYA CHOQUE, RAÚL (Raúl). A Bolivian, born in the city of Oruro on December 31, 1939. He was an activist in the JCB and a member of its national committee. In 1965, he became a member of the PCML. Quispaya joined the guerrilla force as part of Moisés Guevara's group and he was part of the vanguard detachment. He was killed in the battle at the Rosita River on July 30, 1967, while attempting to assist Ricardo.

RAMÍREZ, HUMBERTO. Leader of the Bolivian Communist Party.

Ramón. See GUEVARA DE LA SERNA, ERNESTO (Che, Mongo, Ramón, or Fernando).

Raúl. See QUISPAYA CHOQUE, RAÚL (Raúl).

REINAGA GORDILLO, ANICETO (Aniceto). A Bolivian, born in Colquechaca, north of Potosí, Bolivia, on July 26, 1940. He was an activist in the JCB and a member of its national executive committee until February 1967. He joined the guerrilla forces at the beginning of December 1966 and was part of the vanguard detachment. He was killed in the battle of Quebrada del Yuro on October 8, 1967.

Renán. See MONTERO, IVÁN (Renán or Iván).

REQUE TERÁN, Colonel LUIS. Commander of the Fourth Division of the Bolivian Army, headquartered in Camiri from May 1967. He played an active part in the 1967 counterinsurgency campaign, specifically in dismantling the guerrilla force's strategic storage facilities.

REYES RIVERA, SIMÓN (Simón Rodríguez). Union leader and leader of the Bolivian Communist Party.

REYES RODRÍGUEZ, ELISEO (Rolando, or Captain San Luis). A Cuban, born in the village of San Luis, province of Santiago de Cuba, in 1940. He was one of the youngest combatants in the Sierra Maestra, where he fought under Che's command. He attained the rank of captain. He was a member of the central committee of the Communist Party of Cuba. He arrived at the Ñacahuazú farm in November 1966 and was part of the center group. He was appointed by Che to the post of political commissar. He was killed on April 25, 1967, in the battle of El Mesón, located between the village of Ticucha and the Iquira River. Che wrote in his diary that day, "we have lost the best man among the guerrilla fighters ..."

REYES ZAYAS, ISRAEL (Braulio). Born in Cuba, in the Sierra Maestra mountains in 1933. He joined the revolutionary struggle in the Sierra Maestra as an illiterate peasant, and attained the rank of lieutenant. He joined Raúl Castro's bodyguard, and became a liaison officer. He was with Che in the Congo, before traveling to Bolivia at the end of November 1966. He was part of the rearguard group, under Joaquín's command. He was the first to be killed in the ambush at Vado del Yeso, on August 31, 1967.

RHEA CLAVIJO, HUMBERTO. Bolivian doctor, who collaborated with the guerrilla forces.

Ricardo. See MARTÍNEZ TAMAYO, JOSÉ MARÍA (Papi, Ricardo, Chinchu, Mbili or Taco).

ROBLES, MOISÉS. Seventeen-year-old Bolivian peasant who served as a guide for the guerrillas.

ROCABADO TERRAZAS, VICENTE (Orlando). Joined the guerrilla forces in early 1967 with the group led by Moisés

Guevara, but deserted within a few days, before the start of armed actions. There are indications that he might have been a provocateur, because it appears that he worked in the Department of Criminal Investigations (DIC). He was acquitted in the Camiri trial of the captured guerrillas.

Rodolfo. See SALDAÑA, RODOLFO (Rodolfo).

ROJAS, HONORATO. A poor peasant, Honorato Rojas lived with his large family on the banks of the Río Grande River. He met the guerrillas during the February 1967 expedition and collaborated with them. At the end of August, Rojas tried to escape, but Major Mario Vargas Salinas forced him to collaborate with the Bolivian Army and betray the guerrillas. He led Joaquín's column directly into the ambush at the Puerto Mauricio (Vado del Yeso), which earned him a place in the Manchego Regiment. Later, he was also given some land. He was shot by an ELN commander on July 14, 1969.

Rolando. See REYES RODRÍGUEZ, ELISEO (Rolando or Captain San Luis).

ROSALES, TOMÁS. A Bolivian, who, after being tortured, was sentenced to death by hanging in the Camiri prison.

ROTH, GEORGE ANDREW. British-Chilean photographer. With a special authorization from the Bolivian Army, Roth was able to move around the war zone and on April 19, 1967, made contact with and was captured by the guerrilla force in the vicinity of Lagunillas. The following day, he left the area, in the company of Debray and Bustos, and was captured by the Bolivian Army. He was freed 80 days later. There is strong speculation that Roth might have been a CIA agent.

Rubio. See SUÁREZ GAYOL, JESÚS (Félix or Rubio).

SALDAÑA, RODOLFO (Rodolfo). Born in Sucre, Bolivia, in 1932. A former member of the PCB, he was among the first to receive military training in Cuba and was one of the four initially assigned by Mario Monje to work with the Cuban liaisons. He actively participated in the preparations for military action and met with Che at the Ñacahuazú farm on November 20, 1966. He was initially assigned to urban work, but in his January 26 diary entry, Che wrote that Saldaña would join the guerrilla force in 15 days, but this did not occur. He was captured in 1968 and set free in 1970, in exchange for the German hostages captured by the guerrilla fighters at Teoponte.

Salustio. See CHOQUE CHOQUE, SALUSTIO (Salustio).

San Luis, Captain. See REYES RODRÍGUEZ, ELISEO (Rolando or Captain San Luis).

SÁNCHEZ DÍAZ, ANTONIO (Marcos or Pinares). Born in Pinar del Río, Cuba, in 1927. From a rural family, he was a construction worker for many years. He fought in the Sierra Maestra, reaching the rank of major. He occupied top military posts and was a member of the central committee of the Communist Party of Cuba. He arrived at the Ñacahuazú farm on November 20, 1966, and was initially appointed by Che as head of the vanguard detachment. Severely admonished for his errors, he was later transferred to the rear guard, as a rank and file soldier. When Che threatened to expel him from the guerrilla forces, he responded by saying: "I'd rather be shot!" He was killed in an ambush on June 2, 1967, in the Bella Vista region, while fulfilling a mission of delivering supplies for the group headed by Joaquín.

SÁNCHEZ VALDIVIA, RUBÉN. A Bolivian Army major when he was captured by the guerrilla forces at the ambush in Iripití. Years later, he admitted to have been the person who provided the press with the ELN's Communiqué No. 1, the only one to be made public. Sánchez had to go into exile, where he established a relationship with left-wing sectors. Subsequently, he rejoined the Bolivian Armed Forces. After leaving active service, Sánchez became a regional leader of the Free Bolivia Movement (MBL) in Cochabamba.

Serafín or **Serapio**. See AQUINO TUDELA, SERAPIO (Serapio or Serafín).

SILES SALINAS, LUIS ADOLFO. Vice-president of Bolivia 1966-69 and briefly president in 1969.

SILVA BOGADO, AUGUSTO. A captain in the Bolivian Army captured during the ambush that occurred on March 23, 1967.

Simón Rodríguez. See REYES RIVERA, SIMÓN (Simón Rodríguez).

SIMÓN, PAUL. Peasant farmer met en route to Muyupampa who cooperated with the guerrillas.

STAMPONI CORINALDESI, LUIS FAUSTINO. Argentine revolutionary and member of the Socialist Party.

SUÁREZ GAYOL, JESÚS (Félix or **Rubio).** Born in Havana, Cuba, in 1936. He actively participated in the underground struggle and later in the Rebel Army, reaching the rank of captain. He occupied top-ranking positions in the revolutionary government and was a member of the central committee of the PCC. He arrived at the Ñacahuazú farm on December 19, 1966, and was assigned to the rear guard. He died in combat on April 10, 1967, in an action in Iripití, in which the Bolivian Army suffered 11 casualties. He was the first guerrilla fighter to fall in combat in the Bolivian campaign.

TAMAYO NÚÑEZ, LEONARDO (Urbano). Born in Bayamo, Cuba, in 1941. He fought in the Sierra Maestra, attaining the rank of captain. He arrived at the Ñacahuazú farm at the end of November 1966 and later belonged to the center group. He survived the battle at Quebrada del Yuro, and together with Pombo and Benigno managed to leave Bolivia via Chile in February 1968. He returned to Cuba on March 6, 1968.

Tania. See BUNKE BIDER, HAYDÉE TAMARA (Tania).

TAPIA ARUNI, EUSEBIO (Eusebio). An Aymará peasant farmer from Alto Beni in Bolivia and a member of the PCB. He joined the guerrilla struggle on January 21, 1967, together with Wálter and Benjamín. He was discharged from the guerrilla forces on March 25, 1967, together with three others belonging to what was known as the reject group and subsequently deserted.

Tuma. See COELLO, CARLOS (Tuma or Tumaini).

Tumaini. See COELLO, CARLOS (Tuma or Tumaini).

Urbano. See TAMAYO NÚÑEZ, LEONARDO (Urbano).

VACA MARCHETTI, LORGIO (Carlos). Born in Santa Cruz de la Sierra, Bolivia, in 1934. He was a member of the PCB and participated in trade union activities. He decided to join the guerrilla struggle while studying in Cuba and upon his arrival at the Ñacahuazú farm, on December 11, 1966, was assigned to the rearguard detachment. He drowned on March 16, 1967, while crossing the Río Grande, when returning from a reconnaissance mission. Che wrote in his diary that Carlos "was considered the best man among the Bolivians in the rear guard due to his seriousness, discipline, and enthusiasm."

VARGAS, GREGORIO. A Bolivian peasant who acted as a guide for the guerrilla force.

VÁZQUEZ VIAÑA, HUMBERTO (Humberto). A Bolivian and Loro's brother, he participated in the guerrilla movement's urban network in 1967. Avoiding persecution, he left the country and participated in the first stage of the reorganization of the ELN in Cuba. He adopted dissident positions that led him to break with the organization and, together with Ramiro Aliaga Saravia, wrote the mimeographed document *Bolivia: ensayo de revolución continental* in Paris in 1970.

VÁZQUEZ VIAÑA, JORGE (Bigotes, Loro, or Jorge). Born in La Paz, Bolivia, in 1939. He was an activist in the PCB, participating in its military apparatus. He was a close friend of Inti Peredo, with whom he participated in various military actions. Along with Coco Peredo, he pretended to be in charge of the Ñacahuazú farm. When his identity was revealed in November 1966, Che asked Vázquez to join the guerrilla force. Following the action at the Coripote farm, near Taperillas, on April 22, 1967, he became isolated and lost. He was involved in a clash with the Bolivian Army, inflicting two fatalities, and was finally wounded and captured on April 29. He was taken to the hospital at Camiri where he was interrogated by top military officials and CIA agents. A month later, it was announced that he had escaped and was tried in absentia together with Régis Debray and Ciro Bustos; by this time, however, rumors were already circulating that he had been killed.

VELAZCO MONTAÑO, JULIO (Pepe). A Bolivian who joined the guerrilla movement as part of Moisés Guevara's group. He deserted from the rearguard detachment to which he had been assigned. He was captured by the Bolivian Army, tortured, and shot on May 23, 1967.

Víctor. See CONDORI VARGAS COCHI, CASILDO (Víctor).

VIDES, MARTÍN. A Bolivian peasant met by the guerrillas en route to Muyupampa. According to Che's comments in his diary, he was the "rich man" of the area.

VILLA, Don REMBERTO. Owner of the Ñacahuazú farm, who sold it to Roberto Peredo (Coco).

VILLEGAS TAMAYO, HARRY (Pombo). Born in Yara, Granma province, Cuba. He was a veteran of the Sierra Maestra and the Congo. He arrived in Bolivia in July 1966 and was in charge of the guerrilla force's final military preparations. He traveled with Che, in two jeeps, from La Paz to the Ñacahuazú farm, together with Tuma, Pacho, and Loro, between November 4 and 6, 1966. He was part of the center group and, after the battle at Quebrada del Yuro, along with Inti, Darío, Benigno, and Urbano, he was able to break through the encirclement; later they were protected by the peasants. With the assistance of the PCB, they first went to Cochabamba, and from Oruro the three Cuban survivors reached the Chilean border, arriving back in Cuba on March 6, 1968.

Vado del Yeso (Puerto Mauricio). Site of the ambush of Joaquín's guerrilla group on August 31, 1967.

Vilo. See ACUÑA NÚÑEZ, JUAN VITALIO (Joaquín or Vilo).

Wálter. See ARANCIBIA AYALA, WÁLTER (Wálter).

Willy. See CUBA SANABRIA, SIMEÓN (Willy).

YPFB. Yacimientos Petrolíferos Fiscales Bolivianos (Bolivian State Petroleum Reserves).

CHE GUEVARA BOOKS PUBLISHED BY
SEVEN STORIES PRESS

The Motorcycle Diaries: Notes on a Latin American Journey
Introductions by Walter Salles and Cintio Vitier
Foreword by Aleida Guevara
"The enormity of our endeavor escaped us in those moments; all we could see was the dust on the road ahead and ourselves on the bike, devouring kilometers in our flight northward," wrote a young Ernesto Guevara as he and his buddy Alberto Granado hit the road on a vintage Norton motorcycle to discover Latin America.

This is his lively and highly entertaining diary of that adventure, featuring exclusive, unpublished photos taken by the 23-year-old Argentine medical student on his journey across a continent, and a tender foreword by Aleida Guevara offering an insightful perspective on her father—the man and the icon. (July 2021). ISBN: 978-1-64421-068-0

The Bolivian Diary
Introduction by Fidel Castro
Foreword by Camilo Guevara
Che's account of the fateful Bolivia mission that attempted to spark a continent-wide revolution. This is Che Guevara's last diary, compiled from the notebooks discovered when he was captured and executed by the Bolivian army in October 1967. It became an instant bestseller. This newly revised edition has an insightful preface by Che's eldest son Camilo, a chronology, maps, and 32 pages of rare or unpublished photos. (December 2021). ISBN: 978-1-64421-074-1

Congo Diary: Episodes of the Revolutionary War in the Congo
Foreword by Aleida Guevara
Introductions by Gabriel García Márquez and Roberto Saviano
Che Guevara's intriguing account of the revolutionary war in the Congo, filling in the missing chapter in his life. Prior to his fateful mission to Bolivia, in 1965 Che led a secret Cuban force that went to aid the African national liberation movement against the Belgian colonialists, after the assassination of Patrice Lumumba by the CIA. (October 2021). ISBN: 978-1-64421-072-7

I Embrace You with All My Revolutionary Fervor: Letters 1947–1967

Foreword by Aleida Guevara

Ernesto Che Guevara was a voyager—and thus a letter writer—for his entire adult life. The letters collected here range from letters home during his *Motorcycle Diaries* trip, to the long letter to Fidel after the success of the Cuban revolution in early 1959, from the most personal to the intensely political, revealing someone who not only thought deeply about everything he encountered, but for whom the process of social transformation was a constant companion from his youth until shortly before his death. His letters give us Che the son, the friend, the lover, the guerrilla fighter, the political leader, the philosopher, the poet. Che in these letters is often playful, funny, sometimes sarcastic, and deeply affectionate. His life was short, and these twenty years, from when he was nineteen until days before his death, show it was also incredibly rich and full. (October 2021). ISBN: 978-1-64421-095-6

Latin America Diaries:
The Sequel to *The Motorcycle Diaries*

This sequel to *The Motorcycle Diaries* includes letters, poetry, and journalism that document young Ernesto Guevara's second Latin American journey following his graduation from medical school in 1953. It reveals how the young Argentine is transformed into a militant revolutionary, ready to commit himself to the guerrilla struggle Fidel Castro and his compañeros are about to launch in Cuba against the dictatorship of General Fulgencio Batista. (January 2022). ISBN: 978-1-64421-100-7

Reminiscences of the Cuban Revolutionary War

Foreword by Aleida Guevara

Originally published a series of articles for Cuban papers, this thoroughly revised edition includes for the first time corrections made by Che himself to his diary on which he based the essays. This book also includes a foreword by Che's daughter Aleidita about how her parents met during the revolutionary war and 32 pages of photos and maps of the guerrilla campaign. (January 2022). ISBN: 978-1-64421-107-6

Che Guevara Reader:
Writings on Politics & Revolution

Edited by David Deutschmann and María del Carmen Ariet García

Recognized as one of *Time*'s "icons of the 20th century," Che Guevara became a legend in his own time and has now reemerged as a symbol of a new generation of political activists. Far more than a guerrilla strategist, Che Guevara made a profound and lasting contribution to revolutionary theory and Marxist humanism as demonstrated in this bestselling book. (February 2022). ISBN: 978-1-64421-112-0

Global Justice: Three Essays on Liberation and Socialism
Introduction by María del Carmen Ariet García
Is there an alternative to the corporate globalization and militarism that is ravaging our planet? These classic works by Ernesto Che Guevara present a revolutionary view of a different world in which human solidarity and understanding replace imperialist aggression and exploitation. (March 2022). ISBN: 978-1-64421-156-4

Guerrilla Warfare: Authoritative, Revised New Edition
Foreword by Harry "Pombo" Villegas
A bestselling classic for decades, this is Che Guevara's own incisive analysis of the Cuban revolution—a text studied by his admirers and adversaries alike. Although often regarded as a "manual" for guerrilla warfare, this book is primarily a political account of what happened in Cuba and why, explaining how a small group of dedicated fighters grew in strength with the support of the Cuban people, overcoming their limitations to defeat the US-backed dictator's army. He also analyzes why the Cuban revolution attained a "continental and international transcendence." (February 2022). ISBN: 978-1-64421-146-5

The Awakening of Latin America
Edited by María del Carmen Ariet García
In a letter to his mother in 1954, a young Ernesto Guevara wrote, "The Americas will be the theater of my adventures in a way that is much more significant than I would have believed." In *The Awakening of Latin America* we have the story of those adventures, charting Che's evolution from an impressionable young medical student to the "heroic guerrilla," assassinated in cold blood in Bolivia. Spanning seventeen years, this anthology draws on from his family's personal archives and offers the best of Che's writing: examples of his journalism, essays, speeches, letters, and even poems. As Che documents his early travels through Latin America, his involvement in the Guatemalan and Cuban revolutions, and his rise to international prominence under Fidel Castro, we see how his fervent commitment to social justice shaped and was shaped by the continent he called home.

Nearly half of this book is published for the first time and pre-dates Che's arrival in Cuba with Fidel Castro's guerrilla expedition in 1956. Also included are his notes for his unfinished book, *The Social Role of Doctors in Latin America*. (April 2022). ISBN: 978-1-64421-164-9